Communic Management

To Anne and Helen

Communication Management

Michael Kaye
University of Technology, Sydney

PRENTICE HALL
Sydney   New York   London   Toronto   Tokyo
Singapore   Mexico City   Amsterdam

Aquisitions Editor: Joy Whitton
Production Editor: Marah Braye
Cover Design: The Modern Art Production Group, Prahran, VIC
Typeset by: Southern Star Design, South Tacoma, NSW
Printed in Australia by: Star Printery, Erskinville, NSW

1 2 3 4 5 98 97 96 95 94

ISBN 0 7248 0207 X

National Library of Australia
Cataloguing-in-Publication Data

Kaye, Michael
    Communication management

    Bibliography.
    Includes index.
    ISBN 0 7248 0207 X.

    1. Communication. 2. Communication-Problems, exercises, etc. 3. Communication in organizations. 4. Communication in organizations-Problems, exercises, etc. 5. Interpersonal communication. 6. Interpersonal communication-Problems, exercises, etc. I. Title.

302.2

Prentice Hall, Inc., *Englewood Cliffs, New Jersey*
Prentice Hall of Australia Pty Ltd, *Sydney*
Prentice Hall Canada, Inc., *Toronto*
Prentice Hall Hispanoamericana, *SA, Mexico*
Prentice Hall of India Private Ltd, *New Delhi*
Prentice Hall International, Inc., *London*
Prentice Hall of Japan, Inc., *Tokyo*
Prentice Hall of South East Asia Pty Ltd, *Singapore*
Editora Prentice Hall do Brasil Ltda, *Rio de Janeiro*

PRENTICE HALL
A division of Simon & Schuster

Contents

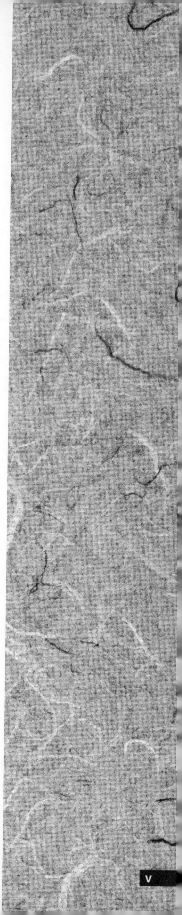

Part IV   Future Development in Adult Communication
           Management 251

**Chapter 11 Adult Communication Management:
            Future Directions 253**

Preface

When I began the preparation of this text some time ago, I was strongly motivated by a desire to bridge the gap between scholarly thinking and practitioner perspectives on human communication. It seemed to me then that much of the contemporary scholarship in the field of human communication was not known by some professional people, and that their work would benefit significantly from such awareness. By the same token, many communication scholars appeared to be developing their theories and their thinking with very little reference to what some people call the 'real world'.

I use the term 'real world' advisedly since I have often concluded that ivory towers are inhabited not only by academics but also by a vast number of people in the 'real world of work'. I am also confident that many readers can recall organisations whose members appear oblivious of major professional developments occurring outside their own place of work.

One is likely to hear expressions such as 'that's not how we do things here' in certain organisations. There are at least two assumptions underlying such statements. One is that 'how we do things here' is the only correct way of doing things; another is that members of inward-looking organisations believe that they can learn little from others in different systems. The rationale often used for such a claim is that every organisation is unique. If this is true, there are no generic learning bases for organisational growth and development since each human system or organisation must be audited and improved on its own terms.

The position I have taken in this book is quite the reverse. We can all learn from others and in particular from others who operate in ways that differ from ours. My own graduate students who work in the broad field of adult education can readily relate to examples from diverse professional areas such as health and nursing, business and management, human resource development, adult learning and teaching, social work and counselling, legal practice, and politics. Of course, whilst this is a book which adult educators, vocational teachers, trainers and staff developers will, hopefully, find particularly useful, it is not intended to be solely a text for trainers and staff developers: it is intended to be of value to professionals from a wide variety of work-related areas.

The lessons we can learn may be either 'how to' or 'how not to' lessons. Both kinds are equally important and they are reflected in various sections throughout this book. If any reader maintains that the only source of relevant learning is first-hand experience in one's own organisation, there is little point in that person devoting any further attention to this book. Many of these lessons, moreover, are relevant for all of us personally, regardless of our field of work.

A question I was asked by reviewers of early chapters was, 'At what level is this text pitched'? Originally, I saw it as an introductory reference for graduate students. However, graduate students derive their thinking from a disciplinary base usually acquired in their years of undergraduate study. What I have tried to do, therefore, is to write a text which allows readers, whether they be in graduate or undergraduate courses, to think as deeply or as plainly as they wish when attempting to fulfil their professional responsibilities as adult communication managers. At the end of each chapter there are suggestions for obtaining further information and ideas to enhance the understanding of serious readers.

This book is not only for university or college students. It is a text which many professionals working closely with other people may find useful and provocative. In its present format, it acknowledges the inextricable connection between theory and practice. 'Communication', a process as natural as breathing, cannot be seen only as a subject of theoretical analysis. On the other hand, an understanding of human communication is inevitably enhanced if the reader can relate real practices to a compellingly applicable conceptual framework.

The wide community of people for whom this book is intended includes anyone whose work involves communication and interaction with others in a wide range of organisations and systems. Its message is not limited to those in supervisory or managerial positions. Indeed, much of it is concerned with how subordinates can manage communication processes when interacting with superiors. As will become evident, one of its themes is that all people in systems are potentially managers of their communication with others.

'Communication Management' has been chosen as the title because it represents a new field of study developed primarily in Australia since the early 1980s. The term refers to how people manage their communication processes through constructing meanings about their relationships with others in various settings. Whilst not all people are managers in the traditional sense, they are managing their communication and actions in a range of relationships—some personal, some professional. The position I have taken is that every person in an organisation, or other kind of human system, has a responsibility for managing communication with other members. In this sense, this perspective is different from standard views on management and organisational communication.

This book is about understanding how people who work together communicate. It focuses on how adults act toward each other in particular contexts and the model proposed is known as 'adult communication management'. As presented in this book, the adult communication management perspective will not be found in traditional texts on management or organisational development. Some of these tend to over-emphasise practice at the cost of sound applied theoretical thinking. Nor does this book resemble conventional communication theory texts which focus more on debates about research methodologies than on issues critical to the beneficiaries of research—people in the world of work.

For this reason, I found that a small but gradually increasing number of colleagues and other professionals with an interest in applied communication shared my view that a new kind of text was needed to address topics and issues which would help people develop communication competence. Over the years, therefore, my thinking has moved from conventional ways of compartmentalising knowledge about communication (e.g. organisational communication, mass communication, political communication and rhetoric) to a broader information base for understanding how people manage their communication processes. This broader base is communication management.

Because of its eclectic orientation, this book draws from a number of contributing fields of study and disciplines. Whilst it has a strong leaning toward social psychology and applied communication theory and research, other sources are educational and training literature, current practical thinking in management and organisational development, learning theory including adult learning theory, and scholarship in human development. I do not claim that this is the 'last word' in applied communication theory. The book represents an unconventional attempt to understand certain phenomena from a perspective which is intended to go beyond traditional models of good practice.

My selection of topics for each chapter reflects what, over the years, numerous professionals have told me are critical aspects of their communication with others. No doubt, it could have included other topics, but it covers a fairly comprehensive range of activities in which communication managers engage. Some facets of communication competence, such as listening, are universal whilst others, such as conducting meetings or performance appraisals, are more often associated with authority. Nevertheless, these skills are potentially valuable to all members of organisations. Sooner or later we are all required to lead and make decisions of one kind or another.

Finally, a word about the structure of this book. Each chapter concludes with recommended reading, key terms introduced in the chapter (defined in the Glossary), activities and discussion questions. Generally speaking, the aim of this book is not to provide definitive answers to the dilemmas of communication managers but to raise questions for further thought, growth and development. In this way, I hope, this book will differ from the more familiar and ubiquitous 'how-to-do-it' approaches by challenging the reader to delve more deeply for an understanding of human nature and communication.

Acknowledgments

There are many people whom I would like to thank for encouraging me to write this book. Over the years, many professionals whom I met as an organisational consultant or as a college and university teacher contributed greatly by sharing ideas and concerns with me. There are too many to name, but I thank them all.

In particular, however, I thank Jesse Delia, Chair of the Speech Communication Department at the University of Illinois and Gerard Egan of the Centre for Organisational Studies at Loyola University, Chicago. Jesse spent many hours with me discussing issues which continued to vex me—issues like whether it is possible to assess people's communication competence at work, and, if possible, how. Gerard Egan's work is central to the adult communication management perspective I have developed, and time and correspondence with him have reinforced my respect for his tremendous contributions over many years to developing systematic approaches to understanding organisational and managerial behaviour.

Of all my colleagues whose vision is to complement and strengthen practice with appropriate applied theory, I specially thank Terry Mohan and Shirley Saunders for their interest and support. Both are exemplars of putting theory to practice and of ensuring that good communication practice is based on sound theoretical principles. I trust that this book will prove to be an additional reinforcement of their commitment to integrating theory and practice.

Nancy Lau's wordprocessing skills helped me immeasurably with format, headings and references, and general presentation.

Lastly, I thank Anne, my wife, and Helen, my mother, for their faith in my ability to create a worthwhile book. Anne has been a tower of strength in critically analysing my thinking on many occasions when I have sought her opinion and advice.

PART I

Communication Management: Theoretical Foundations

Introduction to Communication Management

Communication is something so simple and difficult
that we can never put it in simple words.
T. S. Matthews

Good communication is as stimulating as black coffee,
and just as hard to sleep after.
A. M. Lindbergh

What is communication? Why do people communicate? How do we learn to understand each other so that we can live and work in harmony with others? These are just some of the questions that will come to mind as you read this chapter. You will be introduced to the idea that communication is a process. Our ability to relate well to other people corresponds with our ability to understand and manage this communication process. We will explore one way of explaining this communication process by referring to the self, to **people-in-systems**, to communication as the building and sharing of meanings, and to **communication competence**. These elements combine to make a framework for the concept of **adult communication management**. This concept is our reference point throughout this book, as we examine different ways we can communicate successfully with others.

Learning Objectives

After studying the ideas, arguments and suggestions presented in this chapter you should be able to do the following:

- Explain why communication is inevitable and important in our lives.

- Describe in your own words the meaning of 'communication management'.

- Explain the relationship between *communication management* and *communication competence*.

- Define human communication as a process of building meanings between people.

- Distinguish between *communication* and *communications*.

- List seven assumptions about human communication.

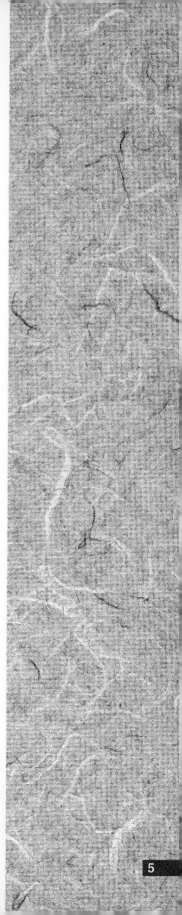

1.1 The Importance and Inevitability of Communication

We live in a world of people. Although at times we feel the need to be alone, we cannot avoid the inevitability of interpersonal encounters. Much of what we do and think is governed by what others do and think and by what we believe others think of us. Our own behaviour is also determined by what we think of others. There are probably very few situations where the influence of other people would count for little.

Our reflection creates hopes, expectations and visions.

When we are alone we may be reflective, fantasising, imagining or planning our future. Our reflection creates hopes, expectations and visions which regulate how we act and react toward others. It is often difficult to separate our private from our professional concerns. For example, our domestic problems may take high priority; once they affect how we function with colleagues, we realise that we are multifaceted creatures subject to various forces operating simultaneously upon us. To this extent, we cannot easily separate our professional selves from our spiritual selves or from our non-worldly selves. Just like James Thurber's character Walter Mitty, we try to be heroic figures, but our circumstances bring us down to earth very quickly.

The several forces acting upon us at any point of time make us what we are. Depending on the intensity of any one of these forces, we become risk-takers or cautious conservatives. In short, we respond to the dominant force of the moment. Our images of ourselves are largely the product of the rationalising adaptive mechanisms we use to manage this force—we become polite when we would rather be retributive, or we feign satisfaction when we really feel dissatisfied or annoyed.

To others who experience us, our observable actions and behaviour communicate our intentions, which are perceived as friendliness or hostility, acceptance or rejection, dominance or submissiveness. *Much of what we intend to communicate is not articulated verbally.* Our nonverbal cues express something of ourselves, particularly our emotions. We are, therefore, ambivalent creatures, often maintaining a semblance of expected conformity whilst we grapple with our personal conflicts. Individually, we are enigmatic and unpredictable. We are constituted of a maelstrom of inner urges and outward manifestations of socialised behaviour. What we communicate of ourselves to others is an image compounded of this mixture. What others glean are mostly the surface qualities we project— those we wish to exhibit. Those who know us well may infer intent beyond the observable realm.

Regardless of others' insights, we persist in moulding images of ourselves for others to decodify. Our words as well as our nonverbal cues are our 'currency' for developing, stabilising, or terminating relationships with others. Even when we prefer to have nothing to do with someone else, we cannot escape communicating our intentions. Unless we live in total isolation from others, we are forced to be communicators. As Watzlawick, Beavin and Jackson (1967) have suggested, 'one cannot *not* communicate'.

The critical significance of communication in the present world is underscored by the depersonalising effects of new technologies that are interactive and 'user-friendly'. Facsimile and computerised work-stations have superseded people as information resources; we can now obtain information without other people being physically present. In some areas, artificial intelligence is supplanting real intelligence, and many people seem to get their work done without other people. Social interaction is becoming limited to lunch breaks and other out-of-work times.

New technologies can depersonalise the workplace

What we must realise is that the heart of communication is not in the surface message but in the meanings or interpretations that we ascribe to the message. When the message is presented in person, interpretations of the message are also affected by how it is presented. This interaction of message, presentation and interpretation shapes the unique character of the communication process. Our meanings—interpretations of stimuli—thus form the bases for our communicative actions and intentions towards others. These bases have been called 'strategic choices' by Delia, O'Keefe and O'Keefe (1982). It is clear that we cannot escape the need to communicate, and so we owe it to ourselves and to others to manage our communication competently.

The concept 'communication management' suggests that the ability to communicate well is not one we are born with, but something we can learn and improve on. For example, we can learn to be more capable communicators in interviews, meetings or public forums. The learning process involves more than obedience to a set of predetermined, mechanical procedures; it also requires an awareness of the process variables that may affect the quality of the dialogue taking place. 'Communication management' is thus an umbrella term for conceptualising the range of variables that may contribute to the co-ordination of meanings between people. Such variables include the ways we construe meanings, the strategies we use to infer others' intentions, and our preferred styles of communicating our reactions to other people.

As individuals, of course, we also exhibit differences which can affect the ways we construct meanings about others. For instance, as a male I may react negatively to a female who is avowedly affirmative-action; or my ethnic origins may alienate me from people of other cultures—at least in my own mind. Again, if I am a modest wage-earner, I might believe that my supervisor or immediate superior who earns a much higher salary is unfairly capitalising on my expertise. Individual differences, therefore, may also explain why we communicate with others in a certain way. On this basis, it is now appropriate to examine more closely a process view of communication management.

1.2 A Process View of Communication Management

'Communication management' implies the optimal use of human and technological resources to promote dialogue between people. Egan and Cowan (1979) and Egan (1985, 1988a, 1988b) proposed a people-in-systems model of organisational development. The model consists of two parts. Model A is a comprehensive tool for mapping the strengths and weaknesses of **human systems**. A human system may be something as general as a community or neighbourhood, or as specific as an institution, or family group. In essence, Model A is diagnostic—it determines whether

human systems
Networks of communicating people that range from units as small as nuclear families to large organisations, communities and neighbourhoods.

people and other resources in systems or organisations are being used to best effect. Egan also suggests that good communication among people is critical for the efficient functioning of human systems. Thus, Model A helps us to see organisations and other human systems from a human communication perspective.

Model B focuses on the strategic management of change in human systems. It consists of a set of organisational decision-making procedures and is a development tool for making appropriate changes. At present, Model A is more fully developed than Model B; it incorporates a range of design, human-resource and situational variables and has an accomplishment orientation.

One important implication to emerge from Model A is that the competent management of communication processes in human systems is crucial to their maintenance and development. This suggests that people in systems should see themselves as managers of the communication processes which characterise professional and personal relationships between members. Good communication managers need all the human communication skills that are relevant to their systems.

Some of these skills, such as active listening or assertiveness, are the special concern of those who study interpersonal communication competence. Other skills, like chairing meetings or public speech-making, are more usually associated with the field of group or mass communication. The importance of these skills varies; for example, questioning skills are vital for interviewing, negotiation skills are crucial in labour management disputes, and problem-solving and conflict-resolution abilities are especially important for counselling.

On their own, skills are hit-and-miss entities, especially without a sound rationale. We can, for example, learn how to be leaders without knowing much about the theories or research on leadership. There are now many leadership training packages. Some of them are soundly based on contemporary research and theory, but others attract disciples simply because their practical usefulness is assumed to be readily demonstrable.

Effective skills are well grounded in theory. Skills can be seen as the evidence of a more complex set of theoretical principles that have been systematically examined and applied by the performer, and communication skills are no exception. They rely just as heavily on research and theory as more familiar psychomotor skills do. Regardless of the performance domain, skills require a strong conceptual foundation. The term 'competency' is perhaps intended to convey more than the term 'skill' since competent people not only know how to do something but also why it should be done a certain way. Skilled people, on the other hand, may not necessarily have an understanding of the reasons for particular procedures or actions. 'Competency' and 'competence' are often synonymous in applied communication scholarly literature. From an adult communication management perspective, 'competence' is equated with general ability and is preferred to 'competency' which is closer in meaning to 'skill'. When pluralised, 'competence' is usually read as 'competencies' and not as 'competences'. Peter (1975), for example, argued that skills constitute only one category of competencies. The major domains of learning, identified by

Bloom (1956) as the cognitive, affective and psychomotor, roughly correspond to the more recently identified competency areas of knowledge, attitude and skill. Practitioners today, in human resource fields such as training and development, tend to use the latter, more pragmatic classifications. However, competencies may be conceptualised at either a professional or technician level. According to Peter (1975:78):

> At a professional level, competency includes understanding the processes involved as well as having performance skills and an academic and theoretical background. This generally accepted concept of professional competence is the basis for differentiating between a professional and a technician. The technician's training emphasises performance skills whereas the professional's preparation includes more theoretical background, academic content, and higher-level abstractions.

The position taken in this book is intended to be consistent with Peter's. Competency approaches aimed to promote effectiveness in communicating with others are described in later chapters within the framework of communication management-as-process.

In this book, communication management applies essentially to the ways adults relate to each other. For this reason, it is appropriate to distinguish adult from non-adult or child communication management. My model of adult communication management is analogous to the Russian matouschka dolls which are encased within progressively larger dolls. Four different sized dolls make up this model. See Figure 1.1 for a diagrammatic representation.

The smallest doll, the innermost part of the adult communication management model, represents the 'self'. Knowing and understanding one's self is a necessary step towards effective self-management. In turn, self-awareness serves as a sound basis for self-analysis and self-examination, particularly when people consider how they affect others through their speech and actions. Thus, the 'self' doll is the intrapersonal component of the adult communication management model.

Encasing the 'self' doll is the 'interpersonal' doll. At this point the focus is on how the 'self' relates to 'the other' (or others). This interpersonal element is best explained in terms of constructivist theory which holds that communication is a process where interacting individuals create meanings about each other and about the nature and state of their relationship. The interpersonal doll draws our attention to the way communicating adults can affect each other and bring about changes in themselves or in those interacting with them.

The third doll is the 'people-in-systems' doll. Here, our concern is with how the human systems or organisations in which people work or function can have an effect on how those people will communicate with others in those systems. This doll also presupposes that people can influence the way these systems or organisations will develop or deteriorate. At this point of the adult communication management model, attention is largely given to understanding and managing the culture of human systems or organisations. In this connection, 'culture' refers to both the 'overt' and the 'covert' rules, norms, values and practices which give those human systems their distinctive characters.

Finally, the fourth doll which encases all the others is labelled the 'competence' doll. It is important to understand that in this model 'competence' is not just seen as an outer layer or casing—communication management competence can occur at any other level of the model. Thus, people are intrapersonally competent when they acquire a realistic understanding of their 'self' and develop some measure of 'self-control' or 'self-management'. People can also be seen to be 'competent' when they construct, coordinate and clarify meanings with other interacting individuals. Lastly, people can be judged 'competent' when they display an ability to change either the systems in which they operate or other people within those systems.

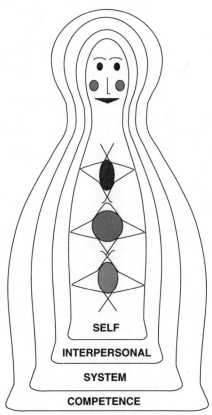

SELF

INTERPERSONAL

SYSTEM

COMPETENCE

FIGURE 1.1

The Adult Communication Management Model

It is suggested that this model of adult communication management may serve as a useful reference point for determining current levels of communication competence and, ultimately, for devising strategies to bring about desired changes in people or the systems in which they exist or work. At appropriate parts of this book, it will be revealed how this model of communication management differs from other more traditional or existing conceptions. For the present, we will focus our attention more directly on the way in which communication management links with the notion of communication competence.

1.3 The Relationship Between Communication Management and Communication Competence

Since the core of communication management is, for our purposes here, the process of co-ordinating the interpretations or meanings construed by interacting people, the term 'communication competence' suggests that interacting people have understood each other's viewpoints and frames of reference. Penman (1985) went a step further, urging that communication competence be viewed in terms of interpersonal *relationships*. The term 'communication' conveys the idea of a sharing of meaning or reciprocity between people. Irwin (1985; 1988) has suggested that 'conceptualisations of interpersonal competence have included relational dimensions for some time'. Communication management therefore involves both understanding and negotiating two or more individuals' meanings.

In certain instances, meanings are rule-bound and literal. For example, in a court of law, evidence is deemed admissible or inadmissible according to that court's rules of admissibility. In meetings, chairpersons following established guidelines assume responsibility for ensuring that relevant information or messages are exchanged.

Real meanings, of course, are personally construed. It was, I think, Dr Seuss's character, Horton the elephant, who said 'I know what I mean and I mean what I say …' when he declared his determination to be faithful. Nevertheless, whilst meanings are individually constructed, the intentions underlying them are often misconstrued by others experiencing the same event or behaviour. For example, two people hearing the Treasurer's Budget speech may form quite discrepant impressions of his or her sincerity or trustworthiness. Such impressions are influenced by values, beliefs and attitudes previously acquired. Thus, preferences for particular political ideologies may serve as a regulatory mechanism for either accepting or rejecting the message being presented. Our memories of broken or kept promises, especially in connection with a personal or professional concern, may also filter certain messages.

It seems, therefore, that communication management requires us to develop receptive as well as expressive abilities; in other words, to decode and encode intended meanings accurately. These general abilities to express and receive depend in turn on one's possession of critical communication microskills such as non-evaluative listening, empathic or reflective responding, interpreting and expressing nonverbal cues, and using language that is unprejudicial and inoffensive. At the interpersonal level, these constitute a range of self-management skills, so communication management is very much a matter of self-management through the judicious application of communication microskills.

An important point should be made here: competence does not necessarily imply excellence. Relatively recent studies have tended to reify the ideal of excellence (McLagan, 1983; Peters and Waterman, 1984; Peters and Austin, 1989), but apart from a few outstanding communicators, people do not, in general, communicate with consistent excellence. The adage 'to err is human' applies in this context.

Individual communication competencies probably vary from one situation to another. Hence, people display differing degrees of competence depending upon a range of relevant variables operating at given moments. The term 'excellence' is probably highly idealistic; people communicate as best they can under the prevailing circumstances. No textbook, manual or training program can guarantee to transform poor communicators into excellent ones. People can, however, become more aware of their own patterns of communicating with others. Such awareness enables people to recognise the need, if any, for change.

The position we take in this book is that individuals cannot be taught to be competent unless they willingly learn, develop and monitor their own changes. Putting this another way, you will not communicate better simply by reading this book. It is what you think and do after studying this field that determines whether you attain excellence or not. Self-management is therefore the key, and the first step in self-management is self-awareness and an awareness of others. Unfortunately, the frantic pace of many modern urban lifestyles has limited our opportunities to reflect on the quality of our relationships with others.

Developing communication competencies to enhance our communication management processes thus requires a quantum leap in our thinking about our associations with others on both a personal and a professional basis. We can hardly resist the rapid tide of social and technological change characterising the world today, but it is imperative that we do not lose sight of our humanity. The mechanisation of society need not mean a corresponding robotisation of people. For this reason alone, the connection between communication competence and the process of communication management is vital and needs to be understood.

The Nature of Human Communication   1.4

There is much debate over what human communication is all about. Dance (1982) edited a collection of essays on different perspectives of human communication, including rules-based, meaning-centred and other theoretical perspectives. At present, the field of human communication theory offers no definitive view or definition that is recognised as superior to others: there is ample scope for investigation.

The theoretical foundation of this book is firmly based on a meaning-centred view of human communication. However, no extant theory provides a totally comprehensive framework for understanding the process of communication management. Perhaps the most rigorous of contemporary theories is the one expounded by Delia, O'Keefe and O'Keefe (1982). This theory, **constructivism**, argues that individually constructed meanings constitute the basis of one's actions towards and interactions with others. Constructivists maintain that people interpret others' intentions on the basis of individually developed **interpersonal construct systems**.

The interpersonal construct is central to our meaning-centred view of human communication. According to Kelly (1955), a pioneer of contemporary constructivist theory, a construct is a bipolar adjective (e.g. tall-short, friendly-unfriendly) by which people determine their impressions of others, and each person uses their own individual construct system.

Constructs may be either physical or psychological. A physical construct refers to an observable feature (e.g. fat-slim, blue-eyed or brown-eyed). Psychological constructs, on the other hand, involve inferred qualities such as sincere-insincere, honest-dishonest and so on. The problem with psychological constructs, of course, is that they are not derived from overtly demonstrable data. From our knowledge of people in certain situations, we can only assume that they are happy or sad, fearful or brave, and so on.

How people communicate is essentially the product of both surface and undetectable information. Most of what we observe of someone is just the tip of the iceberg; the substance of their personality lurks beneath the surface, along with the unobservable urges and impulses that prompt their behaviour. Our communication with others greatly depends on information that is incomplete; we construe others' intentions from data filtered through individual frames of reference which are built from personal or interpersonal construct systems. The key to constructing accurate meanings resides in our sensitivity to levels of consciousness within and without ourselves.

There is no easy answer to the question of how this sensitivity can be developed. Whilst communication can be described as an exercise of the mind, the human mind certainly has its limitations. It does not fully interpret unpredictable emotional behaviour, even in familiar situations. People sometimes exhibit certain moods, for example, for physiological reasons not readily discernible from their behaviour. A person suffering from stress might display all the characteristic symptoms of stress, but it would be difficult to tap their subliminal regions to assess accurately why they feel as they do. In short, the receiver has to rely on cues that are symptomatic rather than explanatory of someone else's condition.

At present there is no certainty about how people decide why others communicate or behave as they do. Current research methodologies focus on methods of observation, direct and indirect, and introspection. Tapping mental and emotional complexities by clinical hypnosis, for example, remains in the avant-garde realm of the unexplored. Human communication has not yet emerged as a totally intelligible phenomenon. At best, present methods of research provide approximations of the motivations that govern people's behaviour.

For the present, it is expedient to accept the notion that, on the basis of our construct systems, we attribute meaning to the intentions, actions and personalities of others. Within the limitations of the cognitive structures which characterise the individual ways we form impressions of others, we make sense of our world. Communication, therefore, is very much a matter of the mind.

Of course, in practical terms, everyday communication is a comparatively straightforward set of acts or events and communicating individuals are often unaware of how others will react to their intended messages. As a manager, for example, I may instruct my staff with a memo, but my message may not be received as I would want it to be. Some of my staff may decide that it should be relegated to the wastepaper basket and ignored.

Much of our everyday communication takes the form of transmitted messages, which are not necessarily acted upon in the way we intend them to be. From a process perspective, therefore, situations of this kind are more a case of miscommunication. Meanings become discrepant rather than shared. Of course, some messages do find their mark, but a process-oriented view of communication cannot be based simply on the notion of message transmission, especially when not all the communicators' meanings are reciprocated.

A generic view of communication allows for signs and symbols that are not only linguistically determined but also idiosyncratically constructed in nonverbal ways. Many of our meanings cannot be readily expressed in words, particularly when what we say represents an acceptable statement rather than our true feelings. Since a good deal of people's meanings are conveyed nonverbally, a comprehensive view of human communication should perhaps be a nonverbal one.

For some time the process view of communication has played a relatively minor part in communication theory-building, overshadowed by the more popular and pragmatic message transmission approaches. Message-centred views of communication developed over the past few decades were essentially elaborations of the one-way model, developed by Shannon and Weaver (1949), whereby messages passed from source to receiver via some medium, in a unidirectional fashion. The assumption is that the receiver understands the message as the sender intended. Later versions such as Berlo's (1960) Source-Message-Channel-Receiver (S-M-C-R) model introduced new concepts of medium and channel. Some conceptualisations of communication also began to feature feedback loops from receiver to source.

All these explanations lacked a consistent, firm commitment to a crucial point: messages acquire meaning only through encoding and decoding people's interpretations of them. McLuhan and Fiore (1967), for example, emphasised the medium as the major force that shaped meanings in messages. But meanings do not reside solely in messages. New information entering our perceptual field can be acquired and interpreted at a literal level, but it rarely remains there. Repeated experiences of the same information allow us to construe personal meanings. The failure of many writers and practitioners, including teachers of communication, to grasp this simple fact may be partly due to the prevailing trend to reduce 'communication' to a practical utility. One example of this tendency has been the persistent definition of communication as a noun so that it is seen less as an activity and more as a product. How often have we heard people say 'I've sent a communication' (e.g. a letter, a telephone message)?

The study of messages, therefore, is probably more aptly termed 'communications'. On the other hand, the study of processes affecting interacting people would more appropriately be termed 'communication'. Some writers (e.g. Mohan, McGregor and Strano, 1992; Taylor, Rosegrant, Meyer and Samples, 1989) have gone so far as to use the word 'communicating' in their book titles to underscore the active, process nature of the phenomenon.

Confusion over what communication means has also been caused by diverse, often incompatible disciplines attempting to focus on a range of common problems and concerns. Like education, 'communication' is preferably described as a field of study consisting of a loosely defined set of issues and unanswered questions. It is probably also true that the field is multidisciplinary rather than interdisciplinary. For example, applied psychologists addressing certain communication problems are unlikely to draw upon terminology and concepts from outside their own discipline. The result is that the present field of communication studies consists of a variety of perspectives, sometimes contradictory, on similar content or subject-matter. Potentially, this is a healthy and promising state of affairs, since the wide scope of the communication field permits inquiry from scholars of many fields. In practice, however, the co-existence of diverse, contradictory perspectives has occasioned contentious debate resulting in a decided lack of consensus on certain issues.

Naturally, theoretical opposites are not easy to resolve, even by zealots trying to unify the field; one of their ploys is to devise a highly selective set of assumptions that excludes other legitimate but non-complementary stances. Some scholars, for example, try to 'psychologise' the field, others draw heavily on sociological theories. The future direction of communication studies depends on whether theorists and researchers are prepared to broaden their narrow disciplinary outlook. Holistic approaches to the study of communication must reflect a spirit of eclecticism and tolerance by contemporary investigators. This is not to suggest that scholars have to compromise their ideals, principles or theoretical commitments in order to promote unity, but to urge investigators to remain open minded. New visions and insights will have some chance of being realised once scholars adopt a more adventurous attitude to multifaceted study, and appreciate the contributions of anthropologists, psychologists, sociologists, philosophers, linguists, mathematicians, economists, artists, and actors as a unique set of resources for the development of a useful theory of communication.

The preceding comments suggest that the quintessential truth about human phenomena is somewhat elusive, since scholars typically design their investigative approaches within their disciplines. Scholarly thinking, therefore, is often confined to concepts central to specific fields of study. The observations above also suggest that such truth will be easier to discover if scholars broaden their thinking beyond their disciplinary confines to newer interdisciplinary perspectives. An example of this kind of broadening is Hofstadter's (1979) cryptic, metaphorical synthesis of musical, mathematical and visual art perspectives to elucidate the concept of infinity. In music, infinity is represented by what Hofstadter describes as the perfect form of musical writing—the canon. Visually, Escher's never-ending staircase is an artistic example of infinity. The science of mathematics has a special symbol for infinity. Thus, infinity can be understood from three different perspectives. Whilst infinity has been traditionally understood from particular disciplinary vantage points, Hofstadter examined three fields in his search for common, complementary themes. His approach exemplifies the one recommended to those studying communication from an adult communication management perspective.

Undoubtedly the present field of communication study contains complementary themes and concepts, but their potential to unify the field has not yet been taken up as a serious challenge since contemporary scholars are usually reluctant to cross the traditional boundaries of interpersonal, speech, organisational and mass communication. The fashionable trend to develop applied theories of communication has also locked investigators into specific needs-dominated contexts: some business communicators, for example, focus on managerial and personnel concerns; and there are communication education specialists who concentrate on explaining and improving instructional practices.

This book, therefore, makes no apology for departing from 'conventional' communication theories to gain insights from other fields. I have, for example, drawn on fiction sources, especially where they have helped to unlock doors to greater understanding.

If a truly comprehensive, practical theory of communication is possible, it should be applicable regardless of context. Whilst this text does not present a fully articulated new world view of communication, it intends to move in that direction. Inevitably, it is based upon several assumptions about the nature of human communication.

Throughout this book, the major assumptions regarding the nature of human communication are:

- *Human communication is fundamentally a social activity*, and therefore mainly concerned with how people relate to, interact with and influence each other.

- *Human communication is also a matter of how people construe images of themselves and of others*. It is affected by how people form impressions of themselves and of others. These impressions result from individual mental interpretations or information processing. In general, communication involves exercising the mind, either consciously or subconsciously. *Communication involves meaning-making*.

- *Human communication is a two-way process*. The Latin derivative 'communis' means 'togetherness' or 'reciprocity'. During the 1950s and 1960s, many human communication researchers regarded the *source* of the message as the only active agent and the receiver of the message as essentially passive. However, receivers are also active as constructors of meaning and, therefore, as communicators. Meaning is not merely an act of decoding but an assignment, by perceivers, of value, importance and interpreted thought to messages received. Effective communication, therefore, occurs when intended messages and receivers' interpretations of these intentions are consistent and reciprocated.

- *Human communication is situational and thus subject to the influence of intervening variables.* Individuals differ in the way they send and receive messages. Many of these individual differences are characteristics which cannot be observed. Our inferences about the motivations of others are, at best, educated guesses based on familiarity and experience. People do not, of course, act in the same way in every situation. They tend to be assertive when they are confident, less so when they are apprehensive.

  Intervening variables include sender and receiver characteristics such as gender, age, intelligence, cognitive style, and personality. They may also be contextual, and include working climate, reward systems, and responses to leadership. The single most confounding variable is **arationality**, the set of unwritten rules that affect role clarity and, therefore, the quality of relationships in organisations (Egan, 1985).

arationality
The unpredictable and undiscussable communication and interpersonal behaviour that characterises the shadow side of organisations and systems. Often associated with organisational politics.

- *Human communication is emotional as well as logical.* Surface meanings are usually articulated in words. I might say to someone 'I love you' without really meaning it. A message is made convincing by nonverbal cues. The way I touch that person may convey my affection more persuasively than my words. My tone of voice and my vocal emphasis may also express something about the value I place on the relationship. For example, if I say '*I* love you', I emphasise my importance as the lover. If I say 'I *love* you', I am reinforcing my feeling for that person. If I say 'I love *you*', you are the sole object of my affections.

  In general, people trust nonverbal messages more than verbal ones. Sometimes our messages are contradictory: these are called 'double-bind' messages. For instance, if I say to my students 'That's an interesting question' and glance at my watch as I say it, my words say that it is an interesting question, but looking at my watch suggests that I am impatient to conclude the class session. At least, that's how some of the students may perceive it. Overall, it is reasonable to suppose that our feelings have an appreciable impact on how we communicate with others. We are rarely devoid of feeling about what we are doing and seldom react to others with clinical detachment.

- *Human behaviour is complex.* Reductionists—for example, of mechanistic or certain behaviouristic persuasions—attempt to split behaviour into convenient observable segments. Some aspects of human behaviour can be isolated, such as reflex actions. What we are and what makes us tick, however, is not accurately indicated by specific cues or words. We are 'whole' beings whose observable actions constitute only a part of our total capacity to communicate and act. The essential difficulty, of course, is that we cannot easily distinguish the mental or emotional processes that motivate our actions, so the accurate interpretation of human communication is complicated by the interplay of unobservable intervening variables. Most studies of human communication are still simplistic since they address surface rather than deep structures of meaning.

- *Human communication is inevitable.* Although much of our communication with others is conscious and deliberate, we also communicate aspects of ourselves to others without consciously intending to do so. For example, the way we groom ourselves and the clothes we wear indicate something of how we see ourselves and how we would like others to see us. Goffman (1959) referred to this communicative function as self-presentation. More recently, Argyle (1976) identified self-presentation as one of three functions central to nonverbal communication.

Much as we may think it possible, it is simply inconceivable, as was intimated earlier, that we cannot not communicate when we enter another person's physical, mental or emotional life-space. True, some people operate in a private 'twilight zone' and fail to attend to observable or nonverbal cues from someone else. Many established relationships have deteriorated for this very reason. Insensitivity has much to do with communication failure since it may generate apprehension or uncertainty. Take the case of a doctor attending to a dying patient. Although the doctor closely monitors the patient's condition, his or her manner in communicating the patient's state to anxious friends or relatives may seem clinically detached, or offhand, and even if the doctor is sympathetic about their feelings, such detachment does little to reduce their apprehension. To this extent, sensitivity is an integral component of human communication competence.

In summary, therefore, the process view of human communication throughout this book is grounded on the seven theoretical assumptions described in this section, although of course these are not the only possible positions. They constitute the philosophical view to which I am committed. The reader is recommended to read Dance's (1982) excellent anthology of various alternative and representative perspectives on human communication theory.

Overview of the Book 1.5

This book is divided into four sections. Part I, consisting of Chapters 1, 2 and 3, focuses on the theoretical foundations of adult communication management. Chapter 2 is primarily concerned with exploring contemporary perspectives on human communication and examines four representative approaches to the process view of communication management outlined earlier in this chapter. The vantage points of relationship, competence, social influence and meaning are analysed in terms of their potential to explain, predict and control communication at both conscious and subliminal levels of awareness. This analysis owes much to the iceberg analogy drawn from the work of Freud, whose pioneer work on the human theory of personality continues to serve as a conceptual model for many contemporary practising psychiatrists.

Chapter 3 details the theoretical foundations of communication management competencies. The notion of self as agent of change is presented here as a basis for the identification and development of personal and professional competencies. In the context of organisation development and change, relationships between communication competence and managerial roles are examined for their potential to improve communication management in work settings.

Part II provides a detailed exposition of critical human communication skills. Chapter 4 focuses on the use of language, especially on the role it plays in meaning-construction and meaning-interpretation. Miscommunication is examined according to common kinds of perceptual and linguistic filters, and the close association between language and thinking is highlighted. Finally, social functions of language are identified, especially current concerns such as managerial etiquette.

Chapter 5 outlines the nature and functions of nonverbal communication. The various subsystems of the nonverbal domain are treated as a field of study in its own right, rather than as a small component of the interpersonal communication field. The chapter explains contemporary views on facial expression, paralanguage, kinesics, proxemics, touching behaviour and the role of clothing in nonverbal communication. It includes a section on the ethics of researching nonverbal communication for those wishing to consolidate the theoretical principles and assumptions developed in this chapter.

Chapter 6 describes listening and assertiveness in terms of the 'Yin-Yang' concept and stresses the importance of empathy, feedback, and the suspension of judgment in listening. The features of assertive, non-assertive and aggressive behaviour are then discussed. Chapter 6 concludes with the generation of strategies for effective listening and assertive behaviour.

Chapter 7 focuses on negotiation and conflict resolution, investigates the origins of interpersonal conflict, and describes the psychological mechanisms that people use when communicating defensively. Methods of overcoming defensive communication (negotiation skills) are suggested, along with strategies for resolving or preventing conflict. The point is also made that conflict is not necessarily counter-productive; it is the essence of a dramaturgical view of human interaction, and an important basis for a problem-solving approach to human communication management.

In Chapter 8, the human communication skills previously outlined are applied to contexts relevant to managers—especially situations requiring equality of opportunity policies. The chapter also emphasises the importance of intercultural variables and how these can be controlled by human communication skills. The increasing rate of technological development is examined in relation to the potential contribution from the human resource development sector of organisations. The remaining sections of Chapter 8 are devoted to practical applications of human communication skills in oral and written presentation.

Part III deals with managerial and personal communication. In Chapter 9 the roles and competencies of human resource managers are examined in relation to day-to-day functions such as interviewing and conducting meetings. Particular attention is paid to the prevention of communication failure by strategies that manage arationality in organisations, and to the concept that a positive organisational climate depends greatly on an awareness of unwanted hidden agendas.

Chapter 10 focuses on issues of personal effectiveness in communication from a human developmental perspective. It analyses the nature of human relationships, the development of interpersonal relationships, and the particular implications of 'culture' at individual and social levels. The unique character of individual 'cultures' and their specific values, attitudes, beliefs, standards and rules are analysed in relation to psychosocial crises, developmental tasks and self-actualisation. Strategies for effective personal growth are also suggested.

Part IV concerns the future. Chapter 11 focuses on understanding, managing and forecasting change. The subliminal aspect of communication management, mentioned in Part I, is reintroduced. In conclusion, the book reinforces the notion that the consideration of people and their needs is crucial for successful communication in organisations.

Summary 1.6

This chapter introduced the concept of adult communication management and, in particular, the importance and inevitability of communication in our daily lives. It proposed a process view of communication management as a basis for establishing a relationship between communication management and communication competence. Finally, the nature of human communication was explained in terms of cognitive processes involving the construction and interpretation of meaning.

Discussion Questions 1.7

1. Describe three occasions when your ability to communicate with others (or another person) was crucial. What would have happened in each instance if your communication management behaviour was unsuccessful?
2. What was your view of communication and communication management before reading this chapter? Has your perspective now changed? If so, how?
3. Are there any deficiencies or weaknesses you would like to bridge as a communication manager? Write them down. How would you redress them?

1.8 Activities

1. Experiment: When you are with someone, try *not* to communicate with that person. Write a brief report on whether you managed this or not. Give reasons for your result.

2. List your strengths as a communicator and next to each item indicate the situations in which these strengths are most obvious.

3. List the situations in which you feel diffident or lack confidence as a communicator. Devise a plan to increase your level of confidence.

4. Select at least one book from the following reading list and read at least the introductory chapter.

1.9 Key Terms

Communication competence
Communication management
Constructivism
Human systems
Interpersonal construct systems
People-in-systems

1.10 Recommended Reading

DeVito, J. A. (1981) *Communication: concepts and processes*, Englewood Cliffs, New Jersey: Prentice Hall.

Hybels, S. and Weaver, R. L. (1986) *Communicating effectively*, New York: Random House.

Myers, G. E. and Myers, M. T. (1988) *The dynamics of human communication: a laboratory approach*, New York: McGraw-Hill.

Roloff, M. E. and Miller, G. R. (1987) *Interpersonal processes: new directions in communication research*, California: Sage.

Taylor, A., Rosegrant, T., Meyer, A. and Samples, B. T. (1989) *Communication*, 5th edn, New Jersey: Prentice Hall.

Contemporary Perspectives of Human Communication

2

All our knowledge has its origins in our perceptions.
Leonardo Da Vinci (1452–1519)

To know all things is not permitted.
Horace (65–68 BC)

How much can we really know about others with whom we communicate? To what extent are our relationships with others based on what is perceivable in us and in those interacting with us? These two very important questions are considered in this chapter as we look at different ways of understanding the process of communication. We examine four theoretical perspectives. First, communication is discussed in terms of human relationships. The various kinds of relationships we have with others are described in connection with our need to understand why these relationships can become stronger or weaker. The second perspective is **social influence**, which involves two important concepts: **persuasion** and **credibility**. The third perspective concerns communication competence and the important question here is 'how can this competence perspective help us determine what to do to improve our communication with others?' Finally, the chapter examines communication as the way people build and share meanings about their relationships and interpersonal interactions. All four perspectives contribute to an understanding of how people manage the communication process.

Learning Objectives

After studying the ideas, arguments and suggestions presented in this chapter you should be able to do the following:

- Give at least one reason why it is difficult to 'know' other people completely.

- Briefly outline how communication can be explained in terms of different kinds of human relationships.

- Describe communication from a social influence perspective.

- Offer at least one meaning of *communication competence*.

- Explain human communication in terms of the building and sharing of meanings between people.

- Show how the four perspectives of human communication are complementary and how they contribute to our understanding of how people manage their communication with others.

2.1 The Tip of the Iceberg

So much of what we do and feel is misunderstood or misinterpreted by others, partly because we do not reveal ourselves totally to others. To our close relations, friends and professional colleagues, we disclose whatever information we think they would appreciate or tolerate. To passing acquaintances we seldom exchange more than pleasantries or trivial conversation.

According to Freud (1938), our base impulses and urges reside in that part of our mind called the 'id'. Our id largely determines the 'libido' or driving force in our lives, but we tend to repress our urges with various psychological defence mechanisms, mainly because our innermost and private motivations are seldom either socially or legally acceptable. People whose behaviour and communication are controlled by their urges run the serious risk of committing criminal acts; for example, individuals who cannot control their sexual impulses may resort to rape or aggravated sexual assault.

Consequently, what we display of ourselves when we interact with other people is a self-image constituted of those features we construe to be socially and legally acceptable. Frequently, what we really want to say or do to others is repressed, at least under 'normal' circumstances. People who hate their immediate superiors at work rarely communicate such hatred directly—usually it is indicated nonverbally. Essentially, however, only a portion of a person's self is manifest. The rest of the iceberg remains submerged.

The fact that we usually communicate with others at a level of partial disclosure suggests that many of our interactions with people are affected by hidden agendas which we keep to ourselves. In some situations we may appear to be negotiating rationally, whilst privately we intend to persuade, manipulate or conquer someone we regard as an adversary—a good deal of human communication is adversarial. Much as we would like all our communication with others to be constructive and productive, good intentions are not always shared. Of course, in many situations good intentions are shared. However, while we may expect other people's good intentions, we cannot be sure these always underlie communication directed at us.

People tend to respond to and interact with others on the basis of observable information, although in many business or political contexts the acceptance of another at face value is often registered as a sign of naivety. Whilst it is important to realise that openness does not always typify human communication, expectations that people will communicate openly often result in great disappointment. No matter how close we think we are to another, we cannot afford the luxury of thinking that we know that person through and through. Does a married person reveal to his or her marriage partner the existence of a lover? How often does a person of mediocre ability admit to anything but the potential to reach a standard of excellence?

Human communication is not always what it appears to be. Although we may not be able to modify the outward appearances of face-to-face encounters, we can acknowledge the likelihood of other variables. Whilst these variables are not usually observable, we must remain aware of them so that we do not accept information at face value—especially not in the world of people management. So often we say one thing when we mean something else, simply to avoid confrontation or hurting someone. For example, it is not easy to discipline a misguided but well-intentioned maverick. Very often, it is a matter of rechannelling their energy, but this is difficult because individual frames of reference may not concur. In other words, managers may not think the same way as employees do, and priorities often differ. People play communication games when they should lay their cards on the table—but this makes them vulnerable. Face-to-face communication does not tell the full story about the people interacting; there is always a degree of uncertainty because of the possibility of undisclosed information.

Bearing this in mind, we shall proceed to examine what is so far known or proposed about human communication processes. The following sections focus on four different perspectives, all of which need to address the caveats outlined in the present section, especially the need to remember that knowledge of other people's intentions is often based on limited observable information.

The Relationship Perspective   2.2

Interest in human relationships is probably as longstanding as the history of the human race. Great tragedians of the past, such as the Grecian Sophocles and the Elizabethan Shakespeare, endeavoured to explain the grand passions and motivations of famous figures. Again, Homer's classic, *The Odyssey*, described the contentions of two mighty nations as a result of an intense relationship between Helen of Greece and Paris of Troy.

Many comparatively recent studies of human relationships in the framework of interpersonal communication theory have been concerned largely with patterns of friendship and acquaintance outside the context of work (Kaye, 1985:43; Monge, Backman, Dillard and Eisenberg, 1982:505). However, the significance of human relationships in organisational effectiveness has been emphasised by well-known contemporary writers (Blanchard and Johnson, 1984; Peters and Waterman, 1984). In their best-seller, *The One-Minute Manager*, Blanchard and Johnson suggest that good managers can say 'the best minute I spend is the one I invest in people'. Investment in people, therefore, is an important aspect of a communication management rationale for the development of professional relationships.

Deterioration and failure in professional relationships is often reported in the media. For example, we hear and read of challenges to leaders of political parties, both at home and abroad. The persistence of such organisational problems led Peters and Waterman (1984) to suggest the principle of *productivity through people*, which entails getting people involved and enthusiastic about their work. As Peters (1987:286) has also suggested, 'truly involved people can do anything!' Managerial effectiveness may therefore depend on an ability to foster satisfactory professional relationships on the job.

To promote productivity through people, managers need to clarify the kinds of roles and attendant responsibilities that individual employees should assume. The term **role** is perhaps easily understood as the 'hat' a person wears at any point in time. For example, Laird (1978) suggested that a training and development manager wears, at different times, administrator, consultant, designer and instructor hats.

We do not, of course, always wear our different hats comfortably. For example, a training manager may feel at ease when performing the roles of consultant or administrator, but less comfortable in an instructor's role, usually undertaken by subordinate training officers. Whilst the ability to engage in subordinate staff activities may well be crucial to a manager's perceived credibility, the fact that some managers occasionally perform certain roles less comfortably than they would like presupposes the possibility that these managers may simply avoid performing these roles so as to reduce any uncertainty or apprehension in communicating with others.

Since the successful performance of roles is an important determinant of stable, viable personal and professional relationships, strategies to minimise **role ambiguity** and **role overload** are important too. **Role clarity** means that people know precisely what is expected of them and what is expected of their colleagues. A good job description contains a clear, precise statement of duties and responsibilities. It can contribute much to the establishment and maintenance of role clarity in organisations.

Just as role clarity is an important determinant of effective interpersonal and professional relationships, role ambiguity can destabilise relationships in organisations. It usually occurs when an individual is identified with two or more individuals or groups that have different or incompatible goals. When individual roles and areas of responsibility are poorly differentiated in team or group situations, people often tread on others' toes by engaging in work or activities which other team members may consider to be related to their own territories. Role ambiguity can also result in the neglect of certain tasks because they are considered by one and all to be 'someone else's job'. Take, for example, a committee planning a conference. If the various member functions are not clearly set out, work may be duplicated, perhaps with discrepancies such as contradictory publicity brochures or catering arrangements. Resultant tension may thus weaken the group's capacity to achieve corporate goals.

Role overload can incur another undesirable possibility. When people wear too many different hats, the additional burdens may weaken their overall efficiency. Role overload poses the risk of moving people away from expertise to mediocrity. Inexpert workers sometimes volunteer to take on extra roles on the pretext that 'if you can't be brilliant, be useful!' In some organisations managers' encouragement of staff members to take too many initiatives can be counter-productive; it can lead to the arational development of role flexibility. This means that individuals may neglect

---

role
Expectations and/or performances associated with positions in human systems. In simple terms, a 'hat' one wears for a specific occasion or circumstance.

role ambiguity
Occurs when we are unsure about the limits and scope of our duties or spheres of responsibility; can result in duplicating others' work or failing to carry out tasks we thought were assigned to someone else.

role overload
Occurs when people assume or are given more roles and responsibilities than they can manage.

role clarity
Occurs when interdependent individuals understand how their particular duties or spheres of responsibility complement or are distinct from those of others.

their assigned responsibilities and decide for themselves what their professional priorities are. This may lead to work simply not getting done. Blame for productivity failure would very probably make relationships deteriorate.

People need to establish different kinds of professional and interpersonal relationships in organisational settings. Six distinct types of relationship are readily identifiable:

Individual to Individual

This kind of relationship exists at peer level and at the status-differentiated level. At the peer level, two employees of the same status in an organisation may, for example, focus their attention on intradepartmental or interdepartmental matters of mutual concern. At the status-differentiated level, relationships between superiors and subordinates often, of necessity, develop on a face-to-face basis, and these relationships are put to the test when status difference becomes a lever for the exercise of authority and coercive power. A general manager may have to discipline a staff member, thereby exerting authority and/or power; a union delegate may be able to wield power over a high-ranking executive by resorting to industrial strategies such as imposing work bans or invoking state or federal union support.

Individual to individual relationships may be characterised by degrees of intimacy and disclosure more typically associated with friendship. In relationships of this kind the interdependency between two individuals differs from the type of interdependency found in professional relationships where it is highly task-oriented. Friendships usually require an interdependency that is qualitatively emotional.

Individual to Group

These relationships also occur at both peer and status-differentiated levels. Committee or board meetings have interactions which exemplify a formal kind of individual to group relationship at the status-differentiated level when the chairperson is appointed or assumes the position *ex officio*. In democratically constituted groups where the leader is elected, the relationship between the chairperson and the other group members is sometimes characterised by a greater degree of peer acceptance.

The nature of individual to group relationships varies according to the type of goal or task involved. If the group is task-directed or engaged in some problem-solving exercise, individual to group relationships are likely to be more formal; if the group is engaged in enhancing its maintenance and/or survival, much of the interaction between members will be probably less formal and less subject to meeting management rules.

In some individual to group relationships, the individual, as temporary leader, may occupy a position of lower status than that of the remaining group members. For example, the individual session leader in a training session may have a middle-management position, whereas the trainees may be upper-level executives. In these circumstances specific sessional rules may need to be set out to protect the trainer from the pressure of such a status difference. For example, one sessional rule may be that the senior manager cannot use a staff member's statements in the session as a basis for future disciplinary action. Regardless of whether the relationship is formal or informal, or based on equality or status differentiation, competence in communication management is vital if effort is to be fully co-ordinated.

Individual to Organisation

When collections of people become so large that they lose 'group quality', they become aggregates or crowds. This means that the numbers are so excessive that interpersonal interactions between any of the members become difficult or impossible without a co-ordinator or chair. These individual to organisation interactions or encounters are more often characterised by mass communication properties than by interpersonal communication. For example, lecture courses involving large audiences are claimed to be highly impersonal since audience participation is relatively minimal. Of course, in such situations a good deal of nonverbal interaction and exchange takes place. Thus, communication in individual to organisation relationships may be two-way at the nonverbal level, even though it is usually one-way at the verbal level.

People communicate and relate to each other nonverbally in lecture classes

Since personal exchanges between the individual and audience are highly unlikely in these relationships, the communication flow is almost invariably formal. For example, a union leader addressing a stop-work meeting usually employs rhetoric that is formal rather than conversational. On the other hand, Sunday afternoon demagogues in a city's public domain may invite—or provoke—individual responses.

Another characteristic of individual to organisation relationships is the speaker's ploy of persuasive appeals, which commonly rely on fear, humour, intensity of language (including emotive terms) and reasoned argument. Many entertainers and after-dinner speakers use humour to appeal to their audiences and to get their messages across. Charismatic political leaders and public figures use intensity of language or intimidation to invoke specific audience reactions. Finally, the success of reasoned argument usually depends on the magnitude of the issue or controversy under consideration or debate. Resolutions are often impeded because emotional exchanges prevail over logic.

Group to Individual

Many group to individual relationships are psychologically threatening, particularly when the individual concerned feels confronted and on the defensive—for example, in the selection interview where a panel or senior staff appraise a candidate for employment and pose questions that are 'loaded', leading or framed as a forced choice. The interviewee may resort to psychological defence mechanisms such as rationalisation, projection, repression or displaced aggression to justify his or her stance on an issue. A similar situation arises when the creator of a marketing or advertising concept defends it before a senior management team representing a potential client or customer.

In some group to individual relationships, however, the psychological climate is decidedly one of safety. Certain organisations, for example, have 'support' groups to ensure that individuals are not disadvantaged or discriminated against. These support groups are often elected to give workers sufficient opportunities for participation in decision-making. Groups formed to support or protect the rights of individuals usually have free flows of communication, particularly when strict confidentiality is the rule.

Group to Group

These relationships rarely advance beyond an impersonal or formal level in organisations. They often take place when the solution of a persistent organisational problem requires two kinds of input. In these circumstances, communication flows are usually co-ordinated formally with a chairperson normally acting as gatekeeper. When two groups encounter each other, social identity is likely to predominate over personal identity. Whilst individuals may relate to others by whispering or passing written notes in group meetings, the overt level of communication remains largely formal since comments or questions to individuals are traditionally directed to and through the chairperson. Group to group relationships can also be adversarial. For example, union officials meeting with a senior management team may find it impossible to adopt anything less than an uncompromising stance in order to secure their demands or to negotiate a fair result.

Group to Organisation

When groups or subsystems relate to an organisation as a whole, communication is rarely personal—written messages are the norm. One method in current use is the Delphi technique which typically requires departmental responses from all sections of an organisation to the executive or senior management group's inquiries.

Whilst group to organisation communication can bring into the open significant quantities of information, suggestions or proposals rarely reflect individual initiatives or concerns. More often than not, leaders' selective interpretations of their own group's consensus are conveyed to the managerial decision-makers.

Group to organisation relationships suffer when the organisation's mission statement is vague and not clearly articulated to all its members. One interesting exercise is to ask randomly selected members of an organisation to state its mission. If the mission statement samples differ considerably, the organisation may be in trouble, since its members could be operating according to personal perceptions and interpretations of its goals.

Relationship clarity is attained when expectations about the integration and distribution of work coincide, regardless of whether the relationship is between individuals, between an individual and a group, or between groups. On the other hand, the simultaneous presence of *divergent* expectations is likely to lead to relationship conflict. To maintain relationship clarity in organisations, managers must deal with the following three questions:

relationship clarity
Convergence of people's expectations about the integration and distribution of work.

- With whom must particular individuals communicate so that the work of the system is satisfactorily accomplished?

- In what ways must certain people collaborate or co-operate with other individuals or other units so that tasks are competently managed and performed?·

- How is the work of the system or organisation to be co-ordinated? Organisational structure encompasses more than roles, responsibilities and relationships; authority and decision-making power are also needed to co-ordinate and integrate organisational roles and relationships.

Perhaps it is clear now that the ability to relate well with professional colleagues—subordinates, peers or superiors—is a critical aspect of communication management competence. Failure often incurs 'pinches' or 'crunches' (Sherwood and Glidewell, 1973). Pinches are subtle disruptions of expectations about work roles. Their effect is entropic, usually leading to the tendency for organisations to degenerate and, ultimately, self-destruct. Defensive tactics, for example the avoidance of discussion or reactions such as fear of renegotiation, are typical of pinches.

'Crunches' occur when pinches are not handled well, and are characterised by neglected emotional crises. There are two types of crunches. The first, 'explosion', often results when people in relationships fail to come to terms with a disruption of shared expectations, and their pent-up feelings explode once the relationship crisis becomes unmanageable. The second type of crunch, called 'implosion', usually involves personal conflicts that are not brought into the open, so that people's feelings rankle and become subjective. They then tend to take a course of action governed by these feelings, without discussing it first— they may plot revenge or to 'get even' with someone.

There are at least four ways in which people attempt to handle crunches. Most of these approaches are ineffective, or what Egan (1985) calls *conspiratorial*—for example, the recourse to 'smoothing things over'. Whilst the parties concerned may apologise and agree to let bygones be bygones, or even to agree to disagree, they fail to deal with the issues that gave rise to the conflict, so that the crunch is merely set aside and seldom resolved.

Another ineffective tactic, *resentful termination,* refers to people's decision not to work with or have anything further to do with someone they find difficult to relate to. Unfortunately, this tactic is, in effect, a decision not to seek a solution to the prevailing crunch. It is not a constructive way to stabilise a relationship.

Ignoring crunches can gradually destroy relationships. Letting the relationship die means that dialogue and communication becomes lifeless. Avoidance approaches of this kind lead to the pretence that the relationship is worth preserving.

The best way to manage conflict in relationships is to plan for periodic review and the renegotiation of roles. Revisions can then be incorporated into a relational contract which may be either formal or subject to informal consensus. The contemporary practice of performance counselling can be used for this kind of planned review and renegotiation of relationship problems.

Although relationships can be understood in terms of a continuum ranging from unfamiliarity or zero contact to increasing levels of mutuality (Levinger and Snoek, 1972), in professional and organisational settings human relationships do not necessarily escalate to levels of intimacy. Naturally, where colleagues at work also become close friends, relationships can be identified as 'intimate', since they often involve a good deal of self-disclosure. However, most relationships are of the 'surface contact' kind because most of the dialogue tends to be work-related or task-oriented.

According to Forgas (1985), many relevant variables contribute to the development of personal relationships, including physical attractiveness, social and demographic similarity, attitude similarity and attraction, complementarity of needs, competence and attraction, self-esteem and attraction, positive personal characteristics and attraction, reciprocity and attraction, gain and loss effects in relationships and self-disclosure. Many of these are clearly associated with attraction or 'liking' behaviour, so it is important to weigh the significance of each variable in terms of the degree to which it influences people's liking for each other.

If there is any truth in the age-old saying that familiarity breeds contempt, there is reason to suspect that the importance of attraction as a determinant of stable relationships may decline. On the other hand, whilst complementarity of needs may be less significant a factor in the initial phases of relationship development, it is likely to assume greater importance once attraction between people begins to weaken.

We conclude this section by suggesting that the development and maintenance of effective personal and professional relationships represent special kinds of adult communication management competencies. Several interpersonal skills are examined in subsequent chapters in the context of their role in the development and maintenance of relationships. For the present, however, our awareness of the factors contributing to relationship maintenance or failure provides a valuable starting point in building good relationships.

2.3 The Social Influence Perspective

Scholars in the field of social influence use a set of operational terms such as persuasion, credibility and compliance-gaining. In general, the concentration of research on the persuasive properties of messages and the factors comprising a speaker's credibility extended from the 1940s to comparatively recent years. **Persuasion** was regarded as a process which presupposed some attitude change by others as a desired end-product. According to Irwin (1983:8):

> Research conducted under the banner of persuasion emphasised mechanistic, cause-effect studies of attitude and behaviour changes brought about by message transmission. This type of research became increasingly out of place as dialogic views of interpersonal communication overtook monologic ones, and as acceptance grew for the cognitive power of human beings to process received messages.

Much of the early work on persuasion and attitude change was attributable to the 'Yale group' which included luminaries like Hovland. Reflecting on the pioneering efforts of the Yale group in research on persuasion and attitude change, Miller and Burgoon (1978) reasoned that Hovland and his colleagues had conceived an approach that assumed social influence to be a linear, undirectional process typically associated with mass communication settings. As a result, speech communication theorists and rhetoricians began to pay close attention to the persuasive impact of messages expressed by politicians, religious demagogues and other famous leaders attempting to influence large audiences. In the past two decades, when television as a communication medium became the subject of intense inquiry, investigators like Salamon (1979) and Postman (1986) have examined how the media have shaped and altered the nature of human discourse and presentation from an individual to group communication perspective.

Contemporary theories about persuasion have progressed beyond the identification of the persuasive properties of message and speaker. However, the current tendency to research in isolation the situational variables that can influence behavioural choices has failed to yield a broad explanation of persuasive communication that tries to promote attitudinal or behavioural change (Reardon, 1981). To understand the effect of a persuasive attempt by one person upon another person's belief and attitude system, a complex model of cognitive processing must be delineated.

The recent decline of systematic research on persuasion is not due to a lack of interest by pragmatists in the field. For example, 'compendiums of persuasive devices' as well as 'decalogues for persuaders' have been developed. These compendiums refer to devices like repetition and scapegoating since these have been claimed to work 'much of the time'. The decalogues consist of sets of axiomatic injunctions such as having clear objectives, using language that is unambiguous, appropriate and forceful, and speaking fluently, directly and with vocal variety to ensure clarity and emphasis. Despite the disrepute that a scholarly denigration of early research on persuasion may incite, we should remember, as Callan, Gallois and Noller (1986: 3) suggest, that 'marketing would not be where it is today were it not for the basic research on persuasion conducted in the 1940s and 1950s'. Whether this is a desirable outcome or not is, of course, debatable.

Common examples of people's attempts to influence or persuade others to think, feel or behave differently are abundantly evident. With unrelenting frequency we are enjoined, for instance, to purchase certain products or subscribe to a variety of services offered on a competitive market. Many of these persuasive attempts occur via the media—print, billboards, radio and television. Sometimes, however, persuasive appeals are made personally. Volunteer collectors for charity often make random telephone calls or present their messages in person through doorknock campaigns. Evidence of early exposure of individuals to opportunities for developing persuasive skills can be found in the scouts' bob-a-job drive and in the increasingly popular requests for support of 'thon' ventures such as telethons, walkathons, and mini-marathons of the city-to-surf kind. In all these types of persuasive enterprises, children and adults-in-the-making are becoming sensitised to persuasive appeals and techniques.

The techniques of persuasion have interested philosophers and social scientists since Aristotle. Much attention has been paid to aspects of speech delivery to ensure that the intended message has been well received. Even today, numerous commercial courses on promoting skilful presentation are advertised widely and heavily subscribed. The thin veneer of theoretical rationales characterising these kinds of courses usually provides only a modicum of respectability for their essentially pragmatic, experiential learning activities. In many cases, the hustling such strategies involve is symptomatic of a reliance on the powerful pronouncements of the 19th century elocutionists (Hoffman, 1970). For instance, some modern presentation skills trainers encourage trainees to practise and cultivate gestures or poses evidently typifying characteristics or qualities such as heroic stance, self-assurance, vitality or exaltation.

Early research on the process of persuasion was based on several theoretical positions, most of which emerged from the discipline of psychology. The contributions of learning theory, for example, have been considerable. Nevertheless, attempts to explain the persuasion process in terms of classical or operant conditioning models have been mechanistic, and have therefore ignored the potential effects of subliminal variables. Perhaps one of the learning theorists' most significant discoveries was the association between a receiver's acceptance of a message and the **credibility** of the message sender or source.

credibility (source credibility)
Attitude of a receiver toward a message source; made up of factors such as competence (expertise), trustworthiness and dynamism.

In essence, credibility may be described as the attitude of a receiver toward the source of a message (McCroskey, 1978). High credibility occurs when the message source is competent (or expert), trustworthy (or reliable) and dynamic (Berlo, Lemert and Mertz, 1970). Note, however, that the message receivers need not be regarded as the passive victims of some powerful persuader. 'Persuadees' do, after all, decide either to accept or reject appeals. In short, people do think, reason, feel and act in ways they find comfortable and natural. For example, a person who is not typically assertive may not find it easy to alter their style of action just because a message promises a reward. If the source of the message has high credibility in the eyes of the perceiver, the message is much more likely to be accepted, and therefore acted upon as intended.

How and why are we persuaded? This depends partly on our perceptions of a source's credibility. Our reactions to a persuasive message are also governed by the kinds of appeals we characteristically respond to. For example, if we have a keen sense of humour we will probably react favourably to messages that tantalise our funny bones. On the other hand, humorous messages may have less impact on those who are naturally serious and respond to a more thoughtful or reasoned, logical statement.

Similarly, most of us realise that fear appeals have different effects on individuals. All cigarette packets today carry the warning that smoking is a health hazard. Nevertheless, many persistent smokers do not appear to have been sufficiently deterred by this fear appeal. Even the tactic of citing the late film star Yul Brynner (who died of lung cancer) has not entirely succeeded in reinforcing the anti-smoking message.

Fear appeals can be subtly persuasive

Two other examples of fear appeal occur in the television commercials and community awareness campaigns concerning AIDS and random breath testing. In both cases, audiences have been threatened with the dire consequences of persisting in illegal or medically dangerous behaviour. Although many individuals acknowledge the soundness of such warnings, their behaviour patterns are not necessarily changed by deterrent messages alone; additional information to impress upon receivers the attractiveness of safer, more acceptable conduct is probably necessary. Humorous variants of slogans originally intended to be serious have perhaps weakened the potential of messages to produce attitude or behaviour change—for example, the bumper sticker referring to the low-budget Mini-Moke vehicle produced by the British Motor Corporation: 'Moking is not a wealth hazard.'

Closely associated with fear appeal is the persuasive device of emotive language. Taken out of their more familiar contexts, words like 'rape' still evoke images of brutality and violence. For example, a politician may be accused of 'raping the country' when new taxes are proposed or when public spending is cut. Germaine Greer (1971:16) described a male-dominated society as 'the castration of women'. Emotive sexual terms like rape and castration can be very persuasive when applied to social practices, actions and issues.

Although most of us would like to think that we are usually creatures of reason, we do not necessarily become persuaded by messages that are syllogistically or logically correct. Unless trained to detect logical fallacies, we are often naively prone to accept persuasive messages at face value and thus to internalise faulty reasoning. You may find useful the writings of such authors as Fearnside (1980), Beardsley (1979), Crossley and Wilson (1981) or Thouless (1976) on the topic of reasoning.

Currently, researchers and theorists addressing issues of social influence have moved away from the concept of persuasion to considerations of **compliance-gaining** and **compliance-resisting**. In 1984, the summer issue of the journal *Human Communication Research* featured articles on sequential-request strategies in compliance-gaining (Dillard, Hunter and Burgoon, 1984), contingency rules theory, context, and compliance behaviours (Smith, 1984), the discourse of requests with respect to the assessment of a compliance-gaining approach (Tracy, Craig, Smith and Spisak, 1984), and compliance-gaining message selection behaviour (Boster and Stiff, 1984). Despite these new orientations, the term 'persuasion' has continued to occur (e.g. O'Keefe, 1990; Dillard, 1993; Roskos-Ewoldsen and Fazio, 1992; Leichty and Applegate, 1991).

In general, the study of social influence has not diminished despite the attempts by some contemporary authors to create a different concept of this sub-field. What is happening, of course, is a redefinition of persuasion as a process devoid of machiavellian strategies. Elsewhere I have suggested that it is reasonable to apply knowledge from social influence research to the facilitator role of training and development professionals (Kaye, 1985). One way this has been done is through the technique of 'process consultation' (PC) where communicative ability is essential. Lange (1982) has claimed that both communication and persuasion are central requirements in process consultation. There is an emphasis on client involvement and at various stages of this involvement either the client or the facilitator may need to use persuasion. These stages may require initial contracts or agreements, the establishment of the facilitator's competence and credibility, and finding ways to overcome resistance to consultation.

compliance-gaining
Producing messages intended to influence others' attitudes, behaviour and communication.

compliance-resisting
People's approaches to resisting or combating the influence of compliance-gaining messages directed at them.

2.4 The Competence Perspective

Competence is an elusive term. What does it mean to be 'competent'? Professor L.J. Peter studied it comprehensively, and Peter and Hull (1975) developed the 'Peter Principle' which states that 'In a hierarchy every employee tends to rise to his [sic] level of incompetence'. More recently, Peter (1986) developed his theory of hierarchiology which explains how and why individuals climb or descend bureaucratic ladders.

As a starting-point, let's ask whether competence in communicating with others can also fall prey to the Peter Principle. For example, does communication competence at middle-management level follow through to the upper level? Can additional training guarantee competence in new as well as familiar situations? In short, can competence be transferred from one context to another?

It is true, of course, that certain communication competencies are generic. Many job advertisements now require applicants to possess 'good' and 'excellent' communication skills. Although these skills are rarely referred to in any more specific way, the skills usually required involve listening, managing and interpreting nonverbal behaviour, assertiveness, negotiating, persuasion, and oral and written language (Kaye and McArthur, 1993).

One of the main problems with the competence perspective is that some scholars and many practitioners still believe that communication competencies can be treated in behavioural or measurable terms. However, good interpersonal communication involves attention to feelings as well as to words and actions. Developing some basis for appraising one's competence in the reception and expression of emotional cues, for example, is in one sense more complex a task than the generation of criteria to evaluate competence in written communication.

Another problem with the competence perspective is that competence is often equated with excellence, yet a competent person may not necessarily excel in his/her job. For example, a director may be able to keep the organisation running, without showing much creativity or innovation. In this sense, the director is competent, because the organisation continues to function, but not excellent since the organisation is not moving toward new challenges or goals.

During the 1980s competence emerged as one of the principal research and pedagogic concerns in the field of interpersonal communication (Bostrom, 1984; Parks, 1985). Early work in this area focused on the identification of the relevant skills, including empathy, suspension of judgment, ownership of feelings and thoughts, self-disclosure, and behavioural flexibility. These skills were closely associated with listening ability and are still regarded as integral elements.

From the practitioner's point of view, the most significant issue is performance indicators: what characterises a skilled communicator? There is no simple answer. It is apparent, though, that communication competence is a relational phenomenon (Irwin, 1985)—a person's communication competence cannot be determined without reference to the effects on the receiver(s). This is particularly true in mass communication situations where audience reaction is the main gauge of source credibility.

One vital point is that communication competence does not necessarily develop as a consequence of awareness of how to communicate. Although it is not difficult to make people aware of their communication deficiencies, awareness does not guarantee their conscious attempt to change. Change will occur only when individuals accept the necessity to change. This will happen only when individuals are motivated, for extrinsic or intrinsic reasons, to alter their patterns of behaving and communicating.

Current research into communication competence is still dominated by 'an ideology of performance' (Irwin, 1985:29), and is still formulating the guidelines or specifications for competent communication. It is also still assumed that following such guidelines will guarantee that readers or perceivers will achieve this competence.

No evidence exists, at present, to suggest that people become more competent in communicating by obeying guidelines or rules. What complicates the issue is that rules cannot apply consistently to each individual. Since communication, particularly interpersonal communication, is a relational process, communication competence must be seen as a set of specific abilities within specific relationship contexts, regardless of whether these relationships are private or professional.

According to Irwin (1985:29), 'increased emphasis will be placed upon situational competence, including communication competence in vocational settings'. This claim suggests that although a core of interpersonal communication competencies can be identified, applications will vary depending upon their specific contexts. The nature of specific relationships will determine how people must act to become competent. In vocational education settings, for example, there are two major communication competencies that inexperienced teachers and trainers feel they need to develop (Kaye, 1992). One is the ability to overcome the fear of facing large groups or audiences—this is a form of 'communication apprehension'. The other is the ability to manage and resolve conflict between themselves and their learners.

Uncertainties of present research should not, however, deter the reader from experimentation. This text, therefore, proceeds on the premise that the reader will play an active part in self-improvement by addressing the issues presented in this commentary.

The Perspective Of Meaning   2.5

Communication implies more than the simple exchange of messages. If it is to be effective, the messages must be carefully encoded or conveyed. The transmitted message must also be interpreted in terms of the sender's intentions. In a very real sense, communication is about thinking. More precisely, it is concerned with the construction of meaning. Generally, people act toward others on the basis of how they construe others' dispositions and behaviour. These constructions (meanings) are, in turn, influenced by individual value systems, beliefs and attitudes. Think for a moment about committed Labor or Liberal voters. Such voters have developed a frame of reference for their thinking and consequent actions. The frame of reference is usually governed by the political values, beliefs and attitudes that have been nurtured by their personal and social experiences.

As communicators, we attribute meaning to events or phenomena that are observable as, for example, spectators at a football match draw their own conclusions about a referee's fairness in ruling on penalties or other decisions. These meanings provide a basis for subsequent communicative behaviour and language, and are eventually incorporated into our cognitive schemes—the mental mechanisms we use to construct meanings about new situations and events. Cognitive schemes are partly made up of word labels to classify experience—usually adjectives or descriptive phrases.

Meaning-centred communication theorists call these descriptive words or phrases *constructs*, and usually define them as *bipolar* adjectives. Some constructs are physical (e.g tall-short), others are psychological (e.g. friendly-unfriendly); the latter apply to our impressions of the actions and dispositions of others. Constructs thus represent the materials we draw upon to attribute meaning to communicative events. **Attribution of meaning** is often causal and applied to answer 'why' questions. For example, we make attributions of meaning as personal explanations or interpretations of why people are verbally hostile or deceptive, or about someone's personality or dispositions. In simple terms, we may conclude that someone behaved in a certain way because that person is stubborn, narrow, or vindictive; or we might decide that some situational element(s) could account for that person's behaviour—for example, an unexpected delay before an interview.

Obviously, explanations of events or actions are often incomplete, so we can only act on available (usually observable) data. In such circumstances, our attributions may conflict with the intentions of the message sender, and we may interpret behaviour inaccurately. Nevertheless, our attributions form the basis of our subsequent communication and action.

For contemporary meaning-centred communication theory, accuracy in constructing meanings remains the central and most critical issue. Much of the research on accuracy has tended to focus on individual difference variables such as cognitive complexity, age and age-related developmental concerns, male-female differences and a number of 'self-related' notions like self-monitoring. As well, accuracy in encoding and decoding nonverbal cues has received considerable attention (Rosenthal, Hall, DiMatteo, Rogers and Archer, 1979; Cook, 1984). Whilst the quest for determining bases of accuracy in constructing meanings continues to be vexatious, the reality remains that construed meanings will be acted upon by communicators, regardless of whether those meanings are accurately or inaccurately formed.

The present interest in the meaning-centred perspective of human communication theory is largely due to the work of scholars at the University of Illinois. Their theory, known as *constructivism*, is comprehensively

attribution of meaning
Explaining or suggesting reasons why people behave or communicate as they do.

explained by Delia, O'Keefe and O'Keefe (1982). The constructivist theory is essentially an eclectic one, weaving together principles and concepts drawn from several established theoretical positions. Thus, constructivism relates construct theory (Kelly, 1955) to the 'naive psychology' basis for contemporary attribution theory (Heider, 1958). In turn, the relationship between construct theory and attribution theory is set in the context of human development. The developmental orientation derives from Werner's (1957:126) Orthogenetic Principle, which holds that through human development, cognitive systems or schemes become more complex, more organised and more abstract.

Note that constructivism has been described as the most thoughtful research enterprise to be developed in the field of 'thinking about thinking' (Tompkins, 1982:79–81). In this review of eight contemporary theories of human communication, Tompkins said:

> . . . we have only one candidate for the status of a full-blown theory, and that candidate is constructivisim . . . only the constructivists have in the main generated their own philosophy of science, their own philosophical anthropology, their own research strategy, and their own research data. (pp. 80–81)

To summarise, constructivism may be regarded as a theoretical basis for understanding and explaining the meaning-centred perspective of human communication. Constructivism's social cognition orientation underscores the importance of interpretive processes as determinants of subsequent actions and communicative behaviour. As well, individually constructed meanings constitute the substantive impetus for impression formation and related person perception processes.

A Theoretical Framework for Developing Communication Management 2.6

The preceding review of four representative theoretical perspectives on human communication has outlined their distinct orientations to explaining interpersonal communication processes and how their complementing features enable us to understand how people interact and relate to each other. It is hoped that the four approaches clarify adult communication management principles.

Any holistic view of communication management must take into account that certain variables—thoughts, feelings, values, beliefs and attitudes—may never become accessible as data sources for interpreting communicative acts or events. People's perceptions of why others communicate as they do are therefore always likely to derive from imperfect (i.e. incomplete) information.

On the other hand, the four approaches provide some structure for people to interpret and explain how and why interpersonal communication processes are managed. We have some idea, for example, how and why relationships are begun, maintained, and terminated; but we do not have formulas to account for exceptional cases where only some of the facts are available or known.

Again, it is highly probable that communication competence can be defined, although situational variables may make this difficult if general rules for excellence are expected. An important point is that communication competence is closely linked with understanding relationships since it is in relationships that our competence in communicating is often determined by others. A person's communicative competence may very much depend on the eye of the beholder. Thus, the competence and relational perspectives outlined in this chapter may be considered complementary.

Social influence involving compliance-gaining and compliance-resisting may also be regarded as a set of competencies that apply to interpersonal relationships. Several well-known communication skills, such as listening, assertiveness, negotiation and conflict management, can be readily associated with social influence processes in human relationships.

The meaning-centred perspective is especially relevant to communicative competence and social influence in interpersonal relationships, since it maintains that communication is essentially a process of reciprocated interpretations of events and interactions. Thus, individually constructed meanings of self, of others, and of self with others, form the bases for strategic choices in interpersonal encounters. Moreover, meanings may involve our own or others' ability to communicate in certain relationships. For example, people may attribute poor listening practices on their own part or on the part of others to some resultant communication failure.

Competent communication managers, therefore, may find meaning-construction a useful concept to explain actions of self and others. Their competence largely depends on their sensitivity to verbal and nonverbal cues, and on how accurately they interpret messages in ways intended by those they perceive. Finally, the strength or weakness of any relationship influences how accurately people construct meaning.

2.7 Summary

This chapter has provided an overview of four contemporary perspectives on human communication: social influence, relationship, communication competence, and meaning-centred. The chapter noted that perfect understandings of why people communicate as they do remain elusive, principally because disclosures vary and in any case are not always made consciously. Nevertheless, the four approaches provide a structure for understanding and explaining human communication and relationships. Competence in acting upon these understandings forms the basis of the following chapters.

Discussion Questions   2.8

1. How would you have explained the concept of 'communication management' before reading this chapter?

2. Before reading this chapter, how did your personal understanding differ from or concur with any of the theoretical perspectives it presented?

3. In what way(s) can your present understanding of communication management help you to continue to develop your ability to communicate with others?

4. What steps would you now take to be a better communication manager?

Activities   2.9

1. Think of a person you like. Take 5 minutes to write a description of that person. Then spend 5 minutes writing a description of a person you dislike. In each description underline every psychological construct (adjectives or phrases describing their psychological qualities). Count the number of constructs you have used: this number represents your index of cognitive complexity. Each time you form an impression of someone you will tend to use your construct system to create some meaning about that person.

2. List the skills and attributes you think communication managers should possess or develop. On a scale of 10 (10 = totally competent; 0 = totally incompetent) rate yourself in terms of (i) the level you think you should reach to be a good communication manager; and (ii) what you believe is your present level of competence. If, for any of your listed competencies, there is a gap between (i) and (ii), this represents a 'need'.

3. Note what steps you would take to fulfil any identified needs.

4. Compare these steps with any relevant suggestions made in the following chapters.

2.10 Key Terms

Attribution of meaning

Compliance-gaining

Compliance-resisting

Credibility

Interpersonal relationships

Persuasion

Relationship clarity

Role

Role clarity

Role ambiguity

Role confusion

Role overload

Social influence

2.11 Recommended Reading

Dance, F. E. X. (ed.) (1982) *Human communication theory: comparative essays,* New York: Harper & Row.

Forgas, J. P. (1985) *Interpersonal behaviour: the psychology of social interaction,* Sydney: Pergamon Press.

Infante, D. A., Rancer, A. S. and Womack, D. F. (1990) *Building communication theory,* Illinois: Waveland Press.

Littlejohn, S. W. (1992) *Theories of human communication,* 4th edn, California: Wadsworth.

O'Keefe, D. J. (1990) *Persuasion: theory and research,* California: Sage.

Trenholm, S. (1986) *Human communication theory,* New Jersey: Prentice Hall.

Communication Management Competence

3

Personally I'm always ready to learn, although I do not
always like being taught.

Winston Churchill

There is nothing permanent except change.

Heraclitus (540–475? BC)

How can we learn to be competent communication managers? What should we do to take control of and responsibility for our professional and personal development? In this chapter we discover the importance of self-awareness in developing our competence as communication managers. One especially important requirement is to be honest with ourselves, so that we can become better at 'being in touch' with ourselves and others. In turn, we will be able to establish some control over our interpersonal worlds. How much control we gain will depend on our progress as communication managers. We will also learn that people at work need to be artful as well as skilful in their communication with others. Managers should aim to be 'transformative managers' whose essential role is to help others achieve their goals. We will come to prefer the idea of managers being leaders rather than efficient bureaucrats—leaders who can understand and manage the covert as well as the overt cultures of their organisations, and who can monitor their own performance and develop appropriate strategies for self-improvement.

Learning Objectives

After you have studied the ideas, arguments and suggestions presented in this chapter you should be able to do the following:

- Identify at least two ways in which people can become more competent at communication.

- Give examples from your reading and experience of communication that is 'appropriate' in specific situations.

- Explain why it is important to apply communication skills with 'integrity'.

- Identify gaps in your own repertoire of communication skills.

- Devise a strategy for bridging these gaps.

- Understand the difference between a 'leader' and a 'manager' and be able to recognise when managers are acting as leaders and when they are not.

- List at least three characteristics of 'transformative managers'.

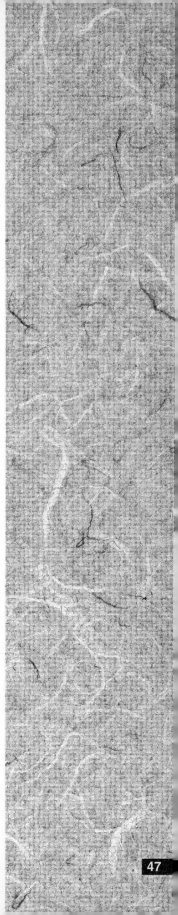

3.1 Self as Agent of Change

Learning may be defined as change resulting from training or experience. In this sense, the learner is the *change agent* or the person doing, acting and experiencing. The successful learner is one who has changed as a result of exposure to ideas, facts, opinions, attitudes, beliefs, feelings or events, and can show that what was formerly unknown or not possible is now known or possible. In short, the learner as change agent can demonstrate some gain in knowledge, thinking, feeling, or acting.

All people are, in a general sense, communication managers committed to learning about ways of enhancing their role-related competencies. Specifically, communication managers must be able to understand and manage with skill their processes of communication with others. The deepening of their understanding—leading, hopefully, to improved strategies for communicating with others—may be taken as evidence of learning or change. Thus, communication managers must realise that becoming more competent means becoming more aware and more involved in learning from one's experiences.

Essentially, the change agent is the learner and not a teacher or instructor. One does not become more competent at something simply because one has been taught to be more competent. This is certainly true of the communication manager. It is also true that the development of a learner's competence does not depend solely on the performance qualities of the teacher, but on personal resolve and perseverance with practising and applying the required skills.

Many self-related notions provide us with a framework for making decisions about learning or change. Self-knowledge embraces all self-related notions such as self-image, self-concept, self-esteem, self-disclosure and self-monitoring; but many other self-related notions are relevant to the development of communication management competence—for example, self-attribution, psychological self-protectors (commonly known as ego-defence mechanisms), self-presentation and self-regulated behaviour. All these variables affect how and why people act as they do in the presence of others; moreover, they constitute data that complement other related perspectives.

It should be understood, at this point, that this focus on self as agent of change should not detract from one's obligation to grasp someone else's perspective if one is aiming to be a competent communication manager. Competent communication management is a relational concept: it requires us to understand our own and others' potential and influence. Thus, in order to change, to grow and to develop as communication managers, we need to acknowledge and recognise the perspectives of all interacting parties.

Our need to understand ourselves greatly depends on our ability to be honest with ourselves, to recognise our strengths and shortcomings, and to perceive the dominant external and internal forces that influence our thoughts, feelings and actions. Unfortunately, our tendency to self-justification is a common obstacle here. Our wish to have others overlook, excuse or forget something we regret doing or saying is likely to make us defensive or perhaps less than honest, or we may behave as though our indiscretions never occurred, even though our credibility has been seriously shaken. We may continue to operate normally, believing that we are still liked and accepted, when our self-determined breach of trust persists in others' minds. When this happens, our capacity to be learners or agents of our own change is weakened.

Perhaps our greatest obstacle to communication competence is our inconsistent ability to be honest with ourselves, since it affects our honesty with others. We must keep alert to all the consequences and effects of our communication that will facilitate or inhibit our abilities to perform as effective change agents.

Competent communication management requires people to be honest with themselves

The next section examines a range of personal communication skills, and the principle of being honest with one's self remains paramount. It also proposes that communication competence arises from the learner's own reflection rather than from instruction.

Personal Development Competence

3.2

Personal development is a term that draws ridicule from some quarters, as indicating a remedial bag of tricks used to help people function 'normally'. Others regard the term as a pretentious label for an assortment of lunatic fringe activities. Typically, many business managers equate it with parapsychological therapeutic practices of dubious relevance for a world of practical decision-making.

> **personal development**
> *Aspects of a person's development that do not concern task performance or professional competence.*

As part of the quest for communication competence, however, personal development has high status, partly because most interpersonal communication skills are generic rather than situation-specific. Since personal development extends beyond work-related contexts, its managerial-organisational applications are discussed separately in the next section. As well, we need to remember that personal development takes place at all stages of our life, not only at work. Our personal development, therefore, includes our learning to be successful as interpersonal communicators in many different situations as well as our quest for deeper understanding of our individual nature and characteristics.

Central to the notion of communication competence as a basis for our ability to relate to others, regardless of context, is the issue of perceiving oneself and others accurately (Cook, 1984). Our competence in any communication skill such as listening depends greatly on our ability to interpret accurately our own and others' intentions during an interpersonal encounter. People often miscalculate their own and others' true intentions, mainly because they select certain verbal or nonverbal cues instead of appraising all the information expressed; and, as suggested earlier, real intentions do not always surface. Hence, accuracy of perception requires one to ascertain more than the observable data.

Searching for accurate meanings by probing the unobservable domain is a difficult task. Nevertheless, relationships that deepen professionally or personally probably demand reciprocal concessions of disclosure. We cannot expect others to understand us if we project only surface information about ourselves. Nor are we likely to understand why others think, feel or act as they do if they remain reluctant to provide honest clues about their intentions.

A primary personal development competency in communication management, therefore, is the ability to find clues that are not immediately apparent. Most people can only rely on their sincerity to open up a relationship that encourages the expression of true feelings. I was once accused by two of my program managers of directing my energies toward other members of my faculty, thus failing to support their endeavours in program management. As it turned out, my colleagues' grievance really had little to do with my support of their program. They had been refused sabbatical leave by a committee to which I belonged, and it was not my alleged lack of support for their program but my complicity in the committee decision that annoyed them. I could not resolve this issue simply by reassuring them about their program management efforts. Over dinner one evening I discovered the real reason for their discontent. Perhaps I was in no better position to resolve it, but I was nevertheless able to understand it, and this gave me a basis for developing a strategy to communicate with them in the future. Probing beyond the observable clues had given me a more accurate picture of their intent.

Just how we develop greater accuracy in revealing the true intentions of others is largely a matter of managerial sensitivity. Equally difficult is the task of accurately interpreting and acknowledging our own motivations. So often we are blinded by our own feelings, by our perceptions that others fail to appreciate the pressures on us, and by our conviction that we are merely obeying rules, that we use these reasons to excuse our actions towards others. Our belief that others do not understand these pressures on us, and our negative evaluations of those whom we manage, probably lead us to conclude that we are *'right'* because we have obeyed bureaucratic dictates. As managers, what we have failed to accept is that we may have projected sympathy and support but inwardly maintained biases and prejudices that governed our strategies of communication management.

Probing others' real intentions requires one to suspend judgment until any problem is given a fair hearing. Being non-evaluative is a tall order, particularly when managers are responsible for getting work done—do busy managers have the time to find out why individuals need counselling or help?

Being non-evaluative is not always easy

According to Peter (1986:180), 'a major problem in management is that competence in an executive or a bureau chief is primarily an abstract idea. An executive or a chief administrator should be paid to think, to decide, and to manage. He [sic] should deal primarily with intangibles, such as concepts, assumptions and values'. Unfortunately, managers laden with paperwork, phone calls and meetings tend to do less thinking or conceptualising than they should. Being an innovative communication manager, therefore, means being able to develop a set of vital communication skills, including the ability to give feedback, to clarify interpersonal meanings, to summarise one's own and others' thinking, and to suspend judgment until all available information has been considered. In essence, effective communication managers are good at listening rather than telling, good at perceiving rather than judging or guessing, and good at eliciting information whether it concerns themselves or others. Above all, they allow creative ideas (including their own) to surface and be acknowledged.

Recognising the creativity of another is indeed an integral facet of communication competence. Sieradski (1988) argued that understanding creative processes reduces professional conflict. We must accept that not every breach of establishment rules harms an organisation's mission; on the contrary, mavericks can give new insights to problems, so nurturing creative talent is symptomatic of competence in communication management.

Sometimes our own creative limitations prevent us from recognising or encouraging true talent, especially if we fear that the organisation's harmony could be upset by individuals challenging its rules or established procedures. Longstanding members of organisations often tend to resent newcomers telling them how things should be done, and very few organisations encourage creative individuals to make radical changes before they are firmly convinced of the consequences. Since few managers condone change merely for the sake of change, they need to be able to listen intelligently and sympathetically before assessing innovations proposed by others. Perhaps this is a personal as well as a professional competency.

The ability to perceive our own and others' behaviour accurately is vital, but accurate perception accounts for only part of the communication process. People's perceptions influence their behaviour toward others. Ultimately, it is the way people act and behave toward each other that determines the success or failure of each relationship and reveals the extent of their communication competence.

Sometimes our actions are at odds with our perceptions. We may think in one way but act in another, apparently contradictory, way. For example, I may form an unfavourable impression of my next-door neighbour, but not act in any way to suggest this; or I may seem to encourage acquaintances who want to become friends, even though I would prefer these acquaintances to drop out of my life.

There are various reasons for inconsistencies between our actions and our perceptions. For example, we may conceal our true feelings to avoid conflict. Quite often, depending on the kind of people we are, we opt for a no-conflict form of communication where true perceptions and feelings are both postponed and suppressed. In effect, this course of action becomes a course of no action. As a result, the relationship usually deteriorates because its future is placed in a state of uncertainty, unless the people concerned are content to play the game of pretending to enjoy each other's company.

On some occasions, perceptions do not match actions because the perceivers have ambivalent motives. Some people stay on friendly terms with others not because they genuinely want to be friends but because the relationship may be useful for professional or financial reasons. As already stated, what is observable in people's actions and use of language is not a firm basis for understanding why they act or speak as they do, or for understanding what kind of people they are. Communication competence, therefore, in terms of personal development, requires us to increase our sensitivity to discrepancies between our actions and intentions and to ambiguity or deception in the communication patterns of others.

Perhaps the most important practical skill for developing sensitivity of this kind is careful listening. This is not a revolutionary notion—in Shakespeare's *Hamlet*, Polonius advised his son Laertes: 'give every man thy ear, but few thy voice; take each man's censure, but reserve thy judgment'. To be a good listener, one must realise that listening is not something that comes naturally. It can be poorly or highly developed, depending on the amount of effort put into it. The listening skill involves the discipline of suspending judgment about another's message until it has been accurately interpreted. Chapter 6 discusses this skill in more detail. At this stage, it is sufficient to emphasise that it should not be taken for granted but practised whenever possible. Because listening is something we learn to do, the more we practise the skill, the better listeners we become.

There are other personal development skills we should acquire, practise and refine—for instance, being assertive (or standing up for our rights), negotiating, managing conflict, and understanding our own and others' use of words and body language. All these skills can be learned in order to increase our competence as communicators.

What we have been considering suggests that communication competence involves our ability to establish personal control over our environment. This concept of personal control was developed by Powers (1973) and subsequently supported by Carver and Scheier (1982) and Parks (1985). According to these theorists, communication is a developmental phenomenon, ranging over nine levels from developing control over the ability to receive sensory information, to mastery of language, to developing communication strategies consistent with one's ideals and principles. The nine-level hierarchy also permits the evaluation of specific and general competencies at any level. According to Parks (1985:187), 'we can evaluate competency in general by tapping the individual's own competency judgements'. Self-judgments, therefore, reinforce personal control and, in turn, the necessity for self-knowledge and honesty with one's self.

We conclude this section with the thought that our personal development of communication competence amounts to our total development as a communicative being. Listening, for example, is hardly a situation-specific skill—even at home or with friends, the rudiments of good listening still apply, so practising them anywhere can enhance our performance in meetings and interviews. We now turn to the professional requirements of developing competence in communication management.

Professional Development Competence   3.3

Many scholars in the fields of applied social sciences, management and communication agree that the best organisational systems are characterised by good communication between the various members within those systems. According to Egan (1988a:157), 'effective communication is the lifeblood of the system, the energizer, the productivity enhancer. Communication breathes life into relationships in organizations, institutions, and communities'. An analysis of jobs advertised in twenty Australian public and private sector organisations revealed that 'good communication skills' were considered essential for a wide range of positions (Kaye and McArthur, 1993). The data for this analysis was drawn from newspaper advertisements and follow-up telephone interviews with recruiting personnel. The positions ranged from paraprofessional technician to middle-management. In another study, Athanasou, Pithers and Cornford (1993:37) surveyed 236 people from occupations in business, industry, higher education and the public service and found that 94% of respondents emphasised the importance of 'communicating ideas', while 91% regarded 'working in teams' as essential for doing the job well.

The ability to work in a team is an essential part of communication competence

Even though many people seem to get their work done without the presence of others, it is still difficult to imagine any profession that would give low priority to good communication skills. People do not work well in a vacuum. They are required to interact and communicate with other people, either formally or informally. Nevertheless, the type and amount of communication competence required varies from one position to another. Some personal skills may develop further in work-related contexts. On the other hand, some communication skills not usually required at work may need to be developed for their work role by training or study.

Organisations and systems which are reactionary and unprogressive tend to assume that people acquire job-related communication skills simply by doing the job, and making mistakes and then learning from these mistakes. However, it is wrong to assume that people know when they make mistakes or fall short, or that self-discoveries will repeatedly occur through the process of incidental learning. Learning requires a systematic approach to think through and process one's experiences.

At all levels of appointment in human systems or organisations, competence in communication management is crucial. Skill requirements vary, however, depending on the position. Subordinates, for example, will undoubtedly find it useful or necessary to be able to stand up to their superiors in a dispute or personality clash, or to challenge unfair treatment or criticism. Managers and supervisors, on the other hand, may need to develop skill in helping their staff to perform to required standards. This kind of help sometimes involves difficult tasks like disciplining a staff member or terminating their employment.

Regardless of the particular context and professional relationship, our ability to perform these tasks greatly depends on our ability to communicate well, which involves understanding what to say or do as well as being able to say or do it. The competent communicator not only knows what to do or say but also why certain things should be said or done. In professional settings, therefore, the people who can make a difference to their organisations or systems are invariably those who can communicate *appropriately*. This ability is the trademark of what Dunphy and Stace (1990) call **transformative managers**, who have in common a belief in people. As Dunphy and Stace (1990:163) put it, transformative managers

> . . . know that change will only occur through people and therefore they place great value on personal relationships; they spend time in planning how to select, deploy and develop people; they spend more time getting amongst their people rather than trying to manage from the remote fastness of a head office. They tend not to limit their contacts within formal hierarchies, but move about their organisation, listen to people at all levels, be seen by them, and speak to them, as far as possible, on a face-to-face basis.

transformational (transformative) leaders *These leaders create a new vision for the future of their organisations, communicate it to the public, stakeholders and the organisation's members, and carry out the vision throughout the organisation.*

In face-to-face encounters, transformative managers demonstrate confidence in their staff members' abilities, and spend a good deal of time giving them emotional support by way of public and personal acknowledgment of their abilities.

It is now apparent that successful human relations in professional settings involves more than learning basic communication skills like listening or negotiation, even though these skills form the core of communication competence. Nevertheless, we need to complement them with certain beliefs and attitudes. For example, as Dunphy and Stace (1990) suggest, managers should demonstrate belief in the abilities of their staff members; and a manager should like being with other people. The 'lone wolf', preferring solitude to the distraction of working alongside others, is more task-directed and less concerned with developing communication competence. The gregarious person has the great advantage of liking to be with people.

Besides enjoying the company of others and believing in their abilities and worth, competent communicators know when to praise and when to withhold praise. For instance, when their subordinates' contributions cease to be anything more than routine repetitions of some earlier initiative, indiscriminate praise or encouragement will reinforce their mediocrity. As a result, their superiors' encouragement will lose its impact and value.

In one sense, the development and manifestation of communication management competence in the workplace is both an art and a set of skills. The skills can be learned but there is no certainty that people will communicate well simply as a result of performing them routinely.

Communication managers must continue to refine and improve their abilities to communicate appropriately with others. Communication as an art involves a dedication to thinking through and reflecting on interactions and professional relationships with other people in their organisations or human systems.

One of the pitfalls of staff development and training programs in communication skills is that participants often expect the program's bag of tricks to solve any problem that might arise in the workplace. If this expectation is reinforced by the program, people are likely to communicate in ways that are mechanical, rigid and insensitive. The program, therefore, should be seen for what it is: to help participants understand the basics of communicating with others. It should not be seen as a means of developing creative communication managers. Creative communication is the product of dedicated practice and thoughtful reflection. It is not gained in a few days of training but is developed over a lifetime.

A useful way of differentiating *professional* from *personal* development competency needs is to identify the context in which the set of communication skills is to be applied. For example, the skill of conflict management is exercised less formally—certainly quite differently—in a personal setting like the home than it is in the workplace; and professional competency needs may vary from one place of work to another. For example, organisations with strict, inflexible work practices and employment conditions may give less scope for creative communication than organisations that are receptive to change.

For these reasons, it is difficult to produce a definitive list of professional communication skills because their application varies, depending on the setting. Let's take the recruitment or selection interview as an example. Although skills like listening and questioning are important in all kinds of selection interviews, interviews for a grocery store assistant, an orthopaedic surgeon, and a financial analyst in corporate business all require different applications. Broadly speaking, however, there are certain functions which most managers have to carry out. In large organisations, some of these functions are commissioned to specialist consultants. What are these functions?

As Dunphy and Stace (1990:206) observed, 'ultimately organizations are people'. People are hired and fired. They are counselled about their aspirations to climb the organisation ladder. They are promoted if they perform well, and disciplined or advised to improve their performance if they show little sign of progress. Performance appraisals or reviews occur regularly. Those who are highly rated are envied by some of the weaker performers. Rivalries develop between those rated as achievers and those who don't seem to have what it takes.

Communication managers have to handle all these events and must be able to communicate their intentions and decisions confidently, unambiguously and resolutely. As well, they need to understand and be at the forefront of change so that they can help their staff members adapt to changes in organisation policy or new technology. We now move to a closer consideration of communication management in organisation development and change.

Communication Management in   3.4
Organisational Development
and Change

In a second bestseller, *A Passion for Excellence: The Leadership Difference*, Tom Peters and Nancy Austin argued that effective and ineffective organisations could be distinguished by the quality of their leaders (Peters and Austin, 1989). The best leaders, Peters and Austin say, **manage by wandering around (MBWA)**. These peripatetic leaders help organisations become 'adaptive' because every challenge to change is confronted head-on. Much of the MBWA leader's power is derived from being in close touch with the thinking and feeling of staff members, and spending a lot of time communicating with them. Successful MBWA leaders are highly competent at communication, but their competence involves a lot more than basic skills. According to Peters and Austin, these skills are only powerful if they are used with *integrity*: 'virtually every device we suggest is doomed to be useless unless applied with integrity' (Peters and Austin, 1989:34). Earlier in this chapter I argued that communication managers should use their skills *appropriately*. It is my opinion that integrity and appropriateness are complementary aspects. In any system, the achievement of its mission greatly depends on the genuine commitment of its members to that mission statement and its corresponding goals. This is integrity, for it connotes a real belief in what the organisation or system stands for.

If belief is to prevail, it needs to be supported by some appropriate means of communicating it. An example of inappropriate communication of belief is the stating of religious messages in journals or other print media with non-religious readerships. On the other hand, the placing of equal opportunity clauses in advertisements may be appropriate but lacking in integrity if the

MBWA
Managing by wandering around.

Competent communication managers should communicate appropriately and with integrity

organisation will continue in practice to promote a policy of inequality of opportunity by favouring certain individuals over others because of characteristics such as gender, age or ethnicity. Hence, communicatively competent individuals in organisations need to possess basic communication skills, believe in the importance of these skills, and use them appropriately according to the demands of the situation at the time.

Organisational change is seldom accidental or random. It usually occurs when influential people change, learn new skills, synthesise new knowledge or develop new attitudes. Such change does not occur merely as a result of new policies pronounced from on high, but upper level managers do play a significant role in the promotion of organisational change. In most systems change from the bottom up is much rarer than change from the top down.

It is also important to note that in unprogressive organisations communication between staff is often confined to particular subsections or departments. For example, the accounts and salaries department may rarely communicate with the staff development department or the personnel department. In an analysis of a large multinational organisation in transition, McKenna and Yeider (1991) reported the consultants' identification of several problems, particularly one that the consultants called 'the individualistic view taken by managers':

> . . . each manager interviewed gave the impression that his or her concern was with his or her department and what happened in other departments was of little consequence. After all, the management system instructed and rewarded them for meeting only those individual goals to which they had agreed at the beginning of each year. (McKenna and Yeider, 1991:57)

When organisations change, therefore, the more communication there is between different parts of the system, the greater the opportunity for people to understand others' perceptions of the change, and how they are coping with it. This kind of sharing of perspectives and perceptions helps them to adjust to corporate expectations and to adapt personal goals to new organisation goals.

There are, of course, several variables that can affect how far people are prepared to change *themselves* to fit in with the new order. Some of these variables include their own characteristics—for instance, their age or stage of career development. Do people well advanced in their career development and opportunities tend to resist change more than less experienced staff with everything to gain by being flexible and adaptable?

As many of us may have realised, older workers are often expected to 'fill gaps', and even take on less challenging work to stay employed. This may be because some people's patience with routine tasks develops over time. On the other hand, since their critical thinking and verbal skills sometimes improve with age and experience, older people may be better equipped to come to terms with changes in the workplace.

If there is any truth in Hayakawa's memorable saying that 'there is only one thing age can give you, and that is wisdom', then many older people have a potentially crucial communication role to play in their organisations. The trouble is that this potential is often neglected by managers who look to younger colleagues for ideas and inspiration. As someone else once said, 'old age is when you know all the answers but nobody asks you the questions'. On the other hand, it is also true that just by growing older people do not necessarily become wiser. To communicate wisely, individuals need to spend time processing and reflecting upon their experiences. Hence, good critical thinkers are also often good communicators because they can skillfully assess information and arguments.

What other personal characteristics can enhance people's communication competence in organisational development and change? In some aspects, women appear to have greater expertise than men. For example, much of the research by Rosenthal and his colleagues (1979) suggested that women, regardless of their ethnic or cultural origins, are superior to men in the interpretation of others' nonverbal cues, particularly *negative* nonverbal cues. On the other hand, the evidence for differences between females and males in the expression of nonverbal cues is less conclusive. On this point, Rotter and Rotter (1988:140) noted that 'the comparative ability of males and females to encode emotions is complicated by the specific emotion being expressed and by perceiver characteristics'. Their study also revealed that whilst women were generally superior to men in recognising disgust, fear and sadness, in the case of anger 'there was no overall difference in accuracy between male and female subjects' (p. 146). They suggested also that males express anger more openly, although in general women are probably better at expressing emotion. The recognition and expression of nonverbal emotions will be examined in detail in Chapter 5.

Just as individual characteristics can have a powerful effect on the nature of communication in an organisation, *situational factors* can too. To be more specific, it is difficult for people to develop their competence in communicating with others in the system if they are constantly thwarted by task-oriented superiors with little understanding of the significance of good working relationships.

In many cases, communication with people in other parts of the organisation is a luxury because workers barely have enough time for this. Many managers, often for reasons beyond their control, delegate new tasks to staff members before previously designated work has been satisfactorily completed. In these circumstances, workers' communication with others tends to focus on issues of inequality and disadvantage rather than on constructive, creative approaches to their current projects. In short, negative feelings often predominate over motives to succeed in new areas of endeavour.

Other situational factors that can affect people's motivation to communicate with workers in different parts of the system include the organisation's reward system (e.g. promotion, bonuses) and working conditions (e.g. leave, compensation for illness). These are 'quality of life' factors, and when the quality of life in an organisation is wanting in some respect, its staff morale is prone to suffer. For this reason, it has been suggested that an organisation's business mission should incorporate a people-oriented mission (Egan, 1991:38).

Deteriorating morale may lead to a decline in productivity. The symptoms of this kind of decay become manifest when people compromise their standards of communication to gain advantage over others. They become adversarial rather than supportive, and their prime motive in communicating with others is to acquire information, particularly if organisational change involves some deterioration of working conditions such as retrenchment of staff, or reduced career opportunities.

In relation to organisational development and change, therefore, competence in communication is essential to manage both desirable and unwelcome changes. In times of organisational uncertainty, skilled communicators will thus be in the strongest position to grapple with the unpredictable elements of change. These unpredictable elements constitute what Egan (1988a, 1993) calls the **shadow side** of organisations: 'the ability to manage the shadow side of the organization often makes the difference between a successful or unsuccessful manager or between a mediocre and an excellent manager' (p. 9).

This discussion has focused on how people in organisations need communication competence so as to understand and manage processes of change regardless of whether the changes are orderly or unpredictable. It is now appropriate, therefore, to consider how communication competence applies to managerial roles in organisations.

shadow side
Also called the arational *side of human systems; characterised by uncertainty, unpredictability; is 'undiscussable', covert and usually informal.*

3.5 How Communication Competence Relates to Managerial Roles in Organisations

The concept of 'role' is usually understood in terms of *expectation(s)* or *performance.* If I identify one of my roles as 'manager of the household accounts', I will be expected to do certain things because that role carries with it certain *expectations.* For example, I will probably have to check monthly statements of account from banks, credit card agencies, and department stores. I will also be expected to keep a record of all receipts which I may have to produce when I claim income taxation rebates. As well, I may have to keep track of the balance of monthly income and expenditure to ensure that the budget is not overspent. All these expectations I have to meet come with the role of 'manager of household accounts'.

I might also be judged on my *performance* of that role. In other words, apart from doing what is expected, I may be judged on how well I carry out the expected tasks. As manager of the household accounts, how thoroughly and accurately did I check all the monthly statements of account? How diligently did I record all expenditures? Did I maintain a file of receipts for taxation purposes? How well, overall, did I perform what was expected of me?

One of the most convenient ways of understanding the concept of 'role' is to think of it as a kind of hat one wears. For example, you wear different hats depending on what is expected of you. At certain times you might wear the hat of a parent; at work you wear your professional hat; at a community education class you wear the hat of an adult learner or student; on weekends you wear the hat of sporting coach for a team of children. Whatever hat you are wearing, you are likely to be judged in two ways: on whether you are doing what you are expected to do, and on how well you are doing it.

Despite differences in job-specific areas, managers generally have to perform several similar roles. Most significantly, they are expected to act as leaders, providing direction and vision for their staff. The leadership role may be performed in autocratic, consultative, or delegative ways, depending on the manager's mode of communicating with staff members (Vroom and Yetton, 1975; Vroom and Jago, 1988). Over several decades, leadership has been studied and understood from perspectives that range from a distinctive traits basis, to leadership styles, and (more recently) situational and contingency models. A functional view of leadership is useful here; it poses the question 'what do leaders do which non-leaders (or followers) don't do?' Once these functions are identified, they can be seen as competencies associated with the role.

There is, however, an essential difference between the concept of 'leader' and that of 'manager'. In Bennis's book *Why leaders can't lead* (1991), the difference between leaders and managers is explained as follows: *while managers do things right, leaders do the right things*. Let's take an example to illustrate this difference. A department store manager, who has been receiving complaints from numerous customers about the poor quality of service in the store, decides to identify the sales staff about whom most complaints are made, and then terminate their employment. Certainly, this decision is a bureaucratic one but it does not necessarily mean that the manager has acted with the initiative or vision of a leader. By contrast, a leader might consider several viable options for resolving the problem of poor customer service. These options may have been based on a comprehensive understanding of the poor customer service—perhaps it was not only the fault of some staff members but also the result of inadequate company incentives, lack of effective training or support, or a weak organisational sense of mission.

A manager acting as a leader would decide which of those reasons or combination of reasons could account for the problem before deciding on an appropriate course of action. On the other hand, the bureaucratic manager, by taking a convenient course of action, has opted for an efficient if not necessarily appropriate solution. 'Doing it right' (efficiently) does not mean that the right thing has been done. In fact, a totally inappropriate decision can be efficiently executed. The main goal is to decide on the right thing to do, so while it is easy for us to loosely equate 'leader' with 'manager', some managers may never become leaders and some potential leaders may be denied promotion to management.

Let's analyse the leadership role of managers from a functional perspective. Yau and Sculli (1990:35), who derived their manager development strategy partly from the earlier work of Mintzberg (1973), argued that leadership skills primarily involve an ability to deal with subordinates as well as the skills of motivating, training and helping subordinates, and dealing with problems of authority and dependence. There are undoubtedly other skills you could add, but for the moment let's work through this list as an example.

Taking each skill separately, ask yourself two questions. First, what level of skill is required for an effective leader? Consider, for example, the skill of training staff members: how proficient does the manager have to be? When you analyse what training involves, it becomes clear that managers must be able, among other things, to plan training, state training aims and objectives clearly and unambiguously, select appropriate training strategies, and evaluate learning performance and outcomes. Collectively, these subskills represent the 'skill of training subordinates'.

Now, using a scale from 0 to 10, where 0 means the required level of skill is nil, and where 10 indicates the highest level of skill required for the leadership role, decide on the skill level required for training staff members. Note that many skills need not be rated at the extremes of the scale. If you find it confusing or off-putting to use numerical scales, try developing a scale of your own in which the intervals are differentiated; for example, use several intervals or points ranging from a very high level of skill through moderate to low or minimal levels.

Next, ask yourself the second question: what is my current level of performance for this skill? In answering, use the same scale you used to answer the first question. Once you have rated yourself on the second question, you will have two measures. The first indicates your perception of the skill level required to perform the particular role effectively. The second measure is your perception of your current level of performing that skill. If your perceived level of functioning is lower than the required level, you have a gap that represents a need or deficiency which you should redress if you are to operate satisfactorily as a leader.

In some instances the gap may be so small as to be hardly worth worrying about. For instance, on the numerical scale the difference between a rating of 9 and 8 suggests that the current skill level is very close to the required level. On the other hand, a difference between a required level of 9 and a current level of 5 suggests that the gap is serious. The final step is to decide how to remedy the deficiency, perhaps by training programs or with a non-training solution.

The above procedure is just one way in which people can identify which needs must be met to perform their roles competently. With special reference to managerial roles in organisations, it is apparent that some of the most essential skills are concerned with relating to and communicating with staff members. As Egan (1993:105) observed: 'communication skills are basic to effective management'. However, Egan also noted that 'few managers are proficient in them'.

One should not assume that managers communicate only with subordinates. Any progressive organisation that encourages as much communication as possible between members from different parts of the system wants its managers to communicate with superiors and peers as well—managers must be competent in communicating upwards, sideways, and downwards. Nevertheless, downward communication naturally assumes a special significance for leadership.

We conclude this section with the reminder that the best organisations or systems allow all their members to communicate freely with each other. In some rigid bureaucratic systems, staff are required to communicate only through their immediate superior(s). This unilinear form of communication was once typical of many systems and there are still some organisations which insist on all things being done through formal chains of command and lines of authority. Extreme formality, unfortunately, may result in a good deal of initiative being lost down the line because of unintentional (sometimes even intentional) delays or opposition at various higher levels of management.

The term 'manager' derives from the Latin words *manu*, meaning 'by hand', and *agere*, meaning 'to do' and connotes genuine involvement in the supervision of work and people. The development and refinement of interpersonal communication competence is essential for the effective performance of managerial roles in organisations. In the following chapters particular communication skills and their application in various contexts, including managerial settings, will be considered in greater detail.

Summary 3.6

This chapter began with a discussion of the notion of self as agent of change, and emphasised that the learner, not the facilitator, is the agent of change. The implication for the development of competence, the theme of this chapter, is that one is not taught but learns to be competent. This is especially pertinent to the development of competence in understanding and managing communication processes.

The next two sections differentiated personal from professional communication management competencies. In some respects, all communication competencies derive from one's personal development. Professionally, some of the generic communication abilities apply in special ways to job-specific activities such as formal meetings or interviews. A method of determining communication competence in professional settings is to ask whether the particular communication skill is being used and applied appropriately.

Then came a discussion of the importance of communication management in organisational development and change, in which the point was made that communication benefits organisational development and change so long as it is used not only appropriately but with integrity. As well, communication competence means the ability to deal with uncertainty and unpredictability. Effective managers were differentiated from less effective managers in terms of their ability to deal with the 'shadow side' of systems.

The next section analysed the relationship between communication competence and managerial roles in organisations. It outlined the concept of 'role' in terms of expectations and performance, considered the leadership role of managers and relevant skills, and described a simple procedure for identifying needs for further skill development. These skills were related to the broad area of communication competence. It was then argued that the best organisations are characterised by free flows of communication among all their members.

Part II discusses in detail several vital human communication skills. It considers how people use language and nonverbal cues, the need for effective listening and assertiveness skills, and strategies for negotiating and managing conflicts. Although there are other skills, such as questioning, these are regarded as the most relevant to communication competence in general.

3.7 Discussion Questions

1. If communication competence is learned rather than taught, identify some ways of learning it.

2. Describe some of your roles in which you are required to be competent in communicating with other people. Detail the skills and the skill levels you need to perform those roles satisfactorily.

3. From your own experience, list some examples of appropriate communication in organisational settings. Explain why they are appropriate.

4. Why is it important to apply communication skills with integrity? Give a couple of examples of how they can be used with integrity?

3.8 Activities

1. Using the procedure suggested in this chapter, identify the gaps you perceive in your communication skills for two of your roles as a communication manager.

2. Devise a strategy for bridging the gaps you have just identified.

3. Describe an organisation or system, perhaps one in which you have been a member, which you consider as effective or ineffective. Give reasons for your opinion.

4. In any capacity you can specify, indicate the steps you would take to ensure that you are performing your leadership role effectively and living up to other people's expectations.

Key Terms 3.9

Integrity (of managers)
MBWA—Managing by wandering around
Personal control over the interpersonal environment
Personal development
Self-knowledge
Shadow side
Transformative manager

Recommended Reading 3.10

Bennis, W. (1991) *Why leaders can't lead: the unconscious conspiracy continues*, San Francisco: Jossey-Bass.

Dunphy, D. and Stace, D. (1990) *Under new management: Australian organizations in transition*, Sydney: McGraw-Hill.

Egan, G. (1993) *Adding value: a systematic guide to business-driven management and leadership*, San Francisco: Jossey-Bass.

Kaye, M. (1992) 'Communication competence', in *Developing a competent workforce: adult learning strategies for vocational educators and trainers*, Gonczi, A. (ed.), Adelaide: National Centre for Vocational Education Research, 80–104.

Mitchell, T. R., Dowling, P. J., Kabanoff, B. V. and Larson, J. R. (1988) *People in organizations: an introduction to organizational behaviour in Australia*, Sydney: McGraw-Hill.

Peters, T. and Austin, N. (1989) *A passion for excellence: the leadership difference*, Glasgow: Fontana/Collins.

Rasberry, R. W. and Lemoine, L. F. (1986) *Effective managerial communication*, Boston, Massachusetts: PWS-Kent.

Vecchio, R. P. (1988) *Organizational behavior*, Chicago: Dryden Press.

PART II

Human
Communication
Skills

The
Use of
Language

A

If thought corrupts language, language can also corrupt thought.

George Orwell

If you scoff at language study . . . how, save in terms of language,
will you scoff?

Mario Pei

Language is the light of the mind.

John Stuart Mill

When I use a word, it means just what I choose it to mean —
neither more nor less.

Lewis Carroll (Charles Lutwidge Dodgson) (1832–1898)

Why do we use language? How does language function in our lives? Experience tells us that the words we use and the way we use them have profound effects on our relationships and communication with other people. In this chapter we learn that our language enables us to classify our thinking and to construct meanings for our world of people, ideas, objects and happenings. Some examples of how people speak to each other nowadays demonstrate how language is ever changing and developing in our society. Some of the chapter focuses on sexism and racism and on how we can prevent careless lapses into these discriminatory uses of language. We also consider how the construction of written messages can lead to miscommunication and to inappropriate responses. After returning to the relationship between language and thought, the chapter concludes by reflecting briefly on how language enables us to act appropriately in different social settings, especially on how it determines etiquette in unfamiliar professional, diplomatic or workplace contexts.

Learning Objectives

After you have studied the ideas, arguments and suggestions presented in this chapter you should be able to do the following:

- Explain the difference between denotation and connotation.

- List three functions of language and provide an example for each.

- Identify examples of sexist and racist remarks and indicate how these could be restated so they are no longer discriminatory or offensive.

- Give examples that show how language is dynamic and how it has changed over the years you have been using it.

- Show how poorly constructed written messages can lead to mis-communication and inappropriate reactions.

- Demonstrate how people in other English-speaking countries or communities may find it difficult to understand or interpret certain Australian idiomatic expressions.

- Explain the relationship between language and the process of thinking.

- Indicate how we conform, through language, to socially acceptable norms and etiquette.

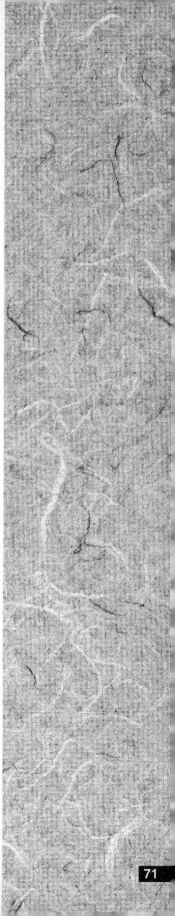

4.1 The Nature and Functions of Language

All our image-making is bound up with our use of language. When we construct images of others we activate a system of words to form impressions of people. Even when we meet people for the first time, we tend to size them up as friendly or unfriendly, interesting or dull, warm or distant, intelligent or unintelligent, and so on. In effect, we use words to classify our experience of people, events, and places. The words we use to make our judgments and classifications of people are often expressed as logical opposites—as sincere or insincere, honest or dishonest, fair or unfair, and so on.

Our judgments are probably based on more than either-or types of classification because we modify the adjectives or descriptors we use. For example, instead of thinking of someone as being either approachable or unapproachable, we tend to think of them as *quite* approachable, or *fairly* approachable; we create our own methods of classifying the people and events we encounter. These methods are like roughly developed scales with intervals loosely defined by words such as very, extremely, moderately, mildly, and so on.

Language, therefore, is something we use to classify thought. Words become symbols to denote people, objects, events, places. Note that words by themselves, out of context, do not always carry significant meanings. They are often merely convenient labels to identify classes of objects, places, events or people. Meanings conveyed by words alone tend to be literal rather than emotive. When people interpret their experience by assigning meaning to words, language becomes not only a tool for classifying thought but also a vehicle for communication.

In using language to communicate with others, individuals construct two different kinds of meanings. The basic level of meaning is known as **denotation**, which is the literal description, or dictionary definition. For example, for many people the word 'supervisor' denotes 'someone in charge of another'. However, meanings can develop to signify more than the basic denotation, and this type of meaning is known as **connotation**. For example, to someone who has unpleasant associations with superiors in the workplace, 'supervisor' could connote authoritarianism, abuse of power, exploitation, lack of worker participation or consultation, and an absence of fair play. Similarly, the word 'politician' probably denotes a person involved in government to most people. For those with favourable experiences of politicians the word may have connotations of responsible, civic-minded, hard-working servants of the community. For others, the word might carry cunning, self-seeking, predatory and greedy connotations.

Connotations, therefore, are mostly formed from people's personal experiences. Whilst denotations carry meanings that are common to all people, connotations vary from person to person depending on their feelings, beliefs, attitudes and thoughts. In some ways, connotations are

denotation
The literal definition of objects or phenomena according to commonly understood and agreed terms.

connotation
Concepts and ideas one indirectly associates with specific people, objects, events or phenomena.

Political leaders have various effects on individual audience members
Source: Fairfax

like values and may be favourable or unfavourable. As people interpret their experiences, they go through a process of deciding whether the objects of their perceptions are good or bad, right or wrong, suitable or unsuitable and so on. Thus, connotations are, in a sense, people's evaluations of their particular experiences.

Connotations are often emotionally charged. For instance, for many people the word 'apartheid' connotes brutality, oppression, and racial hatred. The degrees of emotional intensity tend to correspond with people's first-hand or second-hand experiences of it. Those who have lived in South Africa when apartheid was rampant are most likely to have stronger feelings about it than those who have only heard or read about it.

Regardless of the level of meaning we give the words we communicate with, our use of language is also linked with the intentions of our messages. For example, when a mother says to her child, 'Hurry up and wash your hands. Dinner's on the table', she intends the child to follow her instructions. The intention is made even more explicit if the words are accompanied by nonverbal cues such as tone of voice and volume. Intentions conveyed this way correspond to what some refer to as the functions of language. The mother summoning her child to dinner illustrates the imperative function of language.

Apart from using language to instruct or direct, all people use language to convey information, written or oral. This informative function of language occurs in a broad variety of situations ranging from informal conversations to formal classroom, lecture hall, boardroom, theatre and church venues. Many people regard the informative function of language as the main, if not the only, function of language.

Nevertheless, although language is the main vehicle for the communication of information, it is not the sole means of information exchange. For example, information about our emotional states and interpersonal attitudes is often signalled by our facial expressions and by vocal qualities like intonation, rhythm, inflection, and enunciation. The functions of nonverbal cues will be discussed in more detail in Chapter 5.

A third function of language is concerned with the expression of emotions and feelings. The expressive function of language is often associated with forms of literature like poetry or drama, and especially with self-expression. Of course, people also express their feelings to others. Radio and television sports commentators, for example, get carried away very easily with the hype of close games and contests. Similarly, people discussing or debating a controversial issue or topic can become quite heated.

Generally speaking, people use language for instructing, informing, or expressing feelings. Naturally, there are other reasons for using language— for example, it has an interrogative function, for drawing verbal responses from others. The interrogative function complements the informative function, since one is concerned with seeking or soliciting information, and the other involves generating information. The interrogative function can also be seen as a subset of the informative function.

Language enables people to classify their thinking and experience. This process is complex since meanings, especially connotations, are not only drawn from words in isolation but also from how they are placed in cultural and social linguistic structures; the syntactical and grammatical composition of written and spoken sentences can shape meanings.

This chapter does not aim to examine linguistic concepts and principles comprehensively. Interested readers may find it useful to follow up some of the references at the end of this chapter. This chapter is concerned with how people construct meanings and interpret the intentions of others, how miscommunication can arise, and how inappropriate language may sometimes be construed as a breach of etiquette.

4.2 Constructing Meanings with Words: Speaking

One of the distinctive features of speech is that meanings are constructed aurally: people act and communicate according to what they hear. Sometimes, of course, speech is accompanied by visual reinforcers. For example, people presenting papers at conferences often use overhead projectors to display their messages, so that their audience can interpret the presentation both visually and aurally.

Another important difference between speaking and writing is that speech is not always as tightly worded as most written messages are. Formal speeches and presentations may, of course, be carefully scripted, but the face-to-face or oral communication of people at work tends to be less rigid than their written memos. Oral communication is usually planned in general rather than detailed terms. For example, although a manager may plan a series of points to present at a committee meeting, the exact wording is seldom determined until the time comes. By contrast, written messages are constructed in significantly more detail and are not subject to change once they are issued.

There are various points which communicators should remember when constructing spoken messages. First, their spoken messages tend to have more spontaneity than their written messages. Because of this, there is relatively little time for speakers to adjust their thinking in mid-sentence. Once the spoken comment is made it is not easily undone, whereas written messages can be redrafted several times until its intention is expressed as well as possible. It is a good idea for people to remind themselves to think before they speak. However, we still say things that can unintentionally hurt, embarrass or anger others. Off-the-cuff comments often betray people's lack of tact or sensitivity when interacting with others, and can seriously damage professional and personal relationships.

'You look good today! You should always wear blue and not that ghastly geriatric brown you wore yesterday.'
'That's a great suggestion! Until now, I was beginning to think you didn't have what it takes.'
'You don't mean to tell me *you* wrote that report?'
'How can an intelligent person like you agree with that idiot of a manager?'
'That was a good game of tennis. Too bad you missed so many returns of my serve. Have you thought about switching to golf?'

TABLE 4.1

Examples of careless remarks that could damage relationships

From your own experience, you can probably recall comments like the ones above; most of them are back-handed compliments that seem to praise until they are followed by some derogative remark. In the workplace, the recipients of these kinds of comments are likely to develop suspicion and distrust about those who spoke to them in this way.

At this point, the shadow side of organisations will probably exert a profound influence on the future communication among its members. For example, without necessarily retorting assertively to those who delivered these back-handers, the slighted individuals might explore covert ways of 'getting even' with them, perhaps by making derogatory remarks behind their backs to other colleagues. These remarks may be fanciful or based on half-truths. Suppose a manager, who is frequently observed in the company of a fellow worker, indirectly insults a colleague; that colleague might spread the rumour that the manager is having an affair with another staff member.

Speculating about other people is, of course, something which many people are prone to do. In such instances, meanings are not created from facts but from people's imaginations. Without really observing what others are doing, some people are inclined to fill in the gaps with merely possible explanations. When these tentative explanations are taken as fact, their communication to others can injure relationships. In short, trust between people in systems is unlikely to survive if rumours are allowed to go unchecked.

Language is dynamic—it changes constantly and in various ways according to social and cultural trends. In speech, new expressions and buzzwords constantly arise. Sometimes the new vocabulary is specific to particular professions, organisations or fields of study. For example, in some life assurance organisations, 'financial services' are now known as 'financial products'. The notion of product as service is relatively new and suggests (to these organisations, at least) greater substantiality.

Another way in which managerial language has changed in recent years has been the growing practice of using nouns as verbs. Most people in systems today at one time or another use the term 'to liaise with'. Decades ago one would not have found this in any English dictionary because the correct usage was considered to be 'to make liaison with'. Below is a list of other examples of nouns currently used as verbs.

TABLE 4.2

Nouns used as verbs in modern organisations

Noun	Current usage as verb
action	to action a policy directive
access	to access information
diagram	to diagram the concept
format	to format a book
impact	to impact on management
size	to rightsize an operation

Think of other examples you have encountered in your professional experience. You will undoubtedly notice a similar trend to transform nouns into verb forms. For example, the word 'priority' has led to 'prioritise'; from 'strategy' we now have 'to strategise'. Other examples include verbs such as 'professionalise', 'marginalise', and 'lateralise'. When using personal computers, individuals are required to 'initialise' their floppy discs.

Another recent tendency of managers' spoken language, particularly in times of turmoil or recession, has been to resort to euphemism. Times of financial crisis, for example, are referred to as 'economic downturns'. Redundant staff are no longer retrenched but 'disemployed' or 'dehired'. 'Budget cuts' are now called 'financial streamlining procedures'. Military terminology also shows the same tendency—a planned attack on the enemy is more commonly called a 'tactical military offensive operation'. Soldiers killed in action are referred to simply as 'losses' or 'M-I-A' ('missing in action'); an atomic bomb is a 'nuclear device'.

Spoken language has also changed in other ways over the years. For instance, with the advent of assertive feminism, women have come to object to terms of endearment used by their superiors. Words like 'sweetie' and 'honey', once tolerated or even considered acceptable, are now often considered to have sexual connotations, and many women employees regard the use of such terms by male employees as a form of sexual harrassment. Many women see the male-female worker relationship in terms of 'sexual politics' where the struggle for power represents a struggle for gender-based dominance in the workplace.

Many organisations today provide guidelines for the use of non-sexist language. They suggest the substitution of 'person' for 'man', the plural form of nouns and pronouns to avoid references to masculine pronouns like 'he' or 'him', and the use of gender-inclusive synonyms such as 'police officer' for 'policeman' and 'policewoman', or 'flight attendant' or 'cabin crew member' for 'steward' or 'stewardess'. Some guidelines also warn against patronising expressions and sex-role stereotyping. For example, it is preferable to say 'My assistant will take care of that' instead of 'My girl will . . .' and 'teachers have families to support' instead of 'teachers have wives and children to support'.

Sometimes the same type of behaviour in men and women is described in different terms. For instance, men intent on their career paths are usually called 'ambitious' but women in this category are sometimes referred to as 'aggressive'. Stereotyping of this kind can extend to a patronising sexist comment like 'the client's behaviour was typically female' instead of a specific description of her behaviour.

All organisations are now required to enforce legislation against gender-based discrimination, which includes sexist forms of address. Some organisations, however, continue to overlook male employees' persistent use of sexist language. Many of these males are in male-dominated occupations like plumbing, building or vehicle trades.

It is curious that in women-dominated occupations like nursing or office management (including secretarial work), discrimination against males is evidently rare. The dearth of reports of discrimination against men by women in all probability signifies that increased opportunities exist for men to enter traditionally female-held types of occupations. The few examples of women using sexist language tend to refer to male genitalia in derogatory terms. Although words like 'dick-head' or 'prick' are often used by men referring to other men, women seldom disparage other women in terms of female sexual organs. Men, on the other hand, often refer to people, regardless of their gender, in terms of female genitalia. So long as people continue to use sexist language, communication in the workplace will be in danger of breaking down.

Our speech can betray our true values. Even if we guard against words that are likely to offend others, occasional slips of the tongue can still reveal what we really think or feel. For instance, the way people refer to different ethnic groups can be seen in the following examples.

TABLE 4.3

Examples of terms of abuse for cultural groups

Nationality/ethnicity	Terms of abuse
Italian	Dago, wog
English	Pommie, limey
Chinese	Chink
French	Frog
Pakastani	Paki
Japanese	Nip
German	Hun, kraut, Gerry/Jerry
American Hispanics	Spics
American Blacks	Niggers
American Whites	Honkeys
Australian Aborigines	Abos

Some of the examples above (e.g. nip and kraut) derive from World War II, but some older Australians continue to use them. Many younger Australians may find these terms strange, especially as our cities are assuming a more cosmopolitan, multicultural character. The prejudices underlying the use of derogatory ethnic labels will probably fade once Australians begin to form an *inter*cultural rather than a *multi*cultural identity. Elsewhere I have suggested that an 'intercultural' society has different ethnic groups influencing each other through the sharing of diverse cultures. By contrast, in a 'multicultural' society, different ethnic groups often form separate communities of their own and remain untouched by the cultures of other groups.

Slips of the tongue also occur when religious prejudices surface. Catholics, for example, are often labelled by non-Catholics as 'tykes', and Irish Catholics are called 'micks'. Some refer to Jewish people as 'yids' or 'kikes'. Christians generally, and in particular fundamentalist Christians, have been called 'bible-bashers' or 'holy rollers'. All these kinds of terms when used in the workplace can jeopardise relationships and communication. The extract on page 79 illustrates this point.

Without doubt, spoken messages containing offensive words can seriously impair personal relationships even if those messages are not intended to be provocative. Insensitive people often simply don't realise that they may be offending others by their choice of words; for them, such words are not even offensive. For example, people who blaspheme are

Scene: a group of male staff members at lunch discussing the events of the week at work and other general matters.

Alex: How the hell did that crawling dago Luigi get promoted to supervisor? Why couldn't it have gone to a true-blue Aussie?

Joe: Maybe because Luigi and that do-gooding bastard foreman Ron are both tykes that go to the same church.

Fred: Nah, it's more than that. This company just doesn't appreciate honest-working 'real men' like us. I mean men with balls—men who can stand up to the nonsense that people like Ron dish out.

Phil: Next time it'll be someone like that coon Rasheed who sucks up to anyone in authority.

Fred: Who knows? They might give the next promotion to a bloody sheila who's prepared to have it off with the right people.

Joe: If you ask me they'll give it to one of those yellow-eyed computer whizz kid chinks on the second floor. They're getting to be a dime-a-dozen. They'll probably give it to a chink bird.

Alex: You may be right, but when Ron gets kicked upstairs I know who my money is going to be on. Not on any of us hard-working bastards. Someone like that wog Theo. He's not here with us, is he? Right now he's probably pissing in Ron's pocket.

Joe: Now there's a pair of little queers for you. I'll bet they both watch that game that sheilas should play instead of watching proper footy like league.

Phil: Oh, you mean soccer. That's strictly for wogs and wimps.

At this point an attractive young female office worker enters the lunch room. Most of these men give out wolfwhistles.

Fred: Hey honey! How'd you like a bit of a cuddle with a real stud?

often unaware that this makes others feel uncomfortable or angry. Some non-Christians use the word 'Christ' as an expletive. In such instances, there is usually no denotative meaning but the word is typically associated with states of surprise, amazement, horror, frustration and other related feelings. When used indiscriminately, blasphemous words, therefore, become little more than recurrent modifiers of speech. Clearly, the use of this kind of blasphemy in the presence of people who use the same word with respect can weaken or even destroy relationships.

In general, the way people speak to each other indicates the nature and intensity of their interpersonal relationships. Those who use potentially offensive language give the impression that they are indifferent to or even disrespect others' values; furthermore, they in turn invite disrespect and disapproval. No worthwhile communication is likely to occur when a relationship is characterised by mutual disrespect.

Communication scholars recognising how language can cause offence to specific community groups have begun to study **politically correct language** (e.g. Carey, 1992; Dennis, 1992; O'Keefe, 1992; Burgoon and Bailey, 1992;

politically correct language
Language acceptable to all groups in a human system. 'Political correctness' has been traditionally associated with radical leftist movements, e.g. in feminist scholarship.

Whitney and Wartella, 1992; Gross, 1992; Henderson, 1992; Glasser, 1992). The general idea behind politically correct language is that words should be carefully chosen to avoid offending any specific sector of the community. Desirable as this may be, politically correct language is not always appropriate for every sector. 'Antipols'—those who oppose the concept of political correctness—argue that people should be able to say what they want and that what may be construed as sexist or racist to some would not necessarily be sexist or racist to others (Asante, 1992:144–46). One thing is certain: the debate about political correctness (PC) is in its infancy. As one writer has noted, 'the "PC" debates have yet to really hit the discipline of communication' (Grossberg, 1992:148).

Appropriate spoken communication, therefore, involves the careful choice of words that are not potentially offensive. When it is accompanied by skilful sentence construction, there is every chance that intended meanings will be appropriately shared, co-ordinated with clarity, and reciprocated without misinterpretation.

Section 4.2 examines some of the distinctive features of written communication, and how meanings can change according to different structures.

4.3 Constructing Meanings with Words: Writing

Because meetings, particularly informal meetings, can be very time-consuming, people at work often find it useful to communicate with their colleagues in writing. Written messages like memos have certain advantages over spoken messages. They can be read over and over again, whereas spoken messages may be imperfectly remembered. However, written messages are not invariably more permanent than spoken ones which can also have permanent effects on those who receive them. Take for example a manager disciplining a staff member for failing to come up to scratch—the 'shape up or ship out' order is not likely to be forgotten quickly. Statements like 'I'm afraid I've got some bad news for you' preceding the announcement of some personal tragedy or the loss of a job also probably ring in people's ears for a long time.

Written messages, of course, can be equally devastating. A letter terminating employment can be just as horrific as being told the news by a superior at work. Naturally, conveying this kind of news in a letter seems a more impersonal way of communicating because written messages are sometimes expressed economically. Moreover, written messages have an aura of finality about them. Putting something in writing often gives the message a 'legal' status. Perhaps this is why many managers will only follow up written, not orally communicated, complaints.

Why do people in organisations sometimes write messages to each other when they can communicate readily by telephone or in person?

Much depends on how accessible others are, and whether directly speaking to someone can achieve any more than communicating in writing. Nowadays, electronic mail appears to have superseded many other forms of communicating amongst members of organisations. For example, routine tasks are easily assigned through concise memos. Requests for information, reports on staff members' performance, and recommendations about salaries or promotion are all made the same way.

Of course, if memos are poorly constructed, those who receive them may respond inappropriately. Ambiguous or contradictory wording in written business communication often signals uncertainty or conflict in the author's mind, and confuses the receiver of the message. Here's an example.

INTERNAL MEMORANDUM

To: All section and department heads

From: I.M. Vaig, Human Resource Development Manager

Date: 1 April 1994

Re: 1995 staff training needs

The Human Resources Division invites all section and department heads to indicate training and development needs for their staff in 1995. As soon as these submissions are received, estimates of cost will be forwarded to section and department heads for verification and approval. Alternatively, section and department heads may wish to provide their own cost estimates and indicate training and development funding allocated within their particular budgets. Some indication of preference for internal or external training and development consultants would be helpful although this information is not strictly required.

Submissions, preferably in writing, should be forwarded to U.R. Slack, Senior Training and Development Consultant, HRD Division, within the next few weeks or as soon as convenient. Section and department heads wishing to make their own arrangements for training and development of their staff in 1995 do not need to follow the procedures suggested in this memorandum. However, should they wish to avail themselves of HRD services at a later date, they would be well advised to make a submission in the near future.

Your co-operation in making your submissions promptly will assist the HRD Division in planning to meet the future training and development needs of your staff. For this reason, we ask that your submission reach the HRD Division by <u>Friday 13 April at the latest</u>. Action on submissions received after that date may be subject to unavoidable delays.

I M Vaig
cc U R Slack

TABLE 4.5

Poorly worded memos can be confusing to the receiver

There are two main weaknesses in this memo. First, its requirements are vague—for instance, 'within the next few weeks or as soon as conveniently possible'. It would be much better to provide a definite deadline straight away. Later in the memo the deadline (Friday 13 April) is followed by a statement that weakens its urgency. The implication is that submissions will still be considered after 13 April.

Second, there is no reason to provide unnecessary options. What is gained by giving section and department heads the choice of drafting their own estimates or having the HRD division draft them? Intelligent individuals are unlikely to undertake tasks not required of them. Similarly, it is odd that written submissions from section and department heads are not mandatory. Other forms of submission, such as telephone messages, can be unreliable, particularly when they are reiterated from memory by the initial receiver.

Written messages, therefore, are relatively permanent records that can be readily reproduced. For instance, if employees violate a no-smoking rule, they cannot claim that the rule was not brought to their attention, especially when that rule was circulated in writing to all employees, or if there are no-smoking signs throughout the building.

Another reason for committing information to written form is that the confusion of meanings can be significantly reduced, particularly if it is presented clearly and unambiguously. Imagine a group of marketing and human resource managers relying on memory for a discussion of their organisation's mission statement and objectives. The discussion might go something like this:

TABLE 4.6

Important information should be recorded in writing

> *Richard Hedde* (presiding): I think we should now consider the implications of the organisational mission statement for the marketing and human resource departments. I am referring to the mission statement the vice-president referred to at our regular management committee meeting a month ago.
>
> *Sam Keene*: Oh yeah! Wasn't it something about increasing percentages of sales by 10—or was it 20 per cent?
>
> *Mike Shure*: I'm pretty certain it was more like 5 per cent and maybe for only next year.
>
> *Lucy Wright*: You guys are really off-beam. I have the distinct recollection that the v-p said that for sales to increase we need to focus on providing quality service in this organisation. The mission statement was something about quality service, I'm positive.
>
> *Ella Ford*: Maybe Mike was right about the 5 per cent. It could have meant improving quality service by 5 per cent.
>
> *Sam Keene*: How the hell can you measure quality in percentages? If that's what the v-p said we shouldn't waste our time on this any more.
>
> *Richard Hedde*: Now, now, folks. Let's not lose our cool. What we need to do is to recall bit by bit what the v-p spoke to us about last month. Did anyone take any notes at that meeting?

Plainly, this is a ridiculous scenario, yet not completely unlikely. In many conservative organisations, people tend to become suspicious about things like 'mission statements' and 'strategic plans'. Discussions about organisation goals, for example, will not get very far if people have little more than vague recollections of peptalks from superiors. Ideally, every person present should have a copy of the mission statement.

According to Egan (1991), it is vital for all people in a system or organisation to know thoroughly and have a firm commitment to the system's mission. On this point he argues that '. . . it is critical that everyone in a company or institution understand and be guided by the central concepts and policies of the mission . . . The trick is getting the mission to sink into the consciousness of everyone in the company or institution' (Egan, 1991:34-35). Of course, if the mission statement itself is unclear, the discussion will be sidetracked into trying to make sense of it.

When information is presented in imperfect or incomplete form, it is relatively easy for receivers to weaken its credibility by questioning various aspects of it. This can involve people in what is commonly termed the 'fallacy of the straw person', where a portion of an argument is selected and then a case is made out against it to destroy the entire argument. In the example above, members of the group seem uncertain about the details of the previous meeting on the organisation's mission statement. Despite their uncertainty, they continue to debate these poorly remembered details. For example, they debate the legitimacy of determining quality by percentages when this concept may not have been introduced at the previous meeting. This is fallacious reasoning, resulting from a dearth of clear written information. As someone once said, 'that comment is not worth the paper it was not written on'.

Another advantage of communicating in writing is that messages may be readily understood even if they are cryptic. For example, a telegram concentrates on key words and the reader has to 'fill in the missing blanks' to construct its full meaning, as follows:

Telegram: Returning Monday 0635 CO23 contract OK projected sales figures separate settlement details follow   Roger *Same message with blanks filled in:* (I will be) returning (on) Monday (at) 6.35 a.m. (on Continental Flight Number) CO23. (The) contract (was considered) satisfactory/OK (by the client). (I am forwarding the) projected sales figures (under) separate (cover). (The) settlement details (of date, time and place will) follow (the client's confirmation of the contract).

TABLE 4.7

Telegrams contain key words. The full message is longer

It is harder to fill in blanks in oral messages, either because the words are forgotten quickly, or because all the present and missing elements are not as easy to review or piece together as they are in a written message. There are other contexts where written messages are deliberately left incomplete to entice receivers to fill in their own blanks. Take advertising, for example. Some advertisers begin by giving the public the full message. After a while, only part of the message is given because it is assumed that people can complete the original message. In the advertisement for Winfield cigarettes the full slogan 'anyhow, have a Winfield!' became contracted to 'anyhow'. The intention of this device is to condition people to produce associated meanings and connotations, which reinforces the intended message. Here are some other examples.

TABLE 4.8

In advertising certain words connote a larger message

Product	Brief message	Rest of message
Sharp	Simply the best	(when only the best will do)
Ford	Have you?	(driven a Ford, lately?)
Commonwealth Bank	Which bank?	(gives you more?)
NMLA	Because we care	(about the most important person in the world—you!)
Toohey's	How do you feel?	(I feel like a Toohey's, or two.)
David Jones	There's no other store	(like David Jones)

This section concludes with how the meanings of written messages can be misconstrued. First, vague wording usually signals uncertainty of intent. This kind of vagueness is cannon fodder for receivers already prejudiced against such messages, and for fallacious argument. Effective written messages, on the other hand, are clear and unequivocal. Warnings like 'Billposters will be prosecuted' are undoubtedly more daunting than modified versions like 'Billposters may be prosecuted'. In the former instance, there is absolutely no doubt that all billposters who are caught will incur a penalty. The substitution of 'may' for 'will' in the second version, however, suggests that a penalty is just a possibility.

A second characteristic of effective written messages is that their intended meanings are communicated as economically as possible. They communicate only what is necessary, since unnecessary information may reduce the likelihood of the message being responded to appropriately.

Sometimes words are not necessary to convey meaning economically. Most people recognise the familiar prohibition sign that consists of a red circle containing a symbol (e.g. a cigarette) with a diagonal line through it.

A third characteristic of effective written messages is that they have a coherent grammatical and syntactical structure. There is more than one kind of appropriate structure for written messages, of course. Business letters, for example, usually require short, direct sentences. On the other hand, legal documents go into great detail and at great length, to cover all aspects and to avoid leaving loopholes. The full scope of grammatical and syntactical structure is beyond the range of this book, but some texts on the subject are recommended at the end of this chapter.

The next section is concerned with how people assign meaning to the language others use, and what influences their interpretations.

Interpreting the Language of Others   4.4

Most people in systems use language in socially determined and accepted ways, and talk and write much the same way—that is, with a common vocabulary and idiom. When they move from one system to another, confusion sometimes occurs because words and phrases can mean different things in different systems. For example, to educators and trainers the word 'workshop' usually means a learning session for problem-solving groups, but to automotive mechanics 'workshop' means space with equipment for servicing and repairing vehicles. Similarly, to most people in Australia the word 'pension' refers to payments to retired workers, but in Europe it usually means a boarding-house or small hotel.

Confusion over terms can cause embarrassment. For example, the common meaning of the word 'rubber' in America is 'condom', but in Australia it means 'eraser'. Similarly, colloquial expressions are very often misunderstood when used out of context. When Australians say 'Excuse me, I think I've *pinched your seat*', they usually mean they've *taken* someone's seat, but Americans might understand it to mean that one individual had pinched someone's buttocks. Probably all cultures have colloquial phrases and sayings. On page 86 are some typical Australian expressions with their literal interpretations.

The first two examples contain similes based on very locale-specific information and are therefore unlikely to be found beyond certain geographical boundaries. Not too many city dwellers, for example, would easily conjure up images of outside toilets in the country. Similarly, Bondi trams were part of Sydney's suburban transport system up to the early 1960s. It is highly unlikely that teenagers and young adults of today would identify with images of long-departed trams in Sydney's eastern suburbs.

Some organisations generate idiomatic expressions and special vocabulary of their own, to distinguish them from other sectors of the workforce. As a consultant to an international financial institution, I found that people there expected me to understand and use as a basis for intelligent discussion words I had never encountered before. They were

TABLE 4.9

Some Australian colloquialisms and their literal interpretations

Australian colloquialism	Literal interpretation
All alone like a country dunny	As solitary as an outside toilet in a rural area
Shoot through like a Bondi tram	Disappear quickly
Throw a spanner in the works	Confuse an issue
Flat out like a lizard drinking	Working to full capacity
Have a blue with somebody	Get into an argument or fight
Furphy	A rumour or false story
Fair dinkum (?)	True; really?
Fair go!	Give me a chance! or, you don't really mean that, do you?
She'll be apples, mate	It will be OK
Give it a go (have a go)	Try it

surprised when I professed my ignorance of their 'language'. Occasionally, of course, language that is understood by some and not by others in an organisation is simply jargon that is not yet in general use. It is frequently based on current political, managerial, or training rhetoric—for example, 'strategic', 'forward planning', or 'proactively leading'. In some ways, expressions like 'forward planning' are tautological. Planning can hardly be 'backward' looking, nor can people lead 'retroactively'. Sometimes technical jargon is peculiar to a particular department or section of an organisation.

Again, a lot of jargon derives from new vocabulary in high-technology areas such as computing science. Almost daily, it seems, unfamiliar technical terminology is generated. Here are some instances: pagemaker, imagewriter, hypercard utilities, electronic mail, RAM cache, diacritical marks, memory multifinder, serial interface, and customising startup disks. Most of these are probably household words now, since computer terminology is fast becoming 'user-friendly'. Computer literacy is also becoming more widespread in the community as it becomes part of the curricula of schools and colleges.

Perhaps the most extreme instance of needlessly complex jargon I have recently seen is: 'We need to know the performance indicators of the key players in the current scenario'. After spending some moments attempting to decipher this, a couple of my colleagues concluded that the quoted portion means 'the job descriptions of present senior staff members'. Words and sayings exclusive to certain organisations often take the form of acronyms. For instance, people in the pharmaceutical manufacturing industry tend to refer to non-prescription products as OTC items. OTC stands for 'over-the-counter'. To outsiders, OTC can mean 'overseas telecommunications'. You can probably think of other examples of this kind. Whilst these are not, strictly speaking, technical terms, they have an aura of mystique suggestive of technical specialisation and authority. Consequently, outsiders not knowing these abbreviations and sayings may feel excluded and uncertain whether to pretend to understand them or to admit ignorance.

Consider the following meeting of individuals from different organisations at a management convention seminar. They are discussing ways of being kept informed regularly about the activities of the staff they manage:

Manager 1 (Rob): I tend to keep tabs on my staff by following a regular WIGO routine. I don't know of anything that works better. How do you find it, Phil?

Manager 2 (Phil): Well, Rob, I like the YAKIM method. It seems to work with my staff. I'll bet there are others here who would support me on this one.

Manager 3 (Tom): I suppose I must agree with you Rob, because I know I don't go wrong when I use WIGO, although for a while we tried using electronic mail messages or LAMOD. What's YAKIM, Phil?

TABLE 4.10
Unfamiliar acronyms can prevent successful communication

This could seem like a foreign language to people outside this discussion group. Even Tom has to ask what YAKIM is. It is unlikely that everyone would know organisation-specific acronyms like WIGO ('What is going on?'), YAKIM ('You all keep informing me'), or LAMOD ('Let's all meet once daily'). Meaning cannot be fully shared if the understanding of everyone involved is taken for granted.

As a general guideline, listeners should make a point of clarifying with speakers any verbal messages that are vague or ambiguous. However, some people are reluctant to admit their inability to understand other's messages, often because they don't want to seem ignorant or incompetent. Seeking clarification of others' messages tends to be less stressful in social and recreational settings, probably because encounters outside the workplace are usually less formal, and free of officialese.

Sometimes listeners' misunderstanding of messages can be exacerbated by inappropriate words. Section 4.5 describes some of the ways people can miscommunicate with words.

Miscommunicating with Words   4.5

The ways people use words can cause others to misconstrue their intention. Sometimes the message is unintentionally misleading simply because speakers or writers have an inadequate command of the words they are using. An example that comes to mind is the often-found confusion some people have between the verbs 'affect' and 'effect'. It is not uncommon to read individuals' written messages where 'affect' is used to signify 'bring about', or 'effect' to mean 'influence'. Subtle as these differences may be in writing, they would almost certainly be undetectable in speech. Bearing in mind the dynamic nature of language and the importance of the contexts in which messages are conveyed, these kinds of confused usages are rarely serious enough to change intended meanings radically.

It does become more difficult, however, for individuals to judge what kind of follow-up is implied by phrases such as 'be responsive to'. Currently it is fashionable to encourage service providers to 'be responsive to client needs'. In fact, mission statements have been defined as organisations' responses to the needs of their particular receiver systems (Egan, 1985). Does 'being responsive', however, mean that servicing agents should simply follow their clients' orders? If so, there seems to be no real acknowledgment of the service provider's expertise.

Let's take the example of a teacher education faculty, which should be 'responsive' to the needs of both its student teachers and the pupils whom they will eventually teach. This means that teacher educators should be thoroughly aware of current developments in the student teachers' subject areas, and the content and design of the faculty's education curriculum should reflect this. Teacher educators must also be able to help student teachers develop a thorough understanding of the learning process.

'Being responsive', of course, can also mean, in this context, that teacher educators should base their teacher education curriculum on the preferred methods of the future employers of student teachers. What if the views of these future employers differ significantly from those of teacher educators— would the latter then cease to be 'responsive' to their clients? Or are they responsive because they are acting in good faith and asserting their right to exercise responsible, professional judgment? Clearly, the meaning of 'be responsive to' varies according to the preferences of the communicators using this expression, and phrases like this can lead to miscommunication.

Other phrases of this kind include 'to take action', 'to develop a strategy', 'to explore the feasibility of', and 'to highlight significant issues'. All these need a set of guidelines or statement to clarify the intended meaning to prevent unnecessary miscommunication and its potential for conflict.

There are also quite deliberate ways in which people miscommunicate. One common tactic is to report only part of a message. Cinema advertising does this. The following are excerpts of three press reviews of a new movie, *Moonlight Revenge*:

> (*Goshen Times*) '*Moonlight Revenge* is based on the recent bestseller paperback novel by John Argyle. Just as the novel holds the reader spellbound, the film is disappointing in its failure to have the viewer gripped by capitalising on a breathtaking plot.'

> (*Daily Star*) 'Michael Vincent could have played the role of his career as this story in many ways reflects his actual experiences as a teenager. Unfortunately, his lack of talent is all too obvious. The heroine, played by much acclaimed newcomer to the silver screen, Della Laroux, lacked lustre from the start and limped her way through the part in what was anything but a convincing performance.'

(*Pacific Tribune*) 'Roger McLean's direction of the film *Moonlight Revenge* makes one wonder if he actually did direct former hits like *Genius at Work* in 1987 and *Fallen Femme Fatale* a year later. What should and could have been a masterpiece of suspense ended up as soapie trash.'

Here are the excerpts that formed part of the publicity for the film:

'*Moonlight Revenge* based on the bestseller novel . . . has the viewer gripped . . . a breathtaking plot' (*Goshen Times*)

'Michael Vincent . . . the role of his career . . . talent all too obvious' (*Daily Star*)

'Della Laroux . . . a convincing performance' (*Daily Star*)

'Roger McLean's direction of the film *Moonlight Revenge* a masterpiece of suspense' (*Pacific Tribune*)

This kind of selective tampering with messages is a machiavellian device which is not restricted to film reviews. It can be detected in any setting, personal or professional, where people attempt to attain superiority over others in covert or subtle ways, and sometimes one carefully chosen word is sufficient to do this. For example, 'that maligning memo' suggests that the whole memo was derogatory, even if it contained only some slightly disquieting remark like 'your claims are not entirely accurate'.

Other emotive words besides 'maligning' that give a negative impression are 'inflammatory', 'insulting', 'berating', 'demeaning' and 'condescending'. You can undoubtedly think of other single words that create a false impression of the entire message and miscommunicate the true intent of its originator.

Another way in which individuals miscommunicate is by applying linguistic 'filters'. These are mechanisms or language structures through which people channel their thinking and intentions. Examples of linguistic filters include accent, pronunciation, dialect, register, and grammar. By being identified with particular linguistic characteristics, people may be easily labelled or stereotyped. The broad Australian accent, for example, is often associated with the 'ocker' type of person. 'Ocker' in Australia is roughly equivalent to 'redneck', 'hayseed' or 'hick' in America, and in England with the cockney or labourer. The essential image is one of unsophistication and lack of urbanity.

Contriving to create an impression by using various kinds of linguistic filters may not always be construed as miscommunication although it often seems to be a form of self-deception. Some highly educated people, for example, speak to less educated people in broad Australian accents instead of their usual accents, to create the impression that their education has not made them elitist and that they are just as comfortable with less educated people as they are with their peers. In other possibly more familiar personal or professional settings, however, it may be more natural for these people to revert to an educated Australian accent.

The reverse could also hold true for those who would normally use a broad Australian accent. In the company of people who speak with an educated accent, some broad Australian speakers may blunt the edge of their vowels and diphthongs in an almost subconscious attempt to approximate the others' speech and accent. In either instance, this modification of one's speech pattern may create an impression of artificiality and jeopardise the credibility of the message; the communication may be construed as something designed to impress, and not completely sincere.

When they speak, people can be stereotyped not only because of their accents but also because of the way they structure their sentences grammatically, and the diversity of their vocabulary. In many cases the stereotypical image matches a person's true character. Without any deeper understanding of or familiarity with such a person, however, we cannot be totally certain that the stereotype is justified. In such situations, the miscommunication may be due to the perceiver, not the speaker, and to the perceiver's attitude to the speaker's use of language.

Perceivers can misjudge others

Miscommunication does not only occur because of the way people use words. Facial expressions, voice qualities, and body language are powerful ways of generating images. These nonverbal channels can be used to communicate deceptive messages about feelings and attitudes. For example, a person who smiles a lot when having a difference of opinion with someone else may give the impression of being happy and unruffled, even if that person is inwardly agitated. The facial expression, in this instance, has become a mask to cover up the true emotional state. This example of the deceptive potential of certain nonverbal cues also indicates the connection between thought and action; not only the connection between our own thoughts and actions, but also between one person's actions and another person's thoughts about them. Section 4.6 explores another connection, the one between language and thinking, and the role of language in the construction of meaning.

Language and Thinking 4.6

One of the main functions of language is the classification of thought. Language gives people a means of structuring their individual worlds of experience. The categories used to classify thought are peculiar to the particular language being used. How individuals think is probably determined by the nature and structure of their different languages. Some people, of course, know more than one language. Their thinking will be determined by the language they are using at the time. Two linguistic scholars with an interest in semantics, Benjamin Lee Whorf and Edward Sapir, have argued that the language structures and systems which people learn from their particular cultures strongly influence how they view and interpret their world (Sapir, 1921; Whorf, 1956). These semanticists developed what is now commonly referred to as the Sapir-Whorf hypothesis, also known as the Whorfian hypothesis or the Theory of Linguistic Relativity. Their hypothesis consists of two basic principles. The first principle is that *all higher-order levels of thought require language*. In other words, complex thought processes such as differentiation or abstraction require a mastery of one's language.

The second principle is that *the structure of the language people use determines the manner in which they understand their environment*. Plausible as this hypothesis may seem, it has never been scientifically tested. According to Infante, Rancer and Womack (1990:199), 'little if any research has explored the relationship between linguistic structure and actual behavior'. Even if the hypothesis were true, it would be virtually impossible to 'prove' it (Cronkhite, 1976:271).

To illustrate this hypothesis in a non-experimental way, try to imagine what it would be like for an inhabitant of another planet to land on Earth and observe what is taking place. Without a command of any language spoken on this planet, how could this visitor from outer space communicate any personal understanding or perception of Earth? And how could people on this planet discover the alien's interpretation of it?

Consider how thinking in English can differ from thinking in other languages. For one thing, English-speaking people have words for counting each number from one to infinity. Certain non-western tribes, on the other hand, only have words for one, two, and many. As another example, English has only one word for snow, but the language of the Eskimos has eleven words to denote different kinds of snow. Again, English-speaking people qualify nouns with definite or indefinite articles but no articles exist in the Russian language.

English differs from other languages in various other ways. English has three pronouns for gender: masculine, feminine, and neuter, but the French language has only the masculine and feminine categories for it. Latin, the language of the ancient Romans, is highly inflected. The meaning of Latin sentences is determined principally by word-endings. By contrast, the meaning of sentences in English depends mostly on word-order, not word-endings or inflections.

To list many more ways in which the English language is structured differently from other languages would only labour the point that thinking in English is different from thinking in other languages in certain ways. Since thinking is at the core of the meaning-construction process, we can conclude that speakers and users of different languages often make sense of their personal and social worlds in different ways. However, speakers or users of different languages do have some things in common. Universal meaning is probably best exemplified by commonly used signs that denote prohibition, public conveniences and danger, as shown in Figure 4.1.

FIGURE 4.1

Commonly used international signs

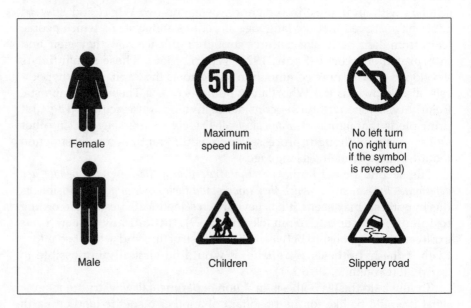

Female

Maximum speed limit

No left turn (no right turn if the symbol is reversed)

Male

Children

Slippery road

Whilst the sharing of meaning between different groups of language users is obviously easier at the nonverbal level, one or two important points should be borne in mind. First, just as there is probably a connection between language mastery and the ability to engage in higher-order thinking processes, people's perceptions and interpretations of their personal worlds provide a basis for their communication and behaviour: perception and thought govern the way people speak, act and behave toward each other. Since language has a powerful influence on how people think about and classify their experience, there is probably a relationship between language and behaviour. Most likely this relationship is an indirect one, mediated by the process of thinking and interpretation. Several decades ago, two other semanticists, Ogden and Richards (1969) proposed a model for the interrelationship between words (symbols), the objects (referents) denoted by those words, and the intervening thought process (reference). They called this explanation 'the referential triangle' (see Figure 4.2).

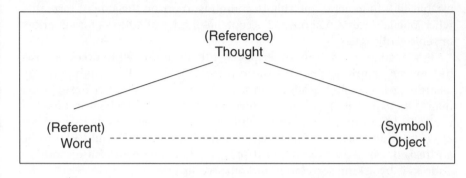

FIGURE 4.2
The referential triangle
Source: Ogden and Richards (1969)

The referential triangle represents a particular part of the interrelationship between the elements of communication considered in this section. The connection the model makes between language, thought and the object of perception could be extended to include 'behaviour' or 'action'. Essentially, therefore, the interrelationship of the elements of experience, language, thinking and individual action may be seen as a linear one where action or behaviour results from the interaction of language and thought.

The following section includes a special situation—where effective communication depends greatly on appropriate thinking. It suggests that managers need to adjust their thinking to the demands of particular situations. It also proposes that inflexibility in managers' thinking could lead not only to a failure to communicate well but also to unintentional breaches of managerial etiquette.

Language in Organisations: 4.7
Managerial Etiquette

Managerial etiquette has attracted relatively little interest from writers on management. This is surprising since there is no systematic or comprehensive set of etiquette guidelines for people to follow when they are appointed as managers. When faced with unfamiliar situations, many sensitive managers tend to learn as much as they can by observing how others act. Without suitable role models, however, uninitiated managers can find themselves embarrassed or stigmatised when they do not behave as expected, or commission inappropriate behaviour.

Acceptable ways of addressing our superiors at work are very much determined by the prevailing culture of particular organisations. In the legal profession, for example, it is conventional to use titles such as 'judge', 'your honour' or 'my lord' when communicating with magistrates. For most professions, however, expectations and practices vary according to tradition and the degree of formality or informality that senior staff have established. In general, the rule-of-thumb is to err on the side of formality when one is uncertain about the acceptable modes of address for superiors or senior colleagues.

It is prudent to address superiors by title until invited to do otherwise, but many people get off on the wrong foot with their managers by assuming the right to begin on a first-name basis. Of course, some managers expect to be addressed formally in settings like boardrooms but prefer to be on first-name terms with their staff members. It is therefore advisable for workers to ask their superiors how they would like to be addressed. Sometimes you can discover what the appropriate mode of address is by asking secretaries and other colleagues.

The art of conversation involves the necessity to know how to address others appropriately, especially in formal circumstances. Ease in conversing with others not only indicates communication competence but also indicates the possession of savoir-faire. It also involves knowing how and when to introduce appropriate topics. It is often necessary to engage in light conversation before gradually moving to meatier matters. Skilled conversationalists know how and when to engage in social chit-chat before turning to more serious topics. People who launch directly into intense conversations with others, especially strangers, may find that such initiatives are regarded as gauche and off-putting.

Finally, it is important to mention that managerial etiquette is most likely to be situationally specific. What is acceptable communication in one situation may well be unacceptable in another, and vice versa. For example, telling jokes or other kinds of amusing anecdotes at the expense of a particular group (e.g. ethnic, religious, gender-based, political, industrial) ought never to be introduced at gatherings where members of that group may be present. It is probably wise to refrain from introducing humour into conversations until it is possible to judge the suitability or otherwise of certain kinds of humour.

4.8 Summary

This chapter has focused on how people use language to construct meanings in speech and writing. It considered the nature and functions of language and the processes by which people interpret the language of others. It was then argued that in the course of interpreting others' messages, people may miscommunicate by 'filtering' what they hear or read. The relationship between language and thinking was briefly analysed, and the linguistic relativity hypothesis and the referential triangle were outlined.

The communication management framework of this book led naturally to the question of how action or behaviour is based on or follows on from language and thought. Finally, the appropriate use of language in organisations was briefly considered—in particular, etiquette in managerial circles.

Chapter 5 considers the nature and functions of nonverbal communication and how the nonverbal domain complements the verbal. It proposes that competence in communication involves knowledge and understanding, as well as performance skill both verbally and nonverbally.

Discussion Questions 4.9

1. Suggest two specific ways in which people in human systems can discourage colleagues, family and friends from using sexist language (e.g. confront the offender directly, report the offender to your immediate superior). State which approach you prefer and give reasons for your preference.

2. List three examples of verbal statements that betray people's bias against particular groups or events; for example, 'the Sydney Gay Mardi Gras disgraces our community'. Discuss how these statements could be reworded so that they are free of bias and prejudice.

3. It is advisable to think before we speak and to weigh our words carefully, but sometimes we have to 'think on our feet'. Describe some occasions when this has happened to you and say how you might manage such unexpected pressures more successfully.

4. Think of an occasion when you have misunderstood what someone else has told you. Why did you misunderstand? What could you do in future to prevent such misunderstanding? Discuss your thoughts with someone else.

5. What kinds of things that people say can cause embarrassment because their words are inappropriate or in breach of etiquette in particular settings? List any examples you have drawn from experience or reading. Now discuss your list with someone and indicate in each case the kind of wording that would have been appropriate and acceptable.

Activities 4.10

1. Next to each of the following words list all your own connotations. For example, next to 'tourist' you might put 'camera freak', 'dressed in poor taste', 'stands on wrong side of escalator', 'sees new places mainly from

the window of tour buses', 'supports local economy' etc. From your positive and negative connotations, describe your overall impression and the value you associate with the target word.

Target word(s)	Connotation
Championship boxing	
Politicians	
Marriage (or divorce)	
Republic	
Royalty/monarchy	
Industrial unions	
Affirmative action	
Rugby league (or other football code)	
Cars	
Money	
Alcoholic beverages	
Violence on TV and in movies	
Graffiti artist	
Work	

2. Draft a letter to your supervisor at work. Express your views on how your department structure could be streamlined to function more efficiently. Show your draft to a friend and discuss its strengths and weaknesses, then redraft it so that any weaknesses are removed.

3. Politicians often use political 'double-speak'. Here are 10 examples:

Statement	Translation
My integrity is beyond question	No-one's found out
Tax cuts next year	Offset by today's increases
The estimated cost is $...	Add two zeros
We have a mandate	Hidden agenda
I promise to	Pigs will fly
What I meant was	Cover-up
It was official business	Dirty weekend
I don't take any notice of the polls	They will forget before the next election
Those donations were entirely a matter for the party	The silly buggers got caught
The Prime Minister/Premier has my full support	I'm gonna screw the mongrel
Source: Sun-Herald, 22 December 1991.	

Compile a similar list for double-speak in other settings with which you may be more familiar. Ask someone from the same setting to compile a similar list and then compare what you have written. To what extent were your two lists similar or different? What does this tell you about the accuracy of your perceptions?

Key Terms 4.11

Connotation

Denotation

Etiquette

Meaning

Miscommunication

Politically correct language

Racist language

Sexist language

Straw person fallacy

Recommended Reading 4.12

Cashdan, A. and Jordin, M. (eds) (1987) *Studies in communication*, Oxford: Basil Blackwell.

Clark, H. H. and Clark, E. V. (1977) *Psychology and language: an introduction to psycholinguistics*, New York: Harcourt Brace Jovanovich.

Jacobs, S. (1985) 'Language', in *Handbook of Interpersonal Communication*, Knapp, M. L. and Miller, G. R. (eds), California: Sage, 313–43.

Kress, G. (1988) 'Language as social practice', in *Communication and culture*, Kress, G. (ed), Sydney: University of New South Wales Press, 79–129.

Lesikar, R. V. (1988) *Basic business communication*, 4th edn, Illinois: Irwin.

Nofsinger, R. (1991) *Everyday conversation*, California: Sage.

Silverman, D. and Torode, B. (1980) *The material world: some theories of language and its limits*, London: Routledge & Kegan Paul.

Wilkes, G. A. (1978) *A dictionary of Australian colloquialisms*, Sydney: Sydney University Press.

Nonverbal Communication 5

Actions speak louder than words.

Anon

We have too many high-sounding words, and too few
actions that correspond with them.

Abigail Adams (1744–1818)

*C*an people communicate without language or words? Do bodily signals tell us anything about peoples' emotions and attitudes? What is 'body language' and what is 'nonverbal communication'? In this chapter we consider how people communicate through their unspoken or unwritten messages which others receive and interpret. We will discover that these nonverbal messages can mean different things to different people, and that facial expressions reveal a great deal about people's emotional states, self-images and their interpersonal attitudes. Nonverbal information is also conveyed by vocal cues, by how people use space, distance and territory, and by physical signals like posture, gesture, touch and movement. We will also see how people's clothing and grooming affects their communication with others. Finally, research on deception, immediacy and intimacy suggests that our nonverbal cues play an important part in determining whether others like us and want to be near us, and in how we reveal true feelings we may be trying to conceal.

Learning Objectives

After you have studied the ideas, arguments and suggestions presented in this chapter you should be able to do the following:

- Define 'nonverbal communication' in terms of its three main functions.

- Distinguish between 'body language' and 'nonverbal communication'.

- Defend the claim that the face is the primary site of emotional activity.

- State what part eye contact or 'mutual gaze' plays in human communication and relationships.

- Explain how our voice qualities can convey our feelings.

- Discuss the significance and function of gestures.

- Define 'proxemics' and list three important concepts established by scholars investigating this field.

- State two important facts about 'touching behaviour'.

- Explain the relationship between clothing and grooming and 'self-presentation'.

- Explain why deception, immediacy and intimacy are of special interest to scholars of nonverbal communication.

5.1 The Nature and Functions of Nonverbal Communication

Although language is usually seen as the principal means of human communication, people's bodily signals provide a good deal of information which may not be stated in words. For example, hand gestures, head movements, body angle (forward or back), and way of touching can indicate something about people's intentions and dispositions. Most of us recognise someone's clenched fist raised to another's face as a sign of aggression. Such familiar signs often enable us to draw inferences about a person's behaviour. The inferences may be based on situational or some other kind of observable information. We might conclude, perhaps, that a person clenching a fist is angry because someone has been provocative, or that their display of anger is symptomatic of their general disposition. Thus we might say that 'a certain individual acted angrily because she/he is typically an angry kind of person'.

Nonverbal cues, therefore, can communicate a great deal about people's motives and personalities. According to Argyle (1976), nonverbal signals principally communicate emotional states, interpersonal attitudes, and images of self. **Facial expressions** and voice qualities are commonly recognised as the main channels through which we communicate our emotional states to others (Davitz, 1964; Ekman and Friesen, 1975; Knapp, 1977). Emotional states can be broadly classified as either 'pleasant' or 'unpleasant'. Emotional states which indicate 'pleasantness' are often equated with 'positive affect', whilst emotional states signifying 'unpleasantness' are synonymously coupled with 'negative affect'. Positive affect is usually associated with emotions like 'happiness' or 'joy', and negative affect connotes emotions like 'sadness', 'anger', or 'disgust'.

Secondly, interpersonal attitudes refer to ways in which individuals form images of others. Bi-polar adjectives (friendly-unfriendly) are, in effect, interpersonal constructs which individuals use to create images of other people. It is important to remember that such images or impressions can seriously influence relationships between people and decisions which interacting persons may choose to take about such relationships, especially in work settings. Interpersonal attitudes can have significant bearings on relationship status and outcomes in work-related areas such as formal interviews (exit interviews or staff recruitment interviews), career-path counselling sessions, performance appraisals, and industrial work-practice negotiations.

Presentation of self, another major function of **nonverbal communication**, involves the construction of images of self (Goffman, 1959). There are two aspects to **self-image** construction. First, through their expression of nonverbal cues people indicate how they see themselves. This facet of self-image is partly projected by personal appearance, including the kind of clothing people wear and the way they groom themselves. The combination of hairstyles, cosmetics, scented products, and clothing

nonverbal cues
Body signals and vocal accompaniments of speech.

facial expression
Emotional signals due to muscular activity in the face.

nonverbal communication
The sharing, between two or more people, of facial, vocal, body signals and gestures, including spatial (proxemic) signals.

self-image
The impressions or images we have of ourselves.

conveys to others a great deal about how people see themselves. Of course, we do not judge others by appearances alone. Facial expressions, voice qualities such as pitch, volume, and rate of speech, physical cues like posture and orientation (i.e. forward or backward lean), and gestures all convey one's self image to others.

The second aspect of self-presentation essentially complements the first. It is focused on how individuals would like others to see them. In other words, **self-presentation** involves not only how people see themselves, but also how they would like to be seen by others. For example, smartly tailored leather gear can create an image of power and dominance, or of trendiness, so people who see themselves as dominant or trendy tend to favour it. They usually dress this way to make others think that they are dominant or trendy. Other nonverbal cues including stern facial expressions, booming voices, short tidy hair, and very erect posture can also reinforce an image of dominance.

Note that there is a difference between nonverbal behaviour and nonverbal communication. Nonverbal behaviour does not communicate anything except when people attach some meaning or significance to it. According to Wiener, Devoe, Rubinow, and Geller (1972:186), 'nonverbal communication' implies '(a) a socially shared signal system, that is, a code; (b) an encoder who makes something public via that code; and (c) a decoder who responds systematically to that code'. Nonverbal communication occurs when both encoding and decoding processes are taking place. Behaviour becomes 'communicative' when a person does something deliberately and when an observer infers something from it.

The view of Wiener et al. (1972) is perhaps restrictive. People can *unconsciously* communicate to others something about themselves by nonverbal behaviour. Key (1972:3) argued that although not all communication involves verbal behaviour, there is inevitably some nonverbal element present. It has been suggested, for example, that 'a person may communicate awareness of the rain by uplifting his face to the sky and holding his hands out to catch drops, with or without the accompanying statement, "I think it's going to rain" ' (Harper, Wiens and Matarazzo, 1978:6).

Argyle's (1976) functional view of nonverbal communication differs from other functional classifications. For example, Harrison (1973:94) suggested that nonverbal signs operate at three different levels. In the first place, nonverbal signs define and limit the nature of communication content and interpersonal exchange. Typical nonverbal signs in this category relate to time, place, and other circumstantial factors associated with a communicative act. Secondly, nonverbal signs have a regulative function. For example, certain gestures that are used to signal turn-taking can control the flow of information amongst people. Nonverbal signs operating in this way can provide 'metacommunicative feedback'. **Metacommunication** means 'communication about communication' (Scheflen, 1968). The nonverbal signs, therefore, convey something about an interpersonal encounter. Some tennis players, for example, engaged in a close match, communicate their enjoyment of the contest by smiling.

Harrison has claimed that at the third level 'nonverbal signs communicate content, sometimes more efficiently than linguistic signs but

self-presentation
Our communication based on how we see ourselves and how we would like others to see us.

metacommunication
The hidden 'communication' behind the overt message; communication about communication.

usually in complementary redundancy to the verbal flow' (p. 94). In this case, the communication of content is easier to relate to objective nonverbal phenomena like architecture or domestic interior decoration, than to human interactions.

Leathers (1978) presents another functional view of nonverbal communication: since the basic function of communication is the exchange of meaning, the function of nonverbal communication is related to the purposes of exchanging meanings (e.g. information, persuasion), the accuracy with which they are co-ordinated (e.g. facial communication is more potent than tactile), and the efficiency with which they are reciprocated (i.e. the time and effort they take). Leathers listed six reasons why nonverbal communication has greater functional significance than verbal communication, as follows:

1. . . . nonverbal, not verbal, factors are the major determinants of meaning in the interpersonal context;
2. . . . feelings and emotions are more accurately exchanged by nonverbal than verbal means;
3. . . . the nonverbal portion of communication conveys meanings and intentions that are relatively free of deception, distortion, and confusion;
4. . . . nonverbal cues serve a metacommunicative function that is indispensable in attaining high quality communication;
5. . . . nonverbal cues represent a much more efficient means of communicating than verbal cues;
6. . . . nonverbal cues represent the most suitable vehicle for suggestion.

(Leathers, 1978:4–8)

Most of these claims are justifiable, but there are grounds to challenge Leathers' claim that nonverbal cues are comparatively free of deception. As I suggested in a previous paper (Kaye, 1991), much of the research on deception has emanated from the work of scholars in nonverbal behaviour and communication. In any case, meanings are communicated only in the sense that they are constructed by each person—they are not transferred from one to another.

Since the face has generally been considered the primary site of emotional display or expression it seems reasonable that honesty and truthfulness could be identified through facial activity. Bond and Robinson (1988), however, argued that people can look honest even when they are lying, and dishonest even when they tell the truth. From these assumptions, Bond and Robinson (1988:304) concluded that tendencies to deceive 'originate in fixed features of the mien, an innocent- or guilty-looking visage'. In other words, people's facial expressions may communicate deceptive messages.

Theoretical perspectives of nonverbal communication, such as those of Argyle (1976), Leathers (1978) and Harrison (1973), attempt to explain nonverbal communication in terms of the functional significance of non-verbal cues. Another commonly-found definition is that nonverbal communication is any communication not involving words (e.g. Mehrabian, 1972). According to Knapp (1972:57), 'traditionally, educators, researchers, and laymen have used the following definition when discussing nonverbal communication: "Nonverbal communication designates all those human responses which are not described as overtly manifested words (either spoken or written)" '.

This kind of definition clearly seeks to distinguish nonverbal communication from any form of communication that must be verbal. The problem with simple definitions like this is that they do not account for the fact that verbal messages are inevitably accompanied by nonverbal messages. In short, a receiver's acceptance of the content or text of a message (i.e. 'what is said') often depends on the simultaneous presence of facial and paralinguistic cues (i.e. 'how the message is spoken'). When the 'what' and 'how' do not coincide, the speaker's intentions and credibility are often judged on the nonverbal rather than the verbal message.

Take, for example, the situation where people glance at their watches while talking to others. Their words may suggest enthusiastic involvement in the conversation, but their casual, furtive, or unthinking glance at the time may suggest a desire to terminate the conversation. People receiving such apparently contradictory messages will probably interpret them according to the nonverbal cues—a glance at your watch may be construed as a sign of boredom or impatience.

Nonverbal cues sometimes contradict what we say

The implication of this is that, in future, the relationship and communication between those conversing will be largely determined by the perceiver's attributions of intent to the other's nonverbal messages. Tolerance of another's apparent impatience or boredom, for example, will probably correspond with how well and how closely the relationship has already been established. Glancing at your watch is unlikely to deepen a relationship if it is still in its early stages.

It is also important to distinguish nonverbal communication from **body language**. The nature and functions of nonverbal communication have already been discussed. 'Body language', however, is a term usually

body language
Popular term to describe how people communicate nonverbally.

associated with popular marketers of nonverbal communication theory and research. Notable among the 'body language' authors are Fast (1971), who coined the term, and successors like Pease (1981) and Braysich (1979). Popular writers like these serve a useful purpose in bringing to public attention how people communicate nonverbally. Some of what they have to say is also very entertaining and has even been the subject of special television programs. However, certain concepts and 'principles' promulgated by body-language writers lack either theoretical or research-based substantiation. For example, Pease's book was intended as a working manual for salespeople, including managers and executives. Pease claimed that:

> . . . little useful information was available on body language and, although libraries and universities had records of the studies done on it, most of this information consisted of closely set manuscripts and theoretical assumptions compiled in an objective manner by people who had little or no practical experience in dealing with other human beings.
>
> (Pease, 1981:7)

His book, as he admits, includes many 'how to' features based on his own experiences and encounters with other people. Despite its substantial bibliography, it rarely cites these references in the body of the text. Most of the 'meanings communicated' by specific gestures are assumed by Pease to be universally understood and applied. Because of his belief in his own ability to explain 'body language', Pease claimed that 'any person, regardless of his or her vocation or position in life, can use [the book] to obtain a better understanding of life's most complex event—a face-to-face encounter with another person' (Pease,1981:8).

Sweeping claims of this kind are appealing but seriously flawed. In the first place, although most scholars of nonverbal communication would agree that people do communicate with others by bodily signals, it is doubtful that these signals form part of a bodily 'language'. The social scientist Ray Birdwhistell (1970) theorised that just as the basic unit of speech is the phoneme, the basic unit of action is the **kineme**. The subsequent theory of human movement that developed from this notion became known as **kinesics**. Fast (1971:1) has suggested that 'kinesics' and 'body language' are virtually synonymous although kinesics is the term used by scientific researchers and scholars.

Birdwhistell's research methodology involved the laborious frame-by-frame analysis of human interactions captured on 16 mm film—a slow, meticulous procedure that nevertheless failed to produce anything of practical value. Since the 20,000 or so kinemes identified by Birdwhistell provided no scientifically elegant basis for studying bodily action, the concept of 'body language' was considered by many scholars to be too intricate for easy scientific study; nor is it useful as a non-scientific tool for interpreting others' bodily signals.

Another aspect of the body language issue concerns the meaning of nonverbal cues. Body language authors tend to argue that many bodily signals convey meanings that are readily understood by most people. For instance, a

kineme
The smallest unit of body movement or action.

kinesics
The systematic scientific study of body movements and their role in multi-channel communication.

shake of the head is invariably a sign of negation, a nod of the head indicates assent or approval, and a clenched fist can only signify anger, rage or a threat.

Most of us would acknowledge that the meaning of any bodily signal is very much in the eye of the beholder. To illustrate this point, try a simple experiment. Select a few gestures like a shrug of the shoulders, and have someone perform these in front of a group, preferably people who do not know each other well. Ask them to write down their interpretation of each signal, then compare these interpretations. They will probably vary. For example, a shrug of the shoulders could be interpreted as a sign of indifference, apathy, ignorance, or bewilderment.

In the following sections the major areas of study within the field of nonverbal communication are addressed separately. These areas include facial expression and visual behaviour, paralanguage or the vocal characteristics of speech, body movement and gesture, and communicators' use of space, distance, and territory. Other less extensively investigated areas of study in the nonverbal domain—touching behaviour, and clothing and grooming—are also briefly considered.

Facial Expression and Visual Behaviour　5.2

Of all the channels through which people communicate nonverbally with others, the face is perhaps the most powerful. In literature, allusions to the face abound. For example, the beautiful Grecian Helen who fell in love with the Trojan prince Paris is supposed to have had a face that could launch a thousand ships. In Shakespeare's *Hamlet*, Horatio meets with Marcellus and Hamlet and describes the ghost of Hamlet's father as having 'a countenance more in sorrow than in anger'. The ghost's face was pale and his eyes were fixed on Horatio 'most constantly'. Again, Gratiano, in Shakespeare's *Merchant of Venice*, says:

> There are a sort of men whose visages
>
> Do cream and mantle like a standing pond,
>
> And do a wilful stillness entertain,
>
> With purpose to be dress'd in an opinion
>
> Of wisdom, gravity, profound conceit.

Most people draw conclusions about others from their facial expressions. For quite some time, the face has been regarded as the primary site of affect (Tomkins, 1962; Tomkins and McCarter, 1964). These authors reintroduced the **James–Lange Theory of Emotion** which argued that physiological states precede, and are the basis for, the experience of emotions. From this theoretical principle Harper, Wiens and Matarazzo (1978:78) concluded that 'in studying facial expressions we are, in fact, studying "emotion itself" '.

James–Lange Theory of Emotion
Behaviour and physiological responses are prompted by situations and, in turn, feelings and emotions result from these behaviours and responses.

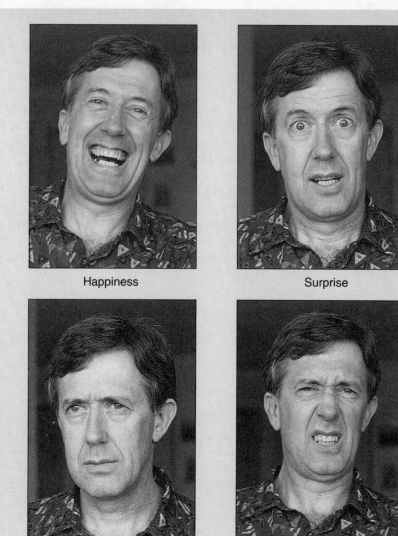

Happiness   Surprise

Worry   Disgust

Emotional states are communicated through facial expressions

Emotion, according to Izard (1971:195), consists of three related elements: 'neural activity, striate muscle or facial-postural activity, and subjective experience'. The second element—the activity of the facial muscles—is an important source of information about the type and intensity of someone's emotion.

There are seven emotional states communicated by facial expressions which appear to be universally understood (Ekman, Friesen and Ellsworth, 1972; Ekman et al., 1980): happiness, sadness, fear, surprise, anger, disgust, and interest. The facial expressions of these emotional states are said to be 'pure', whilst those of other emotional states (e.g. shame, guilt, confusion, satisfaction) are considered to be 'blends'. In general, blends are more subject to varying interpretations than 'pure' expressions are.

Cook (1973:75) has suggested that 'there is plenty of evidence that the six, seven, or eight basic emotions can be recognised from photos or short films or even from live people'. The most common method of determining how people interpret others' facial expressions is to present them with photographs of various facial expressions posed by someone known to the researcher(s) or by professional actors. Researchers prefer actors for this task, since their accuracy in expression is more reliable, although there is always the concern that posed emotional expressions may not truly represent their unposed equivalent.

Photographs can capture emotions communicated by facial expressions

Another problem is that photographs capture only 'micromomentary' information from the face, although interpreting facial expressions recorded on moving film, videotape, or even in live settings, may also be difficult because of the high incidence of blends. In other words, perceivers may be seeing more than pure expressions of happiness, fear, and so on. In real life people's faces probably communicate blended emotional states more often than they do pure ones. To this extent, naturalistic ways of studying and interpreting the facial expressions of others differ from laboratory techniques which require agreement among those selected to interpret, judge or rate the nonverbal information in the photographs. By contrast, naturalistic approaches include direct observation of people or the study of facial expressions captured on movie film.

In more recent times, video has been used to study facial expressions. For example, I have developed a video technique (Kaye, 1986, 1988) to study the facial expressions of college lecturers. This technique involved keeping the facial display message-related while eliminating all other nonverbal information. Videotaped lectures were shown, without any soundtrack, to student audiences. At the lower third of the screen the text of the lecture was synchronised with the lip movements of the presenter. This technique enabled me to study how the facial expressions of lecturers were significantly related to the audience's immediate and delayed recall of the main teaching points in the lecture text. Recall was measured by a short pencil-and-paper test developed for this study. I found that high recall scores tended to occur when the lecturer's face projected an emotional state of 'pleasantness', mainly through smiling.

Through their facial expressions, people also communicate their attitudes toward others. In interviews, for example, interviewees can often sense whether the interviewers are friendly or unfriendly, supportive or dismissive, and so on. Many of these attitudes, as the reader can readily appreciate, closely resemble the kinds of interpersonal constructs people use to form impressions or images of others. Such impressions are formed, moreover, on the basis of nonverbal cues expressed by those being perceived. In the case of the interviewer, therefore, interpersonal attitudes toward the interviewer may be signalled by facial expressions, vocal qualities and volume, body posture and lean, and gestures, including head gestures. Of all this nonverbal information, however, facial expressions indicate emotion most powerfully. A face that smiles a lot with the eyes fully open and only slight muscle activity in the brow region may indicate, for example, an interviewer's enthusiastic, supportive, and non-superior attitude. By contrast, an interviewer may seem hostile, unenthusiastic, or patronising if his or her facial expression is unsmiling, with narrowed eyes and intense muscle activity in the brow region. This impression may be reinforced by other bodily signals such as failure to maintain frequent eye contact—the interviewee might infer that the interview is merely a pro forma exercise.

One important discovery made by researchers during the past two decades is that men and women differ in their abilities to interpret people's nonverbal behaviour and communication. During the 1970s, a team of researchers at Harvard University made a longitudinal study of the sensitivities of men and women to nonverbal cues. This team, led by Robert Rosenthal, developed an instrument known as the Profile of Nonverbal Sensitivity, or the PONS Test. This test was administered to large samples of men and women in many countries. The PONS Test results suggested that, regardless of nationality or culture, men and women interpret others' nonverbal communication in different ways, and that women can decode nonverbal information more accurately.

In addition to gender-based differences in the decoding of nonverbally expressed emotion, there are, according to Woolfolk (1981), age-related differences. For instance, children appear to differ from adults in the interpretation of 'incongruent' messages—that is, when nonverbal cues appear to be inconsistent with verbal content. Adults seem to depend on nonverbal channels (facial expression and tone of voice) more than on the words people use to convey their intentions, whereas children tend to concentrate more on words and tone of voice than on facial expressions when they decipher incongruent messages. This led Woolfolk (1981:202) to conclude that 'the child may have a very different view of the adult's behavior, particularly of the adult's nonverbal behavior. Nonverbal cues which have one meaning to the adult may have a very different meaning to the child or be overlooked altogether'.

So far there is no compelling evidence, on the other hand, that either sex is more capable than the other in the nonverbal expression of feeling.

The claim made some time ago by Friedman (1979:24–25) that 'the research field involving nonverbal skill is not well established' very probably still applies. It also prompted suggestions that information presenters such as university professors or college lecturers could benefit from some form of specialised training in nonverbal expressiveness (Murray and Lawrence, 1980; Scott and Nussbaum, 1981). Perhaps the lack of initiative in developing training programs on nonverbal expressiveness may be due to a lingering suspicion that such programs would resemble the discredited teachings of the 'elocutionists' (Leathers, 1978) or be associated with popular writers' unsubstantiated assertions about body language.

Logically, visual behaviour should be an integral element in the study of the face, since the eye region is one of three distinct facial areas that people attend to when interpreting others' emotional states. Since the eyes are our means of receiving visual messages, we tend to use them to collect rather than send information (Argyle, 1976:229). This is not to deny that we sometimes also use our eyes to affect or influence others. Think of songs with well-known lines such as 'Ma, he's making eyes at me!' or 'Can't take my eyes off you'. Imagine someone glancing coyly at another to attract their attention, or someone 'looking daggers' at someone else. In all of these instances, the eyes are used as a means of projecting one's feelings or attitudes toward others.

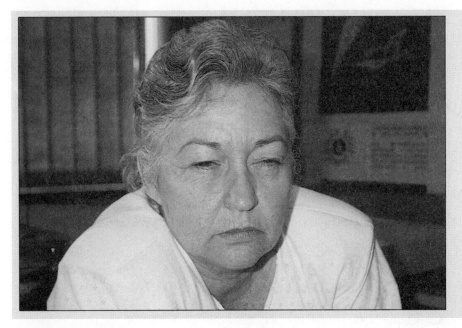

People can say a lot with their eyes

The English language abounds with references to the eyes. Words such as 'stare', 'glare', 'peer', 'peek', 'peep', 'gaze' or 'glance' indicate the levels of intensity and the intentions of eye-messages, and many common expressions include emotionally-charged adjectives: 'a furtive glance', 'a stony stare', 'a steely glare', 'a lingering gaze', 'a cautious peep'. In each of these, an attempt to interpret the intention behind another's visual behaviour is implicit.

Much of the research on visual behaviour has involved the study of gaze and **mutual gaze** (Argyle and Dean, 1965; Argyle and Cook, 1976), which is concerned with how people look at each other when engaged in conversations or other face-to-face situations. Both the *amount* and *quality* of eye contact were studied, and Argyle and his colleagues found that listeners looked about twice as much and twice as long at those speaking to them as did speakers addressing their listeners.

Eye contact is sometimes referred to as mutual gaze. When the interactions of two people are characterised by mutual gaze, certain factors may be assumed to be operating. For one thing, mutual gaze signals mutual liking; for another it indicates attentiveness to others. When two people maintain eye-contact with each other, there is good reason to expect that they have registered more than a passing awareness of each other. It might also mean that each is listening carefully to what the other is saying.

The correspondence of mutual gaze to intimacy, interpersonal attraction, status differences between interacting people, and approach or avoidance behaviours led Argyle and Dean (1965) to propose the concept of 'equilibrium', whereby people try to maintain some balance between forces to engage in eye-contact and forces to avoid it. When two people do not know each other very well, a way of preserving equilibrium is for one of them to move away as the other approaches. Of course, if both persons are attracted to each other, the opposite tendency for both to draw closer together could occur. This approach-approach tendency was labelled 'reciprocity' by Argyle and Dean (1965).

Over the past decade or so, very little further research has been continued on gaze or mutual gaze. Although Argyle (1976) worked on the visual behaviour of schizophrenic and autistic people there has been no systematic study of gaze and mutual gaze in professional work settings. For example, it would be useful to know what type of visual behaviour is optimal in selection interviews, career counselling sessions, or in person-to-person on-the-job training. Unsubstantiated claims about the importance of people maintaining eye-contact in such settings may lead to false assumptions about the nature of communication processes between professional workers.

We shall now consider other channels of nonverbal communication. Section 5.3 focuses on the vocal properties that accompany spoken words.

5.3 Paralanguage and Speech Characteristics

Apart from our facial expressions and our visual behaviour, there are other potent ways in which we communicate information nonverbally; one is through paralinguistic cues. **Paralanguage** represents those aspects of what we say that are not communicated by the actual words used—aspects such as loudness or volume, the rate of our speech (how fast or slow it is), enunciation (clipped or slurred?), inflection (does it rise or fall?), rhythm (regular or irregular?), pitch and resonance.

Voice properties communicate something about our emotions and states of mind. Mehrabian and Ferris (1967) suggested that paralinguistic cues are second only in importance to facial cues in the expression of feeling or emotion. According to their formula, paralanguage accounts for approximately 38 per cent of the total impact of any message. Note that since facial expressions account for about 65 per cent of its total impact, over 90 per cent of its emotional content is nonverbally determined. In fact, Mehrabian and Ferris argued that the impact of spoken words on the emotional component of messages was roughly only 7 per cent.

The word 'paralanguage' essentially means content-free measures of speech. Other terms have been used to denote this; for example, 'extralinguistic' and 'metalinguistic' phenomena (Harper, Wiens and Matarazzo, 1978:20). For all these terms, the essential ingredient appears to be the category of voice (vocal) qualities—that is, content-free accompaniments to speech, such as pitch range, as described at the opening of this section.

Among the most prominent scholars of the vocal properties of speech are Davitz and Davitz (1959), best known for their investigations of the communication of emotion through paralinguistic cues. Their research technique required their subjects to express certain emotions while reciting letters of the alphabet, and observers noted the voice properties that accompanied each emotion. Some emotions were more readily identified than others. For instance, anger, sadness, happiness, and nervousness seemed to be the easiest to decipher from the paralinguistic cues, whereas fear, love, and surprise were most difficult to identify. Subsequently, Davitz (1964) explored the relationship between auditory vocal cues and 14 different emotions expressed in constant-content speech. In this study, the content of the speech remained the same whilst 14 different feelings were expressed. These feelings and their auditory cues are listed in Table 5.1.

An important outcome of the Davitz study was that its evidence supported the hypothesis that people's emotional states are communicated through paralinguistic cues. Moreover, differences in rate, pitch, loudness, timbre, inflection, rhythm, and enunciation were related to the expression of different emotions, as shown in Table 5.1. For example 'joy', which in Davitz' study was rated by expert judges to be a highly positive emotion, is characterised by a voice that is loud, high-pitched, 'moderately blaring' rather than resonant, fast, upwardly inflected, and regular in rhythm. On the other hand, 'anger', which was rated by judges to be the least positive emotion, is characterised by irregular inflection and rhythm, and by enunciation that is clipped rather than slurred.

There are other ways of identifying elements of content-free speech. It is possible, for instance, to relate content-free speech to time factors (also referred to as temporal characteristics of speech). These characteristics include such variables as duration of utterance, and interruptions (especially in 'simultaneous speech', i.e. where two people are talking at the same time). Another type of 'nonverbal' speech phenomenon that is significant in interpersonal communication is silence, since it is much more

Feeling	Loudness	Pitch	Timbre	Rate	Inflection	Rhythm	Enunciation
Affection	Soft	Low	Resonant	Slow	Steady and slight	Regular	Slurred
Anger	Loud	High	Blaring	Fast	Irregular up and down	Irregular	Clipped
Boredom	Moderate to low	Moderate to low	Moderately resonant	Moderately slow	Monotone or gradually falling	–	Somewhat slurred
Cheerfulness	Moderately high	Moderately high	Moderately blaring	Moderately fast	Up and down; overall upward	Regular	
Impatience	Normal	Normal to moderately high	Moderately blaring	Moderately fast	Slight upward	–	Somewhat clipped
Joy	Loud	High	Moderately blaring	Fast	Upward	Regular	
Sadness	Soft	Low	Resonant	Slow	Downward	Irregular pauses	Slurred
Satisfaction	Normal	Normal	Somewhat resonant	Normal	Slight upward	Regular	Somewhat slurred

Source: Davitz, J., *The Communication of Emotional Meaning,* New York: McGraw-Hill, 1964. Reproduced with permission of McGraw-Hill.

TABLE 5.1

Characteristics of vocal expressions associated with the communication of emotions (Davitz, 1964:63)

than a conversational void. Indeed, silence can be as devastating as the spoken word. Singer and songwriter Paul Simon is perhaps best remembered for his song 'The Sound of Silence'. To some this may be a contradiction in terms, but the song celebrates the potency of silence when people communicate. According to Bruneau (1973), silence is to speech as the white of this paper is to this print. Silence and speech are complementary aspects of spoken communication; both aspects provide data for constructing meanings from messages.

The category of silence could also include hesitations and pauses. These types of nonverbal accompaniments to speech are time-related units, and since they greatly influence the fluency of speech patterns, they indicate a good deal about people's communication competence in speech and their feelings.

According to O'Keefe (1990), lack of speech fluency can influence people's judgments of a speaker's credibility. He suggests the following as typical examples of nonfluencies: '. . . vocalized pauses ("uh, uh"), the superfluous repetition of words or sounds, corrections of slips of the tongue, articulation difficulties, and the like' (p. 134–35). There is, furthermore, some evidence that as speakers display increasing amounts of nonfluencies, they tend to be perceived as decreasingly competent. On the other hand, observers' judgments of their trustworthiness do not appear to be significantly influenced by speakers' lack of fluency.

It is not difficult to think of instances where hesitations, pauses in speech, and definite or prolonged silences are likely to have profound effects on the quality and outcomes of communication between people. In job interviews, for example, applicants may be perceived to be lacking in confidence or incapable of 'thinking on their feet' if they hesitate or pause too often. Conversely, it could be easy to form the impression that an interviewer whose speech is frequently punctuated by hestitation and pauses may seem unenthusiastic about an applicant.

The study of paralanguage has provided reason to believe that full communication is not simply a matter of what is being said, but *how* a message is spoken. Words alone do not tell people how a person's intended message is meant to be understood or received. Speakers' messages are interpreted according to all the information received, including auditory vocal cues communicating information about their emotions.

In all probability, paralinguistic cues significantly influence receivers' attitudes and acceptance of incoming information. For example, in previous research (Kaye, 1986b) I discovered that the paralinguistic cues of college lecturers influenced audience perceptions of lecturer credibility. For instance, the lecturers' paralinguistic cues that the audience construed as unpleasant (e.g. impatience) correlated with low credibility scores on the test devised by Berlo, Lemert, and Mertz (1970).

Although people communicate emotional messages predominantly by facial expressions and voice qualities, there are other ways of communicating nonverbally. Section 5.4 discusses the types of nonverbal information that our bodily gestures can communicate.

Bodily Communication 5.4

Two of the ways people can communicate with their bodies are through posture and gesture. Whilst gestures usually involve a part or parts of the body, posture involves adjustment of the entire body. Some researchers have described this in even broader terms. For example, Ekman and Friesen (1975) refer to two categories: the first is called 'body acts'—observable body movements with easily identified beginnings and ends. Because body acts can be observed in a particular part of the body, or in several parts of the body at the same time, they are virtually synonymous with 'gestures'.

'Body positions' is the second category devised by Ekman and Friesen. In general, body positions are forms of postural communication since they are characterised by an absence of movement over a specific time period. Whilst there is abundant evidence that body positions or postures vary amongst cultures, they probably differ from one context to another. For instance, there are international differences in how people stand or lean when interacting with others. Some of these differences have led to stereotypes such as the laid-back sheriff reclining in his office chair somewhere in the deep south of America, or the bowler-hatted Englishman sitting bolt upright in a train, reading a newspaper.

Body positions or postures may sometimes be determined by the requirements or expectations of highly formal or ceremonial settings. For instance, soldiers on sentry duty are expected to stand erect and still; the

Examples of ritualised gestures

Source: The *Age* (a) and (b)

backcourt tennis linesperson in major international tournaments takes on a crouching position just before service; a cricket umpire at the bowler's end leans forward as bowlers commence delivery.

Gestures may also be ritualised and stylised—for example in sporting fixtures, religious ceremonies, and graduation ceremonies. In basketball the umpire holds his right hand vertically against the middle of his left hand, held horizontally, to signal 'time out'. Religious groups make gestures to invoke divine blessings, such as the sign of the cross; and deans and chancellors at university graduation ceremonies doff their mortar-boards when addressing each other formally.

Gestures are often used to signal 'turn-taking' and 'turn-yielding'. For example, in a class discussion a teacher points to a student to indicate that it is their turn to make a verbal contribution. Turn-taking or turn-yielding in conversations may also be signalled by a glance or by gaze avoidance and head movements such as nodding. Note, however, that certain nonverbal cues, particularly paralinguistic cues such as a decrease in pitch or loudness, often discourage the listener from taking a turn to speak, and certain head movements also indicate turn-taking rather than turn-yielding.

Some gestures are 'incongruous' in that they appear to contradict rather than complement the verbal message. Think back to the watch-glancing example. Gestures are also incongruous when they conflict with vocal and other paralinguistic cues. Thus, a handshake may seem perfunctory rather than sincere if the accompanying words are spoken with an apparent lack of enthusiasm or interest. Greetings like 'Good to see you' or 'It's been a long time' when spoken without a smile and in a flat tone of voice can very easily seem insincere.

Finally, note that gestures differ from one community, locality or nation to another. In a major study of how gestures differ among cultures and national groups, Morris et al. (1979) concluded that gestures could be interpreted in various ways. For example, the 'v-sign' signifies 'v for peace' in one context, in another it signifies 'two', and in another it conveys an obscenity. Morris and his colleagues called these kinds of gestures **multi-message gestures**.

multi-message gestures. *Gestures which may be interpreted in more than one way.*

Gestures communicate different messages in different settings

Morris et al. also found that some gestures seemed to be highly localised whilst others transcended national and linguistic boundaries; for example, the 'ring gesture'—the loop formed by the thumb and forefinger—signifies, in northern France, 'all's well' or 'OK', whereas in the south of France it denotes 'nothing' or 'zero'. In Italy the 'head toss' has significance in some places and none in others: Neapolitans use it but Romans seldom do. These findings led Morris and his co-workers to propose the concept of 'gesture boundaries' to distinguish a nation's cultural divisions, which may also be marked by linguistic boundaries. One important implication to emerge from the concept of gesture

Examples of gestures with different meanings: left: ring gesture; right: head toss

boundaries is that it challenges the popular conception of 'national' gestures (e.g. the French always talk with their hands).

How and when people use gestures depends partly on the amount of space they have to communicate in. Section 5.5 outlines some of the ways in which people use space and territory when communicating with others.

5.5 Proxemics, Territoriality and Space

In our relationships with other people, the way we use space gives them a further indication of our actions and intentions. The study or science of how we use physical and interpersonal space is known as **proxemics**. One of the pioneer researchers in this field, Edward T. Hall, coined the term; he defined proxemics as the study of how people perceive and use space—the 'interrelated observations and theories of man's [sic] use of space as a specialised elaboration of culture' (Hall, 1969:1).

Later, Leathers (1978:48–49) defined proxemics as the study of how we use space to communicate. This extra dimension has prompted researchers to investigate a broad range of related topics, including how people use the spaces between them and others during the course of daily communication and interaction, and how they organise space inside and outside buildings. Indeed, the layout of whole townships and communities has been researched as an aspect of proxemics.

One way to understand the phenomenon of spatial relationships between people is by applying the concept of *interpersonal distance*. The distance between communicating people is closely linked with the physiological and psychological factors operating at the time. Physiological factors include what Hall (1968) termed 'sensory inputs' which include the visual, aural, olfactory, and tactile senses, the amount of heat between

proxemics
The study of how we use physical and interpersonal space and territory, and how this influences the communication of information and construction of meanings.

people and postural-sex identifiers which refer to whether men and women communicate while standing, sitting, or lying down.

A factor that explains how people use distance to communicate something is what Hall termed **sociofugal-sociopetal orientation (SPF axis)**. This measures how directly people face each other: 'sociopetal' means that people look at each other a lot, directly; 'sociofugal' means that people avoid direct face-to-face contact, even to the point of standing back-to-back. Clearly, the sociofugal-sociopetal orientation subsystem is largely concerned with communicative behaviours such as eye-contact.

The most commonly cited classification of interpersonal distance also derives from Hall (1968). It consists of four main types of interpersonal distance: intimate, personal, social-consultative, and public. *Intimate distance* involves activities such as lovemaking and wrestling where the sensory input depends mainly on tactile and olfactory codes. In effect, intimate distance usually involves some form of body contact. *Personal distance* varies from 0.46 to 1.22 metres between people; its 'close phase' is from 0.46 to 0.76 metres. According to Leathers (1978:55), American married couples generally interact within this close range. In communication with someone else (e.g. a neighbour or visitor), the distance may extend to the 'far phase' which is between 0.76 and 1.22 metres.

Communication between people tends to become somewhat impersonal when they are separated by *social distance*. People at work or at informal functions usually communicate at the close phase of social distance (i.e. about 1.22 to 2.13 metres apart). The far phase of social distance gives them enough space to be able to avoid eye-contact if they wish. When they are 2.13 to 3.66 metres apart they can give the impression of being unaware of another person's presence.

The fourth type of interpersonal distance, *public distance*, differs from the other types—communication tends to become decidedly formal and impersonal. At the close phase of public distance (3.66 to 7.62 metres), people can quite easily disregard others without appearing discourteous or impolite, and it is easier than it is at closer interpersonal distances to remove themselves physically from any possible communication with others. At the far phase of public distance (beyond 7.62 metres) paralinguistic cues become difficult to construe unless voices are amplified by a sound system. Without this, meanings are more readily constructed from nonverbal signals, especially facial expressions, gestures, and posture.

The concept of interpersonal distance involves 'territory'—areas possessed or controlled by people. According to Lyman and Scott (1967), there are four kinds of territory: public, home, interactional, and body. *Public territory* refers to places which people can enter or leave freely. Traditions, social customs, and government legislation, however, can prevent certain people from entering public territory. For example, some restaurants or clubs impose specific dress codes, so that people not wearing shoes or ties may not be admitted. In some countries, moreover, racial, religious and gender discrimination persists, despite universal pressure to combat it. There are still schools for boys or girls only, and for pupils of certain religions. This suggests that some public territories are 'public' only in a limited sense of the word, since the territory is restricted to a particular group.

sociofugal-sociopetal orientation (SPF axis)
A concept used by scholars of proxemics to denote a measure of how directly people face each other.

Home territory allows freedom of entry and interaction to all those who claim ownership of it—for example, gay bars and private clubs. In some home territories, members' status is established by reserved tables or chairs, special drinking mugs, or plaques. Some churches have brass nameplates reserving pews for certain families.

Interactional territory means meeting-places where people are able to communicate informally; for example, casual parties, local pool halls or barber shops, and campus lawns or gardens. Unlike other kinds of territory, it does not have a fixed boundary. Depending on such variables as the number of people interacting, the type of gathering, or the nature of the particular setting, the interactional territory may expand or contract according to necessity or desirability.

Body territory, as Leathers (1978:59) notes, consists of 'the space that is occupied and used by our bodies; a very explicit set of rules and norms governs the way we may use our own or someone else's body'. Territorial violation of this kind can cause a relationship breakdown or even prosecution. In the workplace, sexual harrassment policy and deterrents are usually powerful enough to discourage most people from encroaching on other people's body territory.

Regardless of the type of territory involved, norms and expectations can be easily neglected or disregarded. The use of territorial markers is a typical example. In libraries, for instance, readers often leave their briefcases on a particular chair to mark their temporary absence. The effect of territorial marking is to lay personal claim to public space. If another reader were to remove the absentee's briefcase and then occupy that chair, this too could be construed as a violation of another's territory. Territorial marking is an example of 'territoriality'—a person's preference for areas and objects (Altman and Haythorn, 1967). As well, it signifies defence of one's territory. The functions of territoriality in the animal world include protection from predators and the determination of flight and fight distance. Humans also protect their territory by using name plates on office doors, fences, screens, or warning signs with messages such as 'Keep out' or 'Trespassers will be prosecuted'.

How people use space and territory, therefore, signals certain kinds of information about their dispositions and intentions. In earlier sections of this chapter it was also proposed that people's motives and personalities are often interpreted according to their facial expressions and paralinguistic cues, and that these nonverbal cues tend to complement and reinforce each other. The next section examines how touching behaviour is closely associated with these facets of nonverbal communication.

5.6 Touching

Although the topic of 'touch' has been the subject of relatively little investigation when compared with the study of facial expression or vocal communication, it has great significance in our lives. A world without people ever touching is hard to imagine. For one thing, touch signals intimacy. People touch each other to express affection, or to soothe and comfort one another. In intimate situations of this kind, touch is usually gentle. However, we know that touching is not invariably gentle or pleasant. In crowded city streets, for example, people are prone to bump and jostle others. Although this kind of behaviour may be unintentional, it can be unpleasant and can seem aggressive. There has been no systematic research on the negative extremes of touching behaviour. Violent gestures—hitting, punching, kicking, or slapping, for instance—are obviously highly undesirable forms of communication or relationships. They also suggest people's inability to resolve problems or differences by more constructive strategies. For the most part, aggression has been investigated more thoroughly by psychologists than by communication theorists. Within the framework of contemporary human communication theory, it calls for further research; for example, on 'special' or 'atypical communication'.

One way of understanding the domain of tactile behaviour is to use the classification of touching developed by Heslin (1974), which constitutes a continuum with very impersonal touching and very personal touching at opposite extremes. The categories include the following:

1. *Functional-professional*. Here, the tactile communication is 'cold' and businesslike—for example, the department store clothing salesperson who helps a customer to choose a garment.

2. *Social-polite*. Touching in this situation establishes and reinforces accepted social expectations, rules, and practices. According to Knapp (1978:252), the handshake is the best example of this.

3. *Friendship-warmth*. This category includes any form of touching that signifies affection or approachability—for example, the mutual grasping of shoulders at arms' length by two people reunited after a long absence.

4. *Love-intimacy*. This refers to the touch that expresses emotional attachment or attraction—for example, a person fully embracing another, the Eskimo practice of rubbing noses, touching tenderly someone's cheek, or two people 'playing footsies' under the dinner-table.

5. *Sexual arousal*. This category is very closely linked with the previous one, except that the primary focus of touch here is a 'sex object'—sexual arousal is not necessarily integral to love and intimacy.

Some useful studies have been made of the relationship between professional touching and other communicative attributes. For example, Lower (1980) discovered a relationship between 'touch avoidance' and communication apprehension in student nurses, and concluded that males are more likely than females to avoid touching patients of their own gender. On the other hand, there appeared to be no significant difference between male and female student nurses as far as touch avoidance of opposite-sex individuals was concerned. Findings of this kind have important implications for nurse education curricula. Nursing cannot be practised without touching, and Blondis and Jackson (1977:6) commented:

> . . . tactile communication is brief in duration and can be reciprocal; the nurse and client touch each other. Touch is the most personal form of communication. Interpersonally, it is the closest means of relating. Tactile deprivation can result in mental confusion, emotional disengagement and infant death for the patient. Touch is essential for life.

One point we must keep in mind is that the extent to which people touch others or allow themselves to be touched is largely determined by cultural and personal norms. This realisation led Trenholm and Petrie (1980) to coin the term 'body accessibility'. For them, this concept is not only concerned with whether people have ever been touched, but also with the number of people to whom these individuals are accessible through touch. Body accessibility, moreover, assumes that the frequency of touch between people is significant. As already suggested, cultural norms tend to govern the extent of body accessibility between people. In certain professional settings touching may be quite acceptable. For example, doctors have to touch patients, beauticians treat clients' skin, and beach lifeguards apply mouth-to-mouth resuscitation to drowning swimmers.

There are, of course, other kinds of professional settings where touching, especially between males and females, is tantamount to a social taboo. If a male manager puts his arms around a female worker, even though he means to be friendly and not seductive, the gesture may be construed as sexual harassment. Social rules or expectations can also discourage touching in education settings, where teachers must be careful that their touching of students is not misconstrued as sexual intent.

Some research on touch has focused on the quality of touching from the perspectives of both the toucher and the recipient (Pisano, Wall & Foster, 1986), the role of touch as an attempt at influence (Patterson, Powell & Lenihan, 1986), and self-touching (Barroso & Feld, 1986), especially when this occurs in stressful situations like job interviews (Goldberg & Rosenthal, 1986). According to Thayer (1986:10), the element connecting these research orientations is the role of gender: 'experiences with social touch and self touching are generally different for boys and girls, and . . . differences in reactions to touch continue to play an important role into the adult years'.

In summary, tactile communication is a major factor in intimate exchange. It can also influence professional relationships in the workplace, particularly where touching may be construed as a violation of social or cultural norms. The very act of touching can indicate someone's desire to alter a relationship from a professional to a personal one.

5.7 Clothing and Grooming

According to Leathers (1978:85), 'our physical appearance has a pervasive impact on our self-image'. How we see ourselves and how we would like others to see us largely depends on our appearance, especially on our clothing and grooming. There is probably much truth in the ancient Latin proverb *uestis uirum reddit* which means 'clothes maketh the person'.

Self-image is a complex concept. In one sense, people's self-images represent attempts to balance how they see themselves with how they would like to be seen by others. For example, middle-aged men who are apprehensive about getting old often choose clothing that is more appropriate for much younger men because they want to appear essentially youthful.

People who take pains with their clothing and grooming usually do so because they wish to appear attractive to others, although their motive is not necessarily a desire for intimacy. In many instances, just knowing that one is attractive to others can enhance self-esteem. When others notice us, and when they compliment us on our appearance either vocally or nonverbally (e.g. by whistling or with admiring looks), our self-image rises. However, if such compliments are crude or coarse, we may feel uncomfortable rather than complimented, and our self-image may suffer.

The fact that many people take a good deal of care with their appearance suggests that our communication is significantly influenced by our presentation of self. People do not dress simply to keep warm or for the sake of modesty. In many situations, such as job interviews for example, they dress to create a favourable impression on others, and at senior executive or managerial levels in organisations and systems 'power dressing' has achieved a certain vogue. For men, this usually involves accessories such as fashionable ties, handkerchiefs, cufflinks, signet rings, smart attache cases and expensive leatherbound diaries.

Women in executive positions tend to dress in ways that not only accentuate a smart businesslike appearance but also enhance their bodies, with expensive, well-cut clothes and tasteful jewellery. The power-dressing female wants to be seen as a well-presented professional, yet at the same time to subtly project her attractiveness. The picture is complete with the careful grooming of hair. In urban western societies hairstyling for both men and women is a major industry.

Power dressing—an example of self-presentation to impress others

A contrasting viewpoint has been developed by Kanter (1977) who argued that many women dress so as not to stand out from the crowd. In this way, women blend into the background and thus become identified as part of the group. By attracting less attention this way, women are less likely to be seen as 'tokens'. People become tokens when the differences between them and their reference group becomes exaggerated. As token members of their groups, they generally have less power, status or opportunities than other members.

One's body image depends greatly on physique. Earlier research (Kretschmer, 1925; Sheldon, 1954) aimed to establish connections between physique and character or temperament. Kretschmer's classifications of people who were similar morphologically (in physical shape) were threefold: first, the *asthenics*—those who are skinny, bony, and with narrow body shapes; second, the *athletic* types who are essentially muscular; and third, the *pyknic* group—fat people.

somatotype
A description of a person that relates body build with personality type.

Although Sheldon's **somatotyping** (the classification of body types) approximated Kretschmer's (see Table 5.2), perhaps his more significant contribution was to demonstrate a correspondence between body shape and temperament. He linked the 'fat' body type, which he termed *endomorphic*, with the temperament category of *visceratonia* (lazy, unenergetic, placid). The athletic type of build, which Sheldon labelled *mesomorphic*, was related to *somatotonia* (assertiveness and confidence), and the third body type, the *ectomorph*, is the thin, fragile build which he linked to the temperament group called *cerebrotonia*. Cerebrotonics are typically introverted people who prefer mental to outdoor or physical pursuits.

TABLE 5.2

Classification of body types and temperament

Researcher	Body type	Temperament
Kretschmer	Asthenic (thin)	
	Athletic (muscular)	
	Pyknic (fat)	
Sheldon	Ectomorph (thin)	Cerebrotonic (inner-directed)
	Mesomorph (athletic)	Somatotonic (assertive, confident)
	Endomorph (fat)	Visceratonic (lazy, placid)

It is worth considering, at this point, what advantage there is in relating body build and temperament and how this could benefit us in understanding how to communicate with others. People made familiar with these somatotype classifications might at least become more observant of those with whom they communicate and interact regularly.

As much as anything, curiosity might drive people to test the validity of these classifications in practical real-life settings, and if their experience confirms them, they might develop certain kinds of expectations about others from their physical appearance. We should reflect further on the importance of personal appearance in interpersonal communication and consider in particular how our presentation of self affects our communication and interaction with others.

Research on Nonverbal Communication　　　5.8

This chapter concludes with some of the directions researchers and scholars have been pursuing in the study of nonverbal communication during the past decade. Two are definitely worth singling out: nonverbal deception, and intimacy in terms of nonverbal immediacy. Two entire issues of the *Journal of Nonverbal Behavior* were devoted to research on deception (De Paulo, B. 1988, De Paulo, P. 1988), and the same journal published a special issue on nonverbal intimacy and exchange (Patterson, 1984).

Deception

The study of nonverbally cued **deception** is based on the assumption that whilst it may be relatively simple to tell lies, nonverbal information from the face, body and voice can convey a different message. In general, this applies to lies about emotions. According to Ekman (1988:165–66):

> ... usually lies about emotions involve more than just fabricating an emotion which is not felt. They also require concealing an emotion which is actually being experienced. Concealment often goes hand in hand with fabrication. The liar feigns emotion to mask signs of the emotion to be concealed.

deception
An act of purposefully conveying to others information the deceiver believes to be false, and which is intended to benefit the deceiver.

When people try to conceal their real feelings, some element of a hidden emotion may resist being 'masked' and 'leak' clues via the face, body, voice, and speech (Ekman, 1988:174). Some nonverbal signals seem inconsistent with verbal statements and are difficult to interpret. They suggest that the speaker is lying and Ekman (1988) calls them 'deception cues'.

Research on deception has been directed toward a number of diverse issues. For example, Snyder and Higgins (1988) considered deception in terms of excuse-making. I have also used excuse-making as a theoretical framework to explain the deceptive communication and behaviour of adult learners (Kaye, 1991). Since all people at some time or other engage in some form of deception (including self-deception), it is important to determine the frequency and extent to which adult learners make different kinds of excuses.

Other research on deception has focused more on the process itself rather than on its occurrence in different contexts. For example, Hurd and Noller

(1988) investigated differences between male and female ability to detect it, and found no outstanding clear differences. Although De Paulo and Jordan (1982) claimed that children are distinctly poor at detecting dissemblance and deception, Saarni (1988) concluded that children do try to interpret others' dilemmas in concealing emotions from situation cues, and claimed that 'by middle childhood children are capable of subtle insights into how emotional experience and social context are to be integrated' (p. 290).

Since lying and deception are common in human communication (Bella De Paulo (1988:153)), any attempt to understand and interpret interpersonal communication requires a keen awareness of the potential effects of deception on relationship stability. Furthermore, remember that facial, vocal, and bodily cues may often be interpreted as inconsistent with the words being spoken.

Intimacy and immediacy

The study of intimacy has, over the years, been concerned with such phenomena as physical proximity (Hall, 1968, 1969) and eye-behaviour, including gaze and mutual gaze (Argyle & Dean, 1965; Kendon, 1967; Rosenfeld et al., 1984; Rutter et al., 1984). As well, intimacy has been studied in terms of 'immediacy'. **Immediacy** behaviours have been defined as 'verbal or nonverbal behaviours that serve to increase or decrease physical and psychological proximity by signalling some degree of affect or approach-avoidance tendencies' (Hale & Burgoon, 1984:287). Immediacy is signalled nonverbally by physical proximity, posture, body orientation, eye contact or eye gaze, touch, and smiling. McAndrew et al. (1984) found that people's immediacy behaviours are strongly related to their emotional states; these investigators concluded that immediacy behaviours should be studied not only as a connected *system* of behaviours, but within its *context*.

Essentially, therefore, immediacy is characterised by inclusiveness with another person and by orientation and attention to them. Involvement and inclusiveness of this kind is typically expressed by 'the same kinesic, proxemic, and chronemic cues as intimacy but also includes such vocalic indicators as more rapid speech rate, increased loudness, greater pitch variety, shorter speech latencies, and fewer pauses and silences' (Burgoon, 1985: 375).

Research on nonverbal intimacy and immediacy is perhaps more valuable to those interested in romantic or personal-social rather than professional relationships, but immediacy behaviour in work settings is worth further investigation. In particular, if people are unaware that they are expressing nonverbal cues that indicate intimacy or immediacy, they may inadvertently jeopardise their professional relationships. Ambiguity and confusion of this type hinder the development of good communication strategies.

immediacy
The degree of liking or disliking for a person or task.

5.9 Summary

This chapter explored the field of study known as 'nonverbal communication'. It considered the nonverbal role played by facial expressions, vocal cues, gestures, the use of space and territory, touching, and how our clothing and grooming can express how we see ourselves and how we would like others to see us. In short, our appearances to others may be construed as statements of self-presentation.

Finally, we looked very briefly at two comparatively recent research directions in nonverbal communication scholarship: nonverbally cued deception, and nonverbal intimacy and immediacy. Although this research has focused on private relationships, its application to professional practice may be worth consideration.

Chapter 6 examines the importance of effective listening and assertive behaviour. Particular attention is paid to the role of empathy, feedback, and suspension of judgment in the listening process. Listening is also considered as a major component of interpersonal communication competence, and assertiveness is described and explained as the logical complement to effective listening.

Discussion Questions 5.10

1. Try to recall an occasion when your nonverbal bodily signals may have contradicted your verbal message to another person. Describe in detail your feelings or attitudes at the time. What *words* did you say? What effect did your words and *nonverbal signals* have on the other person? What lessons for improving your future communication with others can you learn from this experience?

2. How can this chapter help you to become more competent in your communication with others at work or in your private life? List the ideas you have found important or valuable and discuss them with someone else who has also read this chapter and compiled a personal list.

3. Think of someone you consider to be a highly competent communicator, and someone else whom you regard as a poor communicator. Write down all the attributes that make them, respectively, competent or incompetent. Underline each nonverbal attribute. What is the proportion of nonverbal attributes for each person? What does your list tell you about the importance of nonverbal communication in everyday life? Share what you have learned with someone else who has done this exercise.

4. In what aspects of people's daily lives do words have more impact than nonverbal cues? When do nonverbal cues have more impact than words? Discuss these questions with someone.

5. What kinds of nonverbal cues can get people into trouble at work? Can they be expressed so that they are not offensive?

6. Have you noticed that on some occasions people are 'overdressed' or 'underdressed'? For example, at a formal wedding some people come informally dressed (e.g. in open-necked shirts) or at an informal party

some wear formal attire. What effect does overdressing or underdressing have on others, and on those who are overdressed or underdressed?

5.11 Activities

1. Try this exercise with a partner or a group of friends. Ask your partner or group to face away from you. Recite the alphabet in an angry tone, and ask your observers to write down the emotional state they think you were in. Repeat this procedure with a different emotional state each time (e.g. happy, sad, surprised, impatient), then check how accurately your observers 'read' your emotions and how well you expressed them. Which emotions were easiest and which were hardest to interpret or express, and why?

2. Ask a partner to take a photograph of your face while you are thinking about something that makes you feel very happy. Repeat the exercise, expressing sadness, surprise, fear, anger, disgust, boredom, impatience. Show the photographs to several of your friends and ask them to tell you what your face was showing in each one. How often did your friends' interpretations concur? What reasons can you suggest for their agreements and disagreements?

3. Prepare a short (max. 5 minutes) talk to present to a small group of people you know—for example, people you supervise at work, a charity organisation, a community group, a social or sports club. Decide how you want to present your message—standing before a seated audience, around a conference table, informally in a lounge area, and so on. How far will you be from your audience? After the talk reflect on how well it went: what would you do similarly and what would you do differently if you presented it again? Why? How would you use the space between you and your audience next time?

5.12 Key Terms

Body language
Deception
Facial expression
Immediacy
Interpersonal attitudes
Kinesics
Metacommunication

Multi-message gestures
Mutual gaze
Nonverbal communication
Nonverbal cues
Paralanguage
Proxemics
Self-image
Self-presentation
Somatotyping

Recommended Reading 5.13

Argyle, M. (1976) *Bodily communication*, London: Methuen.

Burgoon, J. K. (1985) 'Nonverbal signals', in *Handbook of interpersonal communication*, Knapp, M. L. and Miller, G. R. (eds), California: Sage, 344–90.

Malandro, L. A., Barker, L. and Barker, D. A. (1989) *Nonverbal communication*, 2nd edn, New York: Random House.

Marsh, P. (ed.) (1988) *Eye to eye: how people interact*, Massachusetts: Salem House.

Morris, D. (1985) *Bodywatching: a field guide to the human species*, London: Jonathan Cape.

Listening and Assertiveness

6

I did not catch your words, sir, if, indeed, they were words.
Sir Robert Menzies addressing an interjector
at an election meeting in Geelong, Victoria

What is more enchanting than the voices of young people
when you can't hear what they say?
Logan Pearsall Smith

How well do we listen and what do we need to know to practise the art and skill of listening? Is listening different from hearing? What relationship does being a good listener have to competence in assertiveness? These questions are the focus of this chapter. We learn why it is important at appropriate moments to know how to listen non-evaluatively and empathically, and considers the role and importance of feedback in the communication process since accurate feedback may be taken as evidence of skilful listening. To complement this skill, communication managers should also develop the ability to stand up for their rights by being assertive. This chapter offers practical examples of assertive communication and suggests how to differentiate these from aggression or passivity. Finally, it proposes some practical strategies for developing our skills in listening and being assertive.

Learning Objectives

After you have studied the ideas, arguments and suggestions presented in this chapter, you should be able to do the following:

- Explain the difference between listening and hearing.

- Identify three essential elements of skilful listening.

- List some of the popular myths or misconceptions about listening and explain why these are misconceptions.

- Argue why non-evaluative listening and empathy are important for communication managers.

- Define 'critical listening' and explain how the ability to listen critically complements the ability to listen non-evaluatively.

- State why the ability to give feedback is an important aspect of listening.

- Explain how developing assertiveness can enhance communication managers' competence.

- Give three examples of situations requiring your ability to be assertive and construct three-part assertion messages for each example.

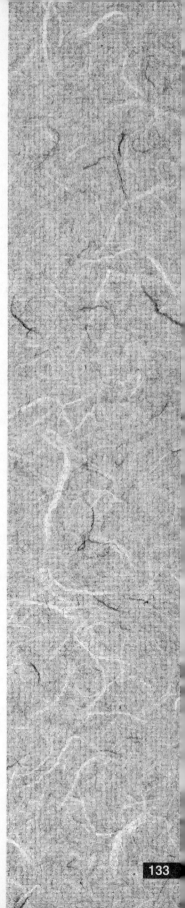

6.1 The Importance of Listening and Assertive Behaviour

listening
Interpreting and attaching meaning to what we have heard.

Of all the skills people need to develop in order to be competent communicators, **listening** is perhaps the most important. On this point, Cooper writes:

> . . . listening is viewed as the primary communication skill, in two senses of the word. It is primary in that it is the first communication skill acquired by a child, well before the ability to speak, read or write. Second, it is primary in that listening is most often used; the greater part of each day (in comparison with speaking, reading or writing) involves the use of this communication skill. (Cooper, 1991:1)

hearing
The physical act of receiving sound.

It is necessary to distinguish between listening and **hearing**. Hearing is essentially the physical act of receiving sound, but listening involves our attention to and interpretation of what we hear. Adler, Rosenfeld, & Towne (1983:145) explain that '*hearing* is the process wherein sound waves strike the eardrum and cause vibrations that are transmitted to the brain. *Listening* occurs when the brain reconstructs these electrochemical impulses into a representation of the original sound, and then gives them meaning'. Listening also depends upon the listener's ability to interpret accurately the speaker's intentions, so 'listening' is an active process.

It has been estimated that people spend between 40 and 60 per cent of their daily lives listening to someone else (Barker et al., 1980; Brown, 1982; Nichols and Stevens, 1957; Verderber et al., 1976; Rankin, 1926). Naturally, in specific situations they spend even more time listening. For example, university students spend much of their learning time in lecture halls, and politicians are required to do a lot of listening when parliament is in session. In our everyday lives, however, we all need to be good listeners, especially when the messages we listen to are critical to our well-being and survival.

There are some common myths and misconceptions about listening. One is that the ability to listen effectively is something people learn incidentally, like learning to walk and talk, in their natural course of development. In fact, many people are surprised that there are training courses on listening. Curiously enough, once these same people have been through such a course they often become the most vocal advocates for the development of competence in listening. Although we are all required to listen from early childhood, few individuals do it well, so one of the major tasks for communication and human relations trainers is to change this popular belief that listening comes naturally.

Another myth about listening is that our gaze or eye-contact is an assurance that we are listening, although it is easy to look earnestly at someone without really listening to them. This is because it is relatively easy to fake attention. In other words, although people may not be really listening, they can give the impression that they are listening. As we shall discover later in this chapter, it is important to make sure, wherever practicable, that people have been listening accurately and comprehensively. In some contexts, the failure to do this can lead to disaster.

There are several common situations in which we may seem to be listening when in fact our minds have wandered elsewhere—in telephone conversations, for example. How often have you heard people on the phone repeatedly mumble perfunctory sounds like 'uh-huh' or 'mmn' while supposedly listening to someone at the other end? Sometimes, they seem even less attentive if they are also doing something else like glancing through the mail, or putting on nailpolish, even though the receiver would be unaware of what they were doing.

One of the most popular myths about listening is that it is a passive process. It comes from the belief that in a speaker-listener relationship the speaker is the sole communicator and the listener is simply a passive receiver. However, listening is a cognitive process, since it involves not only the reception of sounds but also the interpretation of those sounds: when we are listening we attach meanings to what we hear.

Hirsch (1986) presented 10 concepts common to the most frequently used definitions of listening. These include several cognitive components, as follows:

1. a neurological aspect of hearing;

2. interpreting the sounds;

3. understanding the sounds;

4. assigning meaning to the sounds;

5. reacting to the sounds;

6. selectively receiving some sounds and ignoring others;

7. remembering what was communicated;

8. purposely attending to the sounds;

9. analysing the information presented; and

10. using past experiences as a filter of the communication information.

Clearly, Hirsch appears to support the notion that listeners act upon messages they receive. This is evidenced by such cognitive acts, among others, as interpretation, assigning meaning, and analysing information presented. On this basis, it is virtually inconceivable that listening is anything but an active process.

Of the various misconceptions about the process of listening, one of the most disturbing is that all listeners interpret a common message in the same way. However, people's interpretations of a spoken message differ. University students, for example, debate issues raised in a lecture hall. Even though they listened to the same lecture, their discussions after it make it clear that they responded to it differently.

selective listening
The tendency to listen to parts of a message rather than the whole message.

assertiveness (assertion)
The ability to stand up for one's rights without infringing on the rights of others.

Such differences in interpretation and acceptance are sometimes due to **selective listening**. Most of us cannot recall everything said in a lecture, for example—we recall only parts of it. This kind of selective recall usually occurs because we listen for what we want to hear or think may be important. The selective nature of the listening process is resumed later in this chapter.

Assertiveness is an important aspect of communication competence and confidence. Being assertive means being able to stand up for one's rights while respecting the rights of others. In some ways, being a good listener helps us to be confident in being assertive because we become more skilled in constructing messages which listeners will interpret as we intend. Some people have likened listening and assertiveness to two sides of a coin. Bolton (1979) has referred to listening and assertiveness as the yin and yang of human communication. The ancient Chinese yin and yang symbol represents two different but complementary aspects of life (see Figure 6.1). As Bolton notes: 'yin and yang are necessary to each other. The goal of the yin-yang philosophers was the attainment of perfect balance between the two principles' (p. 118). Bolton sees the yin of listening as understanding and accepting other people in times of joy or stress, while the yang of assertion involved disclosing to others one's feelings and needs.

Tao philosophy teaches that all aspects of life can be explained in terms of yang and yin. These are natural polarities like night and day, heart and mind, active and passive, or soft and hard. Dreher (1991) observed that 'this dynamic of yin and yang resembles the Hegelian dialectic of thesis/antithesis/synthesis in which one concept (thesis) inevitably generates its opposite and their interaction produces a new concept (synthesis). The similarity is no accident, for Hegel, too, studied the Tao, lecturing on Taoism at Heidelberg early in his career' (p. 101).

FIGURE 6.1
The yin-yang symbol

Listening and assertiveness, therefore, may be regarded as complementary components of interpersonal communication competence. Both listening and assertiveness, it is suggested, are necessary for effective communication and interaction with others.

Non-evaluative Listening and Empathy   6.2

One of the essential requirements of skilful listening is the ability to suspend judgment about the speaker or the speaker's message. According to Bolton (1979:17), 'the tendency to judge other people is the major roadblock to effective interpersonal communication'. Bolton also describes these 'major roadblocks' as 'common communication spoilers' and 'communication barriers', which usually take the form of *high-risk responses*. As Bolton goes on to say, the impact of these responses on communication is usually negative:

> . . . these roadblocks are more likely to be destructive when one or more persons are interacting under stress. The unfortunate effects of communication blocks are many and varied. They frequently diminish the other's self-esteem. They tend to trigger defensiveness, resistance, and resentment. They can lead to dependency, withdrawal, feelings of defeat or of inadequacy. They decrease the likelihood the other will find her own solution to her own problem. Each roadblock is a 'feeling blocker'; it reduces the likelihood that the other will constructively express her true feelings. Because communication roadblocks carry a high risk of fostering these negative results, their repeated use can cause permanent damage to a relationship. (Bolton, 1979:15)

The ability to suspend judgment is critical to being a good listener. Without this ability we tend to act upon what we want or expect to hear rather than on what was actually stated. For dialogue to be genuinely reciprocal, people must be able to appreciate others' points of view, as well as their own, and receive a spoken message as the speaker intended. Good listeners, therefore, can receive messages without applying judgmental filters such as prejudice or stereotyping.

As noted in Chapter 5, people's judgments of others' spoken messages may be affected by a variety of nonverbal cues. We tend to listen less attentively to someone whose appearance is off-putting, or whose tone of voice seems monotonous and unenthusiastic. When the verbal message is delivered with negative cues of this type, our listening is likely to be selective.

The tendency to judge others is common—we slip very easily into the trap of judgmental listening by letting our personal feelings and beliefs affect our acceptance of others' messages, and these feelings and beliefs can harden into prejudice. Stereotypes and prejudices often relate to specific groups such as women, ethnic or foreign communities, religious organisations, or people with certain political persuasions. For example, it is still not uncommon, even in developed Western societies, to hear comments like 'what would a woman know about management (or government, leadership etc.)?'.

People who are prominent in sport, politics, education, or business are likely to be perceived according to listeners' attitudes to these fields of activity. For example, those not interested in tennis may not be impressed by tennis stars promoting cosmetics—in such cases the advertisement may be counter-productive.

Again, there are some people whose selective listening is influenced (i.e. made selective) because they believe that educated people are snobs, or that religious folk are narrow-minded, or that politicians are opportunistic and devious. Stereotypes of this kind are often encouraged by the media. For example, if the media repeatedly report instances of fundamentalist preachers condemning groups who advocate acceptance of homosexuality or the legalisation of abortion or certain drugs, such listeners are strongly influenced. **Non-evaluative listening** is not easy; it is a skill that has to be practised. First of all, however, we have to know when we are being evaluative; this is a prerequisite to practising this skill.

However, people should not assume that all listening must be non-evaluative. Adjudicators of debates, for example, have to assess the arguments put forward by the debating teams. Oral examinations, too, require examiners to decide what grades to award examinees. In each case, the skill of **critical listening** is required—it has been described as 'listening to comprehend and then evaluate the message' (Wolvin & Coakley, 1988:283). We will take a closer look at critical listening later in this chapter. The point should be kept in mind, however, that there are several kinds of communication situations that require listeners to be critical and evaluative—for example, interviewing or negotiating.

One way to ensure that your listening is non-judgmental is to repeat the message you have just heard exactly as you think the speaker intended it to be understood. This is often difficult to do because our speech rate is slower than our listening rate. Barker puts it this way:

> . . . you normally have a certain amount of free time during the listening process because of the thinking-speaking time differential. Since you can think several times faster than someone can talk, you should have enough time to summarize and evaluate what is heard. While evaluating a speaker's message, you should try to figure out the speaker's view of the world and how that influences what he or she is saying. (Barker, 1984:54)

In other words, when we listen to someone, we also think about the message. Our thoughts about the message can easily become diverted by other thoughts, and when this occurs it is difficult to concentrate on what is being said. Non-evaluative listening sometimes takes the form of an *empathic response* to the speaker. **Empathy** means 'putting yourself in someone else's shoes'. Good listeners reflect the feelings and emotions of those they are listening to, without judging them. Some therapy techniques require counsellors to include the empathic response in their repertoire of skills (Rogers, 1951). An appropriate empathic response would be 'you're really feeling angry right now'; an inappropriate empathic response would be 'your present anger isn't helping you or me one bit'.

non-evaluative listening
Suspending judgment about a speaker's remarks.

critical listening
Evaluating the logic and validity of what a speaker says.

empathy
The ability to understand others' feelings and to express that understanding without censure.

Empathy, the ability to understand and share the feelings of another, is vital to communication competence. It has been suggested by Adler, Rosenfeld & Towne (1983:150) that 'an impressive body of research supports the idea that the ability to empathize is an important element in effective communication for many social roles: business supervisors, teachers, therapists and counselors, and of course friends'. Advocates of empathic listening claim that some people may be helped to solve their interpersonal problems by confronting these problems gradually. This suggests that the essential role of the counsellor or therapist is to help clients understand their problems and to listen empathically rather than give advice.

Skill in non-evaluative listening may be demonstrated by the listener's attentiveness or by empathic responses to emotional messages. Empathy, as suggested, is a key listening skill, but only one of several. The next section of this chapter introduces another significant skill—feedback.

Listening and Feedback 6.3

Without obtaining feedback, speakers do not know how their messages are being received, so it is an essential component of effective, active listening and of interpersonal communication. It gives speakers some indication of listeners' acceptance or rejection of what is spoken, and gives both speaker and listener an opportunity to clarify and co-ordinate meanings.

Let's take the example of solicitors interviewing their clients. It is customary for solicitors, not knowing the precise details of their clients' needs, to begin their interviews with some phrase like 'How can I help you?' Generally speaking, clients take this as an invitation to 'open up' by outlining their legal needs. Solicitors generally continue the interview with some statement like 'Here's the advice I'd give you'.

Unfortunately, advice at this point of the interview may be premature. The client cannot be sure how well the solicitor understands the problem, and if the solicitor does not understand it fully, his or her advice might be inappropriate. What is required here is an intermediate step between listening to the client and proffering advice—that is, the solicitor could check their understanding of the clients' case, perhaps by saying something like 'Well, let's see if I've got this straight, Ms Smith. You were involved in a car accident in which you were found culpable. You believe, nevertheless, that there were special circumstances—wet slippery roads. Must you, therefore, accept responsibility for the accident, or is there some other course of action you could follow?' Statements of this kind allow solicitors to 'get the story straight', and by clarifying the problem together, solicitors and their clients can eventually agree on the precise nature of the legal problem. This type of agreement makes a strong basis for appropriate legal action.

Sometimes, even when feedback is solicited, it achieves very little. For example, many instructors and teachers ask 'Are there any questions?' to check students' understanding, but questions like these are not very useful. Many learners, especially those still unsure of things, keep silent, so the instructor cannot be sure how much they have grasped.

Asking for feedback in this way may even lead to serious consequences. For instance, instructors teaching safety procedures need feedback of a different kind: their learners must restate the safety instructions precisely. One way to ensure this is to ask specific questions such as 'What's the first thing we do before turning on the motor?'; or 'What three checks must we make before engaging the cutting device?' Of course, the final test of whether learners really understand fully occurs when they have to carry out the task by themselves, so restating the safety procedures accurately is not enough—they must be able to perform them.

Another thing worth noting about feedback is that it need not be immediate—sometimes it is even more important if it is delayed. Whilst immediate feedback indicates something about learners' short-term recall of information, delayed feedback tells us something about how much they retain later. In many teaching or training situations it is necessary to check whether students' listening has led them to learn something thoroughly enough to constitute a basis for further learning. In any discipline or field of study basic principles and concepts must be learned thoroughly before learners can progress to more sophisticated levels. For this reason delayed feedback is often essential and may be obtained in various ways. The most common method is to test learners so that instructors can be sure that fundamental concepts have been fully grasped.

One other aspect of delayed feedback is that it indicates some of the thought processes that have taken place between the initial learning and subsequent retesting. During this period most people not only remember what they have listened to but also think more about it. The essence of what was learnt may be understood better—but it can also be changed in the process. For example, when people listen to politicians' claims about their own trustworthiness and about the insincerity of some Opposition member's claims, how do they judge the merit of such speeches? As the media hammer their messages of support or rejection, listeners assess each new piece of information according to images previously formed, and it can eventually take on a meaning not originally intended.

Here's an example of how this might work. Some prominent politician decides to introduce a goods and services tax (GST). Certain listeners are already opposed to this politician because of their own political affiliations. As time goes on, however, the public (according to the media) generally support the new GST. This impression of public support can soften that group of listeners' opposition, and they may change their attitude to the politician.

All this shows how immediate feedback differs from delayed feedback because intervening events and information may change perceptions and opinions. If the discrepancy between immediate and delayed feedback is not noticed or understood by relevant people, quite severe consequences could occur—for example, politicians could lose elections, service organisations could lose clients, companies could lose business, and entertainers could lose audiences.

In organisations feedback has been equated with communication itself (Egan, 1985; 1988a; 1991). When Egan repeatedly asserts that 'communication is the lifeblood of systems', he is essentially referring to feedback from one organisation member to the next, and he points out that it may be either 'confirmatory' or 'corrective'. It is imperative that people know how they are affecting others so that they know where they stand in relation to others in their systems.

Corrective feedback can be subtle

Corrective feedback, of course, is not pleasant as a rule. People do not want to hear uncomplimentary things about themselves, or that others are less than pleased with the way things are going. Learning to cope with criticism and with corrective feedback is therefore an important skill. Unfortunately, as we are usually blind to our own weaknesses and faults, we find it hard to understand the true value of constructive criticism and how to take advantage of it to correct our faults.

Being sensitive and listening to others helps people understand what effect they are having on others in their systems. Even if they do not obtain direct feedback, *indirect* feedback is still valuable. Indirect feedback comes from an unaffected source rather than from anyone directly involved. Sometimes, for example, our speech or actions inadvertently hurt or insult others; if this is pointed out to us, we are at least in a position to change our pattern of communication or behaviour.

We will return to the topic of listening shortly, when we consider strategies we can develop to make ourselves better listeners. Meanwhile, let us turn our attention to assertiveness and how it relates to our listening behaviour.

6.4 Assertiveness: Standing Up for Oneself

Many people discover that they need to work hard at learning how to stand up for their rights. It is not easy to let others know that their speech or action is preventing you from exercising your own rights, and sometimes the need to be assertive is not urgent. For many people the need to stand up for oneself happens only occasionally, so that when they do face the choice of standing up for themselves or keeping silent, they lack confidence. Earlier in this chapter it was suggested that listening and assertiveness can be thought of as the yin-yang of communication. Bolton explains this analogy as follows:

> I like to think of listening and assertion as the yin and yang of communication. Vital relationships involve both asserting and listening. The yang of assertion is the disclosure to another of what the speaker feels, needs, desires. The yin of listening is understanding and acceptance offered to another in times of stress or joy. Now yin, now yang is the way of vital communication. To the degree that a person is underdeveloped in either element, her maturation is incomplete. To the extent that either listening or assertion is missing from either person in their relationship—to that degree the relationship falls short of its potential. (Bolton, 1979:118)

Assertive people have been accorded four main characteristics by Fensterheim & Baer (1989:8):

1. They are not afraid of self-disclosure. Indeed, they feel quite comfortable about expressing their thoughts, needs, and feelings and have no problem with saying 'this is how I feel' or 'this is what I want' or 'this is what I believe'.

2. Assertive people can communicate with others on all levels. As Fensterheim and Baer note, their communication 'is always open, direct, honest, and appropriate' (p. 8) with all kinds of people—friends, acquaintances, family, or strangers.

3. Assertive people have an active orientation to life. Instead of waiting for things to happen they go after what they want. In the film *Dead Poets' Society* the dedicated schoolteacher, Mr Keating, urged his pupils to follow the school motto, *carpe diem*, which means 'seize the day'. This teacher actively encouraged his pupils to make the most of opportunities when they are there to be taken.

4. Assertive people act in ways which they themselves respect—they understand at least some of their strengths and limitations and do not become disappointed when they realise they cannot succeed at some particular task. In such instances they seek new challenges where success is more attainable, and maintain their self-respect and dignity.

It is important to distinguish *assertive* from *aggressive* behaviour. Aggression usually connotes an intention to hurt and may be expressed through paralinguistic cues (e.g. a loud voice), or verbally with hurtful or derogatory remarks. Aggressive people tend to express their feelings and needs and emphasise their rights at others' expense. In short, aggressive people tend to overpower others.

By contrast, assertive people are able to stand up for themselves yet still respect others' needs, feelings, and rights. As Bolton (1979:125) notes:

> . . . the assertive person utilizes methods of communication which enable her to maintain self-respect, pursue happiness and the satisfaction of her needs, and defend her rights and personal space without abusing or dominating other people. True assertiveness is a way of being in the world which confirms one's own individual worth and dignity while simultaneously confirming and maintaining the worth of others.

The key to true assertiveness is being able to stand up for oneself in direct and appropriate ways—in this context 'appropriate' implies an absence of aggression toward another person. Since aggressors violate others' needs and personal space, aggression is an inappropriate way to stand up for one's rights.

Almost daily we encounter situations where we would feel better if we acted and communicated assertively, but for various reasons our words and actions are sometimes anything but assertive. Perhaps this is because few people understand what it means to be assertive. Consider the following examples.

- You are having a quiet evening at home watching television. Your neighbour is having a very noisy party and the noise is starting to irritate and upset you. You feel you have the right to some peace.

- Although smoking is prohibited on suburban trains, someone in your carriage has just lit a cigarette. You feel that your right to sit in a smoke-free carriage has been violated.

- You have been waiting to be served in the local butcher's shop. When the butcher says 'Who's next?' someone who came in later than you begins to place her order. You feel that you were entitled to be served before this person.

- Each time you go to put out your rubbish you find that one of your neighbours has used your bin for his excess rubbish so that there is no room for your own rubbish. You feel that someone is encroaching on your space.

- You get on a city bus and there seem to be no vacant seats. Then you notice that someone is sitting with his feet on the opposite seat. You don't see why you should have to remain standing while he occupies two seats.

- You are in a cinema watching a movie and the people behind you keep talking. You feel you shouldn't have to put up with the film being spoilt by their chatter.

Much of our formal learning and education discourages us from speaking up for ourselves. Fensterheim and Baer suggested that people's inability to be assertive has become a problem of national, perhaps international, proportions:

> . . . parents, teachers, clergymen, and businessmen have unwittingly conspired to produce a nation of timid souls. In early years, many mothers and fathers censor the child who decides to speak up for his rights and thus hinder the child's assertion of self. Teachers reward the student who does not question the educational system and deal sternly with those who buck it. In most cases the church fosters the idea of humility and sacrifice rather than standing up for self. Many an employee learns early in his career that if he 'speaks up', he is not likely to receive a raise or promotion and may even lose his job. Adopted at the office, this attitude carries over to home and social life. (Fensterheim & Baer, 1989:8)

Status can also make direct, assertive communication easier for some than for others. Disagreeing with an employer or superior is harder than contradicting somebody you are supervising. Although assertive people find communication equally comfortable at all levels and with all kinds of people, status and power differences can still affect them. Being successfully assertive also varies from one situation to another. Some people find it easier to stand up for themselves in their homes, but not so easy in less familiar settings like solicitors' or bank managers' offices. This is probably because opportunities to practise being assertive are more frequent in familiar surroundings and less intimidating since we are not so uncertain about others' reactions.

Fear of how others may react also inhibits assertiveness. We may fear being disliked, rejected, or emotionally hurt and we may be afraid to express anger. We can also become conditioned to these fears. Take the example of young children who are repeatedly left out of sporting teams, perhaps because they have not matured physically. The effect on their self-image may be devastating and enduring so that in later years, even when they can compete in sports more successfully, the memory of this rejection may be still powerful enough to make them feel inadequate. One of the consequences of feeling unable to be assertive is the compelling tendency for people to avoid situations where they may need to stand up for themselves. Many people find it very tempting to be submissive and avoid situations that put our assertive abilities to the test. This amounts to self-denial of one's rights. In other words, people who avoid situations where they may need to be assertive are actually precluding for themselves opportunities to practise their assertion skills.

Assertiveness is a skill people can develop with practice. The idea that only some people are assertive while most others are not is probably an assumption that assertiveness is an innate personality trait. It is important, therefore, for people to realise that they can learn to be assertive if they want to. There is no mystery about it and there are guidelines to help people learn and practise it. For example, three-part assertion messages deal with problem behaviour. The first part of the message describes the offending behaviour or communication and usually begins with 'when you':

- when you leave food scraps on the kitchen floor . . .

- when you present me work which has not been checked . . .

- when you make long-distance calls on my home telephone . . .

- when you bring uninvited guests to my parties . . .

- when you borrow my books . . .

In all of these instances, actual behaviours are factually reported. This part of the message is most effective when unnecessary emotive adjectives or adverbs such as 'unthinking(ly)', 'selfish(ly)', 'vicious(ly)', 'insulting(ly)' are left out.

The second part of the three-part assertion message begins with the words 'I feel'. This disclosure of feeling must be direct, honest, and succinct. For example:

- when you leave food scraps on the floor *I feel annoyed* ;

- when you present me with work that has not been checked *I feel frustrated*;

- when you make long-distance calls on my home telephone *I feel angry*;

- when you bring uninvited guests to my parties, in your lack of consideration for me as the host *I feel disappointed*;

- when you ask to borrow my books *I feel reluctant to lend them to you*.

The third part of the message states how the behaviour described in the first part affects the recipient, and explains the feelings disclosed in the second part. The entire message in each case could be completed as follows:

- When you leave food scraps on the floor I feel annoyed *because I will have to clean up the mess.*

- When you present me with work that has not been checked I feel frustrated *because it takes me longer to review careless presentations.*

- When you make long-distance calls on my home telephone I feel angry *because I have to use my special savings to pay for them.*

- When you bring uninvited guests to my parties I feel disappointed *because you didn't bother to ask me if it would be okay.*

- When you ask to borrow my books I feel reluctant to lend them to you *because you have not yet returned any of the books you previously borrowed from me.*

Bolton (1979:144–50) offers some guidelines for developing effective three-part assertion messages.

1. The offending behaviour should be described in specific factual terms. If the description is vague the assertive statement is likely to lose impact. Here are some comparisons between specific behaviour descriptions and vague behaviour descriptions:

Specific behaviour description	Vague behaviour description
When you tell racist jokes	When you are insensitive
When you park the car illegally	When you break the law
When you drink too much	When you lose your dignity
When you don't tidy up your room	When you act like a pig
When you forget our anniversary	When you act selfishly

2. Make sure that the descriptions keep to behaviour and are not inferences about the other person's motives, attitudes, or personality traits. It is all too easy to call someone names or assume what their intentions are. A useful way of checking is to ask if the behaviour is observable; words like 'discourteous', 'negligent', or 'miserly', for example, do not refer to specific behaviours.

3. Make sure that the behaviour descriptions are objective and not judgmental. Emotive terms like 'wrong', 'bad', or 'useless' serve no constructive purpose in assertive messages because they attack someone's character, not their behaviour. It is worth noting that character assassination is a common form of psychological fallacy and in the science of reasoning is referred to as the *ad hominem* form of argument.

4. Behavioural descriptions should be as brief as possible. Make a succinct statement such as 'when you forget to set the table'; unnecessary information complicates the description. For example: 'When you spend too much time watching TV before I come home and you lose track of time and forget your promise to be helpful in small ways like setting the table for our evening meals . . .' As Bolton points out: *'What is not said is as important in an assertion message as what is said.* Don't add peripheral data to your bare-bones assertion. Relinquish side issues and explanations. *The entire assertion message should be compressed into one sentence'* (Bolton, 1979:148).

5. The assertion must be about a real issue. When individuals prefer 'flight' to 'fight' they avoid what is troubling them and tackle some

other less threatening matter. This is a displaced assertion. For example, they might become irritated with minor issues like overspending on unnecessary household items when the real trouble is a relationship breakdown or work stress. As Bolton has noted: 'Displaced assertions keep a relationship in such frequent disharmony and offer such little possibility of improvement that the whole relationship often goes sour. These pseudoassertions that do not deal with the real issues rarely, if ever, help and often hinder a friendship, marriage, or work relationship' (p. 149).

6. Take care that the assertive statement is directed at the appropriate person and avoid making scapegoats of others. When individuals are assertive toward people who are not responsible for offending behaviours, *misattributed assertion* occurs. For example, people treated badly by their superiors at work may confront their peers or subordinates instead; or a schoolteacher may punish only one pupil when in fact several pupils have misbehaved.

These six guidelines apply directly to the first statement of three-part assertion messages. Nevertheless, note that the second part of these messages—the open and honest statement of one's feelings—represents the crux of the assertive intent. As suggested earlier, many people do find it difficult to express their emotions accurately. There are various reasons for this. One is that some cannot easily recognise the depth or intensity of their feelings when they are provoked.

For instance, people may say they are 'disappointed' or 'concerned' when they really mean they are extremely inconvenienced or put out by someone's communication or actions. They use euphemisms like 'concerned' when they really mean something stronger. Sometimes they tone down the message with words like 'somewhat'. For example, 'I was somewhat surprised to learn . . . ' might really mean 'I was appalled to discover . . . '

Of course, the substitution of one emotion for another may not only involve finding a euphemism for a more deeply held feeling. In some cases, people do not even recognise what emotion they feel. For example, someone banging with a hammer might waken someone who was asleep. A reaction like 'you *startled* me with your hammering' might be a substitute for 'you *annoyed* me with your hammering'. Such reactions substitute a secondary emotion for a primary one—in the example above, the primary emotion, anger, was replaced by the secondary emotion, alarm.

Being aware of one's true feelings, therefore, is a kind of defence against involuntary substitutions of feelings. Such awareness is not easy if people develop the substitution habit, especially if they manipulate inappropriate emotional responses from others. A person steeped in self-pity may try to evince pity from someone who has offended them, for example. Unfortunately, the consequence of feeling pity may not be constructive. The offender may not realise that they are stimulating anger rather than sadness. Inaccurate perceptions like these, moreover, could lead to totally unwanted responses toward the offended person, since an apology is more appropriate a response than pity.

A final point to be made about assertion messages is that the third part should focus on concrete or tangible effects. The essential question here is 'How is my life being affected by someone else's actions?' Under the heading of 'life', we could include such tangible effects as invasion of personal space and privacy, demands on our time, energy, or financial resources, and threat to our belongings. As Bolton (1979:153) suggests, such effects are materialistic ways in which we are inconvenienced. Hence people to whom assertive messages are directed are more likely to be influenced by the knowledge that they have cost someone time, money, or space than by vague allusions to being 'put out' or 'disadvantaged'.

Section 6.5 proposes strategies to improve listening and assertiveness, and identifies some of the pitfalls we need to avoid.

6.5 Strategies for Listening and Assertive Behaviour

open listening
The process where listeners try to forget their own concerns and biases so that their response to what is being said is as intelligent and sympathetic as possible.

It is hard to listen attentively to a message that is vague or ambiguous, and skilled listeners clarify speakers' intentions. When a speaker's words do not appear to make much sense, it is very easy to 'tune out', and one way of combating this tendency is to develop the practice of **open listening**. Barker (1984:136) has suggested that 'open listening takes attention focusing one step further, to the point of forgetting for the moment your own concerns and biases and responding intelligently and sympathetically to what is being said'. Open listeners resist the temptation to be self-focused and instead react to speakers with understanding and constructive feedback.

Open listeners are not 'stage hogs' (Adler, Rosenfeld, & Towne, 1983:153). Stage hogs like the sound of their own voices and are therefore not particularly interested in what other people have to say. Take the example of people who have been severely criticised by their superiors, and pour out their anger and frustration to their closest friends. Rather than say things like 'I know exactly how you are feeling. Only the other day, I had a painful run-in with my boss', open listeners would say something like 'Your boss seems to have been tough on you lately. Have you thought about moving to another department?'

One thing people can do to be better listeners is to talk less. Interrupting others in mid-speech is, of course, not only discourteous but also a symptom of poor listening skill; people who try to listen and talk at the same time do neither well. However, there are always times when we need to speak up and be heard. The key is to know when to remain silent and listen, and when to talk.

In our society examples of poor communication occur almost daily. A common one is the failure to listen to someone's entire message. Politicians indulge in so much name-calling, heckling, and other forms of interruption (especially in parliament) that debate seems to have little to do with communication. Some politicians appear to listen mainly to the part of the message that is verbally assailable. When only part of the total message is taken to represent the entire context in this way, such people are prone to the *straw person fallacy*.

Politicians sometimes listen to only part of a message

Sensitive listeners can also tell when brief responses are more appropriate than elaborate feedback. For instance, in **phatic communication**, which includes salutations and greetings like 'How are you?' or 'How have you been?', the expected response is a brief one like 'Fine' or 'Pretty good'—not an invitation to provide a detailed account of your health. Hypochondriacs, of course, may want to elaborate on their imagined illnesses.

There are several annoying listener responses in vogue, such as 'I hear what you're saying'. Whilst their intention is probably to reassure people that the gist of their speech has been understood, to some people they seem patronising. Good listeners can give others feedback without referring explicitly to their intentions, and avoid jargon such as 'I hear what you're saying'.

People determined to improve their skill in listening and being assertive may also find it useful to practise the art of concentration. As Adler et al. (1983:155–56) suggest, focus on the speaker's words, ideas, and feelings. Use the 'extra' time listening gives you to put the speaker's ideas into your own words, relate them to your experience, and think about any questions you might have.

It will help to focus your attention on the speaker if you make every effort to do away with distracting influences. For example, most interviewers find it easier to listen attentively to their interviewees when the setting is relatively free of noise and visual distractions. It can be annoying to attempt an interview disrupted by window-cleaners, painters, vacuum cleaners or telephones.

phatic communication
Aims to build and maintain social relationships rather than transmit information.

Because listening and assertion, as we suggested earlier, are complementary processes, defensive attitudes can jeopardise the quality of communication between people. Defensive people often construe others' harmless remarks as personal attacks, probably because they are insecure in their communication and relationships. Defensive listening, therefore, may lead to a deterioration of communication between people. Defensiveness can also provoke agression from others.

Sometimes what starts off as critical listening turns into a form of strategic ambushing. Whilst critical listening involves not only the understanding but also the evaluation of persuasive messages, 'ambushing' is listening for evidence or information in order to attack the speaker. Ambushing is like legal cross-examining because it is aimed at destroying another's arguments or point of view. Many politicians are expert at strategic ambushing. An example of ambushing can be found in the Gospel according to Luke. When Christ was debating the scriptures with lawyers, scribes and Pharisees, he accused the lawyers of having 'taken away the key of knowledge' because of their narrow-mindedness. Their reaction to this is described in terms of their intentions toward Christ. Thus, it is recorded that

> . . . as he said these things unto them, the scribes and the Pharisees began to urge him vehemently, and to provoke him to speak of many things: laying wait for him, and seeking to catch something out of his mouth, that they might accuse him. (Luke 11: 53–54)

The wording in the Gospel according to Matthew, though slightly different, reinforces the Pharisees' intentions when they 'took counsel how they might entangle him in his talk' (Matthew 22:15). The scribes and Pharisees were evidently listening for opportunities to trap Jesus into saying something which could incur a charge of blasphemy or sacrilege.

One danger associated with ambushing is that the selective listening it involves may lead to false reasoning. For example, the elaboration of words or phrases taken out of context may result in the straw person fallacy mentioned earlier. People who ambush are not so much interested in understanding the intention of someone's message as they are in discrediting it. They do not listen to improve communication and relationships but to generate confrontation and adversarial communication.

Many people believe that if you ignore malicious or unflattering communication directed at you, it will not affect you—'sticks and stones can break my bones but words can never hurt me'. Unlike the ambushers who listen for information which they can use to attack speakers, these insulated listeners avoid things they do not want to hear. For instance, when they are told that their contribution to their organisation's annual report is long overdue they seem to register the admonition but their attention is short-lived because they do not want to acknowledge their deficiencies.

There are several factors common to the communication processes of listening and being assertive: clarity, directness, honesty, patience, persistence, and attention to facts rather than opinions or feelings. Being direct does not mean being abusive; it means not beating about the bush when attempting to persuade someone. Some people are not direct in their communication with others because they become flustered under pressure. Their thinking may then lose clarity, precision, and coherence and this, in turn, affects their messages accordingly. Rather like the Kipling types in the famous poem 'If', good communicators 'keep their heads about them' when 'others are losing theirs'.

Since most systems and organisations have a 'shadow side' in which unpredictable forces operate (Egan, 1993), honest communication is sometimes construed as naive. Deceptive communication, on the other hand, may equip individuals to be better as adversaries of peers and colleagues. Nevertheless, in systems where communication between people is open and based on principles of reciprocity and co-operation, honesty contributes a great deal to the establishment of relationships and workable patterns of communication.

Good listeners are both patient and persistent when attending to what others have to say, and do not interrupt them. If necessary, they clarify speakers' intended meanings. One effective way of doing this is to let speakers 'open up' or continue talking for a while longer. Sometimes it occurs to speakers that their messages are confusing; by continuing to talk, they can modify their messages so that they become clearer.

The qualities of patience and persistence can also apply to assertiveness. If, for example, someone reacts aggressively to an open, direct message, an astute communicator will resist being drawn into a verbal slugging match. It is important to keep cool while maintaining a firm position.

Remember that skilful listening and assertiveness require communication based on facts rather than opinions or feelings. Many contemporary management training films emphasise this approach. People who rely on facts are on safe ground when it comes to proving a point or when it becomes necessary to persuade someone to change their attitude or behaviour. It is much easier to oppose someone's opinion or to counter their feelings with your own than it is to dispute facts.

Let's conclude this section by recognising that when communication is enhanced by skilful listening and/or by truly assertive speech, the people involved ideally interact in a win-win manner. Conflict can be resolved constructively, and this can improve relationships even further. Any organisation moving toward the development of autonomous work teams should pay particular attention to skilling staff in assertiveness. Chapter 7 provides a more comprehensive exposition of how conflict can be managed and resolved.

Summary 6.6

In this chapter we have considered how skilful listening and assertiveness are integral aspects of communication competence. The chapter emphasised the importance of non-evaluative listening, responding with empathy to highly emotional speakers, and providing appropriate feedback to indicate that listeners' interpretations are consistent with speakers' intentions.

Assertiveness was proposed as a complement to the process of listening, and distinguished from aggression. The construction of three-part assertion messages was outlined and several strategies for improving people's competence in listening and assertiveness were discussed.

6.7 Discussion Questions

1. Why is it important not to take for granted our ability to listen? What can we do to ensure that we do not take it for granted?

2. How can we prevent our prejudices and biases from influencing our ability to listen attentively to others?

3. Give two examples of how you could provide constructive feedback to certain people you work with.

4. Think of a situation where you had to stand up for your rights (or think of a situation that might require you to defend them). Construct a three-part assertion message for the person infringing your rights. How does this strategy compare with other possible strategies?

5. Compare the similarities and differences between 'critical listening' and 'strategic ambushing'. Suggest one or two examples.

6.8 Activities

1. Watch a current affairs TV program and listen to a national policy by a politician with whom you do not agree. If you can, make a video or audio recording of the politician's statement. Then summarise what the politician said. Now check the accuracy of your summary by comparing it with your recording, or (if you did not make a recording) with the summary of another person who watched the same program. How accurate was your summary? What does this tell you about you as a listener?

2. You have been standing in line to buy tickets for a concert you are particularly keen to attend. The two people in front of you have just let another two friends into the queue. Decide how you would react to this. Are you satisfied with your reaction? How else could you have acted or communicated?

3. List some situations where you feel you should stand up for your rights. Which ones can you handle to your satisfaction? Which ones would be difficult to handle? Devise a strategy for coping with the difficult situations and try it out if any of them arise.

Key Terms   6.9

Ambushing

Assertiveness

Critical listening

Empathy

Feedback

Hearing

Listening

Non-evaluative listening

Open listening

Phatic communication.

Selective listening

Yin-yang

Recommended Reading   6.10

Barker, L. L. (1984) *Communication*, 3rd edn, Englewood Cliffs, New Jersey: Prentice Hall.

Bolton, R. (1979) *People skills: how to assert yourself, listen to others and resolve conflicts*, New York: Simon & Schuster.

Bostrom, R. (1990) *Listening behaviour: theory and research*, New York: Guilford.

Fensterheim, H. and Baer, J. (1989) *Don't say 'yes' when you want to say 'no'*, London: Futura.

Wolvin, A. and Coakley, C. (1988) *Listening*, 3rd edn, Dubuque, IA: Brown.

Conflict Management, Negotiation and Resolution

The next dreadful thing to a battle lost is a battle won.
Arthur Wellesley, Duke of Wellington (1769–1852)

Do not needlessly endanger your lives until I give you the signal.
Dwight D. Eisenhower

An infallible method of conciliating a tiger is to allow oneself to be devoured.
Konrad Adenauer

Peace is not only better than war, but infinitely more arduous.
George Bernard Shaw

No matter how hard people try to coexist in harmony with others, differences in how they think and see their worlds often lead to some form of conflict. When this happens the opponents are faced with the challenge of managing and resolving their conflict and their differences. This chapter is about the way people manage to resolve conflict, and what qualities and abilities they need to do this. It also considers some of the defensive behaviour and communication that can prevent the resolution of conflict and distinguishes principled negotiation from positional bargaining. In some situations negotiators have to resort to their 'best alternatives to a negotiated agreement'. It is also necessary to know how to develop strategies to resolve or prevent conflict; 'realistic conflicts' are examined as a means of identifying possible win-win solutions. Finally, we explore the constructive use of conflict in problem-solving.

Learning Objectives

After you have studied the ideas, arguments and suggestions presented in this chapter you should be able to do the following:

- Distinguish realistic from non-realistic conflicts and identify examples from your own professional or personal experience.

- Give at least three reasons why people become involved in conflicts with others.

- Explain the difference between principled negotiation and positional bargaining, and from your own experience identify examples of each.

- Define BATNA ('the best alternative to a negotiated agreement') and state how you could identify your own BATNA.

- Explain how and why people in conflict communicate defensively.

- Describe one general strategy for managing conflict and one for preventing it.

- Explain how conflict can be used constructively as a problem-solving device.

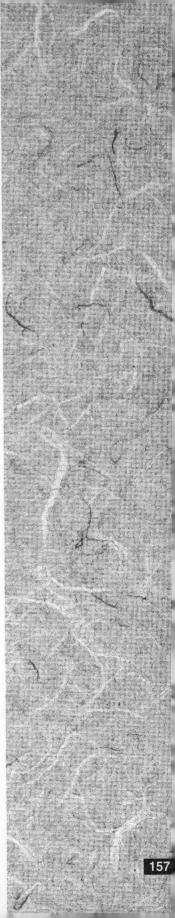

7.1 The Nature and Origins of Conflict

Conflict between people is virtually inevitable. In any situation where people have to co-exist, individual differences in needs, feelings, points of view, or convictions lead to tensions in human relationships. If these tensions persist, people soon find themselves in confrontation.

Not all conflict is interpersonal. In fact, most people have to manage intrapersonal conflicts more frequently. Conflicts within ourselves usually occur when we face choices such as deciding whether to go to a party or stay at home alone to study for an examination; or the choice between an expensive holiday or a new automobile.

This chapter focuses on interpersonal conflict because many people are unaware that there are practical ways of managing and resolving conflict with others, and this makes them vulnerable. Conflict is common—children clash with parents or siblings, school pupils make their teachers angry, people at work find themselves at odds with their colleagues and peers. These are normal conflicts we experience from time to time. To live in a world free of any kind of conflict would mean that everybody thought, felt and acted the same way.

Apart from these normal kinds of conflicts, certain jobs and public images keep some people in constant conflict with others. Barristers, for example, do regular battle in legal courtrooms; politicians conduct verbal attacks on opposition politicians; media interviewers often unnerve or enrage controversial individuals with a high public profile. Perhaps one of the most obvious examples occurs in the field of sport where the conflict may extend to disagreements between performers and umpires or referees. It is now quite commonplace, for example, for champion tennis players to argue with umpires and hurl obscenities at professional officials and the media.

Tennis players sometimes compete with referees as well as their opponents

In some ways conflict is practically synonymous with life itself. Dramatists consider conflict to be the essence of good theatre and novelists seize upon themes of conflict to develop riveting plots. Much historical and religious literature is based on conflict between individuals, armies, nations, and gods. For example, in Homer's epic, *The Iliad*, Achilles fights the Trojan prince Hector; in Shakespeare's *Hamlet*, the Prince of Denmark is at different times in conflict with his uncle, Claudius, his mother, Gertrude, his fiancee, Ophelia, Ophelia's brother, Laertes, and her father, Polonius. Dickens' Ebenezer Scrooge is very much at odds with his clerk, Bob Cratchitt, in the early part of *The Christmas Carol*. The Bible is full of memorable conflicts—Cain slaying Abel, Jacob deceiving his brother Esau, Moses defying the Egyptian pharaoh, David killing Goliath, Solomon mediating two women's dispute over a baby, and Jesus Christ driving out the moneychangers from the temple.

Since conflict is so much part of human life, we can count on it happening at some time in our professional or personal life. As I have suggested previously:

> . . . much as people may detest the prospect of conflict with others, they would do well to remember that conflict is an inescapable part of life. Conflicts are unavoidable regardless of whether they occur at work or at home. Recognising the inevitability of conflict is a good starting point for learning to deal with it when it arises. (Kaye, 1992:92)

Why does conflict arise between people? De Bono (1985:47) suggests that 'people may have to interact in the same situation but they see the situation very differently'. Several factors affect how people approach potential conflict—for instance, the *degree* to which an unfamiliar situation seems threatening or unpleasant. Another factor is that people's *needs* vary. For example, conflict may occur in work teams where some members are motivated by profit whilst others want public recognition for excelling at their work. When such teams are paid by the hour, those trying to make as much money as possible may encourage their teammates to slow down, a tactic that will not appeal to the publicity-seekers who want the job done quickly.

Conflict sometimes occurs because people see it as an inevitable part of their communication with colleagues. Academic theoreticians are challenged by rival scholars; businesspeople conflict with market competitors over products or services; politicians seize every public opportunity to denigrate their opposition. In each case a failure to meet conflict head on can be construed by the adversary as a sign of submission.

Inflexible thinking is another reason why people find themselves at odds with others. The developmental psychologist Jean Piaget called it 'egocentrism' (or 'egocentricity') and claimed that it is more typical of children than of adults, who are more likely to consider other points of view besides their own (Piaget, 1973). Because inflexible thinkers rarely appreciate opinions contrary to their own, they tend to resort to defensive styles of communication by launching a spirited attack on someone else.

Later in this chapter we shall see that in conflict, inflexible thinking of this kind is often accompanied by positional bargaining rather than by principled negotiation (Fisher and Ury, 1986). Bargainers haggle over the cost of goods or services. They do not establish objective criteria to determine the relative merits of arguments. There are many instances where people are strongly tempted to revert to positional bargaining.

Let's think of a couple of examples of inflexible thinkers. One that comes readily to mind is the committed political party member. Really, there is practically no way persons like this will ever change the way they vote at elections simply because their inflexibility of thinking has given them no options to switch their allegiance to another political party. Often, committed political party members of this kind will underscore their devotion to their cause by wearing lapel badges with trendy party slogans or by placing stickers on their car bumper bars or windows.

People of certain religious persuasions are sometimes inflexible about the scientific 'accuracy' of religious accounts of creation, about 'conspiracy theories', or about specific church doctrines. In person-to-person communication with someone of a different religious persuasion such conformists or fundamentalists often find it difficult to avoid conflict because they cannot tolerate arguments that contradict their beliefs.

The world today abounds with inflexible thinkers. There are, for example, international terrorists whose extremist thinking is dominated by particular concepts and causes. Differences between the motives and reasoning of employers and industrial unions frequently harden into positions without compromise. Some financiers and bankers who adhere rigidly to conservative company policy baulk at risk-taking in ventures.

Cautious people can also become inflexible thinkers

Inflexible thinking is a major contributor to interpersonal conflict. Another factor is the influence of peoples' personality traits, especially jealousy, greed, intolerance, lust for power, or the inability to admit to being wrong or beaten. When these personality characteristics effectively set the agenda for communication between people, the prospect of serious conflict is virtually unavoidable.

Besides examining why interpersonal conflicts arise, we should also consider how communication situations can turn into battlefields. This can happen when feelings rather than balanced reasoning govern the communication process. We should not be left with the impression, however, that all forms of effective communication between people should be devoid of emotional content.

When individuals express excessive degrees of feeling, they leave little room for those with whom they are communicating to disagree. Communicating with someone who is passionately defending a position is difficult because emotions complicate an issue and jeopardise the resolution of conflict. Here, the negotiator has to diffuse the other's emotion before being able to reason. Physiologically, heightened emotional states can reduce a person's ability to think critically or logically.

Another source of personal conflict is inconsistency in communication or behaviour. Sometimes inconsistency is simply due to forgetting what has been said or done. For example, two people may verbally agree on a particular procedure for a joint project, yet at some later stage one of the pair remembers the agreement differently; some people claim that verbal agreements are not worth the paper they are not written on! Although failure to recall details is often genuine, it is sometimes a deliberate device used by people who wish to cancel agreements without appearing to do so. When this ploy is seen for what it is, communication and relationships are damaged.

There are many ways people's patterns of communication and behaviour can be inconsistent. For instance, they may seem highly enthusiastic at first about some project, but later on their enthusiasm may seem to have waned considerably. In such circumstances, it is difficult to know just how genuine their interest was in the first place.

Inconsistencies may lead to mistrust as well as conflict between people, and when promises of support and resources are withdrawn the conflict can turn ugly. Although politicians seem able to live with the knowledge that they are not honouring their election promises, few people can expect an easy resolution to conflict caused by broken promises or cancelled agreements.

'By 1990, no children will be living in poverty!'   'I'll give them the mother of all wars!'

For various reasons, promises are not always kept
Source:
Bob Hawke—Lock/Fairfax;
Saddam Hussein—AP/AAP

To summarise: conflicts arise for several different reasons. They can occur when people disagree over meanings, intentions, value systems, attitudes, or beliefs, and when they disagree about their experiences of other people or events.

Before any serious attempt can be made to manage the dispute, it is important to acknowledge that a conflict does exist. This can then lead to a mutually satisfactory resolution which not only restores harmony but strengthens communication and relationships for the future. It has been suggested, too, that 'the important thing is how disagreements are handled' (Stewart & D'Angelo, 1976:247). So, acknowledging a conflict is the preliminary step. The moment of truth comes when the disputants agree on a suitable course of action to work through their differences.

In the next section we look at some typical successful and unsuccessful ways in which conflicting people cope with their differences. The broad term **conflict management** includes 'coping', 'approaching', 'dealing with', and 'handling' conflict successfully *or* unsuccessfully.

conflict management
The ability of people in disagreement to explore mutually acceptable ways to resolve conflict without damaging their personal or professional relationship.

7.2 Defensive Communication: Psychological Mechanisms

Gibb's early paper (still cited in contemporary communication research literature) defines defensive behaviour as 'that behavior which occurs when an individual perceives threat or anticipates threat in the group' (Gibb, 1961:141). Usually, defensive behaviour is accompanied by a strong motive to win, gain ascendancy over others, or impress someone. When such desire and defensive behaviour persist unchecked, they can provoke threatened people into progressively defensive listening.

When people become defensive they interpret others' actions and motives less accurately, even to the point of distortion. Defensiveness is a form of self-protection against threatening or unpleasant situations, and the 'weapons' people defend themselves with are commonly referred to in psychological literature as **ego-defence mechanisms**.

Sigmund Freud, often referred to as the father of psychoanalytic theory, argued that defence mechanisms are internal systems which people activate when their consciences conflict with their instinctive urges. This inner conflict produces a state of anxiety. A defence mechanism, therefore, is used to reduce this anxiety and consequently restore equilibrium. Most people, at one time or another, rely on self-protective tactics, although some can be so disorienting that they render people unable to cope with their worlds in anything like a 'normal' fashion.

ego-defence mechanisms
A psychological term to describe how people alter their thinking and perceptions of unpleasant realities so that they are easier to confront.

One of the most common defence mechanisms is rationalisation—the process of finding an acceptable reason for behaviour that is occurring for a less acceptable reason. For example, people who refuse to lend someone money may give the reason that they do not want to lead the borrower into the temptation of overspending and becoming even more indebted, when the real reason for the refusal is simply their reluctance to part with their money.

By contrast, *repression* is a defence mechanism people use to block out feelings, ideas or memories from reaching consciousness. Often people repress emotions or memories associated with traumatic events. In other words, it may be too painful to relive the horror and unpleasantness of some particular act previously directed at the now defensive person. Typically, people repress former experiences of traumas associated with acts of violence or tragedies, including the loss of loved ones. Repression is usually the first line of defence, especially where anxiety accompanies the memory. In the course of development, children learn to recognise cues that signal danger and corresponding ways to avoid it. Repression is a typical method children use to reduce anxiety so that they can feel safe. Somewhat akin to repression is the defence mechanism of *reaction formation*. In this process, people attempt to substitute a threatening idea with an innocuous one. For example, people who are privately aroused and fascinated by pornography but too ashamed to admit it use reaction formation to justify contact with the objects of their secret desire—they may even become militant crusaders against pornography. In so doing, they create opportunities to study salacious material with the pretext of condemning or exposing it. They might also argue that they intend to educate others about the harm pornography can generate.

Projection, another kind of defence mechanism, is the process of denying one's own unacceptable urges and attributing them to others. For example, some people who are aggressive to practically everybody they encounter maintain that everyone else is hostile. The defence mechanism of projection enables them to blame others for the conflict they cause.

Sublimation, a different type of defence mechanism, involves diverting one's psychic energy from a socially or morally unacceptable drive to an acceptable one. People with strong sexual desires who feel inhibited from expressing them channel the energy of their sexual drive into other, more acceptable, activities like art, music or literature. Sexual energy in such cases is diverted into another form of creative expression.

One of the more dramatic forms of defence mechanism is *conversion disorder*. This is also sometimes referred to as *hysteria*, though the term should not be confused with its more popular everyday meaning of 'running about screaming and generally letting things get out of hand'. When people have inner conflict, physical symptoms such as deafness, blindness, numbness, or paralysis can result. For example, under-developed children obliged to participate in school sport where injurious physical contact can occur may experience pain or immobility; intense fear can even cause paralysis.

With all these defence mechanisms people distort reality in some way so that they can cope more easily with painful or unpleasant situations. The conflicts are not faced directly but by making their actions or communication appear acceptable. As well, people may attempt to create the illusion that the conflict does not exist, or that it does exist but in a less unpleasant or threatening form than it seems to have. Defensive communication does not lead to the effective management or resolution of conflict. The following sections focus on some of the ways people address conflict directly and constructively. Attention is also given to the type of interpersonal negotiation skills people may find useful for managing and resolving their conflicts with others in a satisfactory manner.

7.3 Negotiation Skills

Fisher and Ury (1986) have claimed that 'everyone negotiates something every day' (p. xi). They assume that people usually get what they need from others by negotiation, and cite the following examples:

> Like it or not, you are a negotiator. Negotiation is a fact of life. You discuss a raise with your boss. You try to agree with a stranger on a price for his house. Two lawyers try to settle a lawsuit arising from a car accident. A group of oil companies plan a joint venture exploring for offshore oil. A city official meets with union leaders to avert a transit strike. (Fisher and Ury, 1986:xi)

Despite the variety of situations we encounter daily which require skill in negotiating with others, many people find that their standard strategies for reaching agreements with others do not work well. Poor negotiators may even prolong and aggravate existing differences. Part of the problem is that ineffective or unsuccessful negotiators fail to distinguish negotiation from the practice of bargaining.

There are three basic approaches by which negotiators can deal with dispute or conflict. Two of these represent extreme positions: 'soft negotiation' and 'hard negotiation'. Soft negotiators tend to avoid conflicts at all costs. Their style is to concede and capitulate rather than hold out for better deals for themselves. Hard negotiators are very unlikely to yield any ground. Because they see every situation as a contest of wills, they are determined to get a better deal. A serious consequence of hard negotiation is that interpersonal communication and relationships may be harmed, even irreparably. There are other standard negotiation methods which involve striking a balance between achieving what people want and keeping on good terms with others, but because they are really variations of the soft and hard tactics they bear a closer resemblance to bargaining than they do to negotiation.

principled negotiation
Deciding issues on their merits rather than haggling over them.

The third negotiation strategy, **principled negotiation**, is an all-purpose strategy—it can be used 'whether there is one issue or several; two parties or many; whether there is prescribed ritual, as in collective bargaining, or an impromptu free-for-all, as in talking with hijackers' (Fisher and Ury, 1986:xiii). Developed at the Harvard Negotiation Project, this method does not involve haggling about what each party is prepared to do or concede; it is based on deciding issues on their merits. Principled negotiation, therefore, is distinct from the standard strategies of positional bargaining. Its essential thrust is that people in conflict should look wherever possible for mutual gains. Where there is conflict of interests the criteria for negotiation should be based on standards independent of the will of either side. As Fisher and Ury suggested:

> . . . the method of principled negotiation is hard on the merits, soft on the people. It employs no tricks and no posturing. Principled negotiation shows you how to obtain what you are entitled to and still be decent. It enables you to be fair while protecting you against those who would take advantage of your fairness. (p. xii)

There are three criteria for evaluating any method of negotiation, as follows:

1. Assuming that consensus is possible, the negotiation should lead to a wise agreement. An agreement is 'wise' when it 'meets the legitimate interests of each side to the extent possible, resolves conflicting interests fairly, is durable, and takes community interests into account' (Fisher and Ury, 1986:4). In general, positional bargaining does not lead to wise agreements, largely because it presupposes that contestants will keep to their positions until they are forced to give ground.

2. The negotiating procedures should be efficient. An efficient negotiation approach is characterised by negotiators agreeing upon and following mutually acceptable rules and procedures to conduct the settlement. When negotiation is efficient, time is not wasted on unrealistic or extreme tactics. Positional bargaining, however, is based on the assumption that you ask for more than you really want, so that when you concede a little you still get a good deal for yourself.

3. Relationships between the negotiating parties should be at worst unharmed or at best improved. When negotiations turn into contests of will, relationships between the parties not only become strained but are also likely to be damaged irrevocably—friends part company, people cease to be on talking terms with their neighbours, firms terminate their business dealings with former associates.

In most cases, the damage to relationships is done by positional bargaining. Whilst the negotiators talk about their 'bottom line' and state what they are or are not prepared to do, they transform the task of devising mutually acceptable solutions into a kind of skirmish. In these circumstances negotiators become coercers because their chief aim is to get their opponent to capitulate.

By contrast, the method of principled negotiation is based on four major concepts or guidelines. Each concept concerns a specific aspect of negotiation and the appropriate advice for that aspect. Those who observe these guidelines will find it relatively easy and straightforward to negotiate under almost any circumstances.

- The first concept is about people. Right from the outset, conflict managers who follow principled negotiation must separate the people from the problem. Ideally, negotiators should work collaboratively by tackling a common problem rather than each other. When people take separate stands their egos turn a co-operative problem-solving exercise into a battle of conflicting emotions. For example, managers whose staff members are not performing satisfactorily should quietly point out to relevant staff the standards of performance they expect. By showing precisely how things must be done, they highlight the task, not the inadequacy of their staff's performances. Discussions that focus on tasks rather than people can usually be conducted in fairly calm, rational ways.

Some might say that this guideline only holds good when people are not the problem—what happens when people *are* the problem? Sometimes people seem to be the problem only because someone has failed to appreciate that it is possible to focus on words or actions instead of on someone's presumed motives or intentions. There are many situations where the focus can easily shift from the problem to some person. For example, employees who regularly arrive late for work should be told that their failure to be punctual has become a problem. The principled negotiator focuses on the unpunctual behaviour as the problem, whereas the positional bargainer is more likely to challenge their 'poor attitude' or 'lack of commitment'. Explaining the cause of problems through the attribution of imagined attitudes or motives is not only a counter-productive negotiation tactic but is also likely to be inaccurate. In separating the people from the problem (or potential problem) we should also remember that conflicts reside in people's minds. Successful negotiators perceive how others involved in disputes feel—they can put themselves in other people's shoes. In other words:

> . . . the ability to see the situation as the other side sees it, as difficult as it may be, is one of the most important skills a negotiator can possess. It is not enough to know that they see things differently. If you want to influence them, you also need to understand empathetically the power of their point of view and to feel the emotional force with which they believe in it. (Fisher & Ury, 1986:23–24)

Here are the contrasting perceptions of a real estate agent and a potential home buyer as they negotiate the sale and purchase of a property:

TABLE 7.1

Perceptions of different stakeholders and negotiators often vary

Realtor's perceptions	Home buyer's perceptions
There is a compact bathroom	The bathroom is tiny
The kitchen has charming period features	The kitchen is hopelessly outdated
The garden has a delightful natural appearance	The garden is a wilderness
Carpet has a home-loved appeal	Carpet is very worn
Patio is ideal for outdoor entertaining	There isn't much room to entertain indoors
The living room has a certain atmosphere	The living room is dark and gloomy
The facade has character	The facade needs remodelling

Just because good negotiators understand others' points of view does not mean they have to agree with them. Nevertheless, knowing how others think and feel enables negotiators to revise their own views when necessary. The perceptions of the realtor and the home buyer probably differ according to their needs and motives. Principled negotiators avoid deceptive, ambiguous or euphemistic terms.

- The second element of principled negotiation focuses on interests, not positions. Most conflicts begin as conflicts of interest but can easily develop into conflicts of position. Haggling over positions is typical of positional bargaining and may be appropriate enough in courts of law where positions are either legal or illegal. In other contexts, however, there are rarely only two polarised positions, and through an exchange of interests negotiators can often discover an alternative, mutually acceptable path to resolving the problem.

Among the most powerful of interests are the human needs, so an important question for negotiators to ask is 'why'? For example, why did my supervisor require me as a training specialist rather than someone more experienced and confident to make the marketing presentation to our major client group? Let's have a look at some possible differences between my interests and those of my supervisor:

Supervisor's interests	My interests
Wants to broaden expertise of less experienced staff	Want to continue doing what I do best
Wants to promote a fresh, vigorous new face to client	Want to avoid seeming too inexperienced to client
Wants to give an up-and-coming colleague career opportunities	Want career opportunities in less divergent skill areas
Wants client to accept marketing proposal	Want to win client on issues of training rather than marketing
Wants to impress managing director with this visionary act of staff development	Want to avoid disappointing supervisor by making an unconfident showing

TABLE 7.2

The interests of workers and supervisors may diverge considerably

'Why?' questions can be useful in tapping areas of mutual interest. In the case of myself and my supervisor, there seemed to be some similarity in our needs. For example, my supervisor wanted me to have career opportunities just as I did. My supervisor wanted to impress the client; so did I. What differed were his confidence in me and my confidence in my ability to address the marketing presentation successfully. Also, my preference to remain a training specialist and not diversify in other areas of human resource management seemed at odds with my supervisor's wish to extend the breadth of my experience and expertise in the field.

- Besides focusing on interests rather than on positions, principled negotiators invent options for mutual gain. This is the third concept or guideline associated with principled negotiation. The notion of 'inventing' does not, of course, mean the usual temptation of making premature judgments about the most desirable option. One way of inventing options is to have all negotiating parties brainstorm a set of mutually acceptable alternatives. Techniques like the Nominal Group Technique (NGT) are particularly useful for this purpose (Fox, 1989; Delbecq, Van de Ven and Gustafson, 1975).

  To see how this guideline might be applied, consider the example of a public conflict between the chairperson and an executive board member at a board meeting, where the chairperson has ruled this board member as out of order and has subjected him to several offensive, humiliating remarks in front of the rest of the board. The board member, moreover, has been given no opportunity to counter the chairperson's personal attack.

  By inventing another option, such as speaking to that board member privately after the meeting or at some later mutually convenient stage, the chair could have avoided this public display of aggression. By getting together after the board meeting, these two people could have sorted out their differences in a more positive, constructive way without endangering their professional relationship. They might have come to understand each other better, too, thereby developing their abilities to be empathetic and to invent realistic, appropriate options another time.

- The fourth guideline for the method of principled negotiation is to insist on objective criteria. This means that the basis for negotiation should not be influenced by the will of any negotiating party. Negotiations can break down when one will (or one side) is pitted against another. The best tactic to adopt is to 'frame each issue as a joint search for objective criteria' (Fisher and Ury, 1986:91) so that negotiators can identify common goals and collaboratively work through common problems. The following case study illustrates this.

  > In educational settings, the common goal for both learners and instructors is learning. If learning does not take place, there is no justification for pointless instruction or related activities. Consider the situation where a group of learners consistently arrives half an hour late to a two-hour evening class. The instructor has finally admonished the offenders and has issued a warning that late comers in future will be penalised in their grades. What has happened here is that the instructor has assumed a stand or position without applying any of the elements of principled negotiation. In actual fact, what the instructor and students need to do is to tackle the problem systematically by addressing each of the elements of principled negotiation.

This problem could be approached in the following way:

- What is the problem? The problem is that one-quarter of the face-to-face allocation for instruction is not being used. Hence, the class time each week for students and the instructor to address new material is significantly reduced. Many teachers, however, would see the problem as one of unpunctuality. The point is, of course, that punctuality in itself is not an educational objective. Punctuality is a desirable student characteristic which potentially assists the attainment of the goal of learning.

- What are the interests and needs of the conflicting parties? Whilst the instructor would like classes to commence and finish on time, it is possible that students may find it difficult to arrive by the 5.00 pm scheduled starting time because they don't finish work until 4.55 pm. Travelling from work to college can take up to an hour, especially during the peak hour traffic period.

- Apart from the threat of future penalties, what constructive and mutually-beneficial options can be devised by the conflicting parties? One possible option may be to delay the starting time of the class by half an hour. If this is not possible because of the unavailability of teaching rooms after 7.00 pm, another option may be to hold 90-minute classes each week and then schedule additional two-hour sessions on every fourth weekend. Various alternatives are conceivable so long as the people in conflict are prepared to communicate rationally on the issues concerned.

- Lastly, the students and their instructor need to explore objective criteria for arriving at a solution to the problem of losing face-to-face time in class each week. Examples of objective criteria might include room availability (as previously suggested) or the teaching commitments of the instructor who may have another class at 7.00 pm. In some fields, laboratory assistants may be required and if they are required to be present after certain hours, the college will be forced to make expensive overtime payments. Many objective criteria, therefore, are based on issues of practicality rather than on the relative merits of opposing positions.

Source: Kaye, M. (1992) 'Communication competence', in Gonczi, A. (ed.) (1992) *Developing a competent workforce: adult learning strategies for vocational educators and trainers*, Adelaide: National Centre for Vocational Education Research, 99–100. Reprinted by permission of NCVER.

When negotiators are not sure which option is the most beneficial or fairest, they may find it helpful to consider their *best alternative to a negotiated agreement (BATNA)*. The **BATNA** is the standard against which any agreement should be measured. It is, moreover,

> . . . the only standard which can protect you both from accepting terms that are too unfavourable and from rejecting terms it would be in your interest to accept. Your BATNA . . . also has the advantage of being flexible enough to permit the exploration of imaginative solutions. Instead of ruling out any solution which does not meet your bottom line, you can compare a proposal with your BATNA to see whether it better satisfies your interests. (Fisher & Ury, 1986:104)

BATNA
A negotiation and conflict resolution strategy that determines the best alternative to a negotiated agreement.

Let's consider the case of managers who delegate work to the point of overloading their staff. What is the BATNA of these employees with excessive workloads: To look for employment in another organisation? To lodge a formal complaint with the organisation's ombudsman? To seek support from their industrial union? Whatever it may be, it will become the standard against which the option of a negotiated agreement will be compared. In other words, will these workers be better off negotiating a reduced workload instead of seeking employment elsewhere, or lodging a formal complaint, or seeking union support?

Interpersonal negotiation skills, as we have seen, are important tools for managing, resolving, and even preventing conflict. Where conflict has already developed between two parties, the principled negotiation approach can ease or de-emphasise existing differences. It has been recommended over the more traditional methods of positional bargaining mainly because neither soft nor hard extremes are chosen as solutions.

In the next section we contrast two strategies for resolving conflicts: win-lose and problem-solving. The latter should be seen as a complement to the principled negotiation approach just as the former can be aligned with positional bargaining. When conflict can be reconstructed as an exercise in solving mutually perceived problems, communication and relationships between people are likely to develop and improve.

7.4 Strategies for Resolving Conflict

win-lose conflict resolution strategy
A competitive approach to conflict that assumes that the other party is hostile and intends to defeat its opponent. The parties in conflict consider only their own positions, needs and interests.

win-win conflict resolution strategy or problem-solving strategy of conflict resolution
A co-operative strategy by which conflicting negotiators recognise each other's interests and/or needs and search for a mutually acceptable solution.

There are two basic ways of settling conflicts of interests between people, according to Johnson and Johnson (1982). The first is the **win-lose** strategy whereby one contestant strives to gain advantage over the other so that there is eventually a winner and a loser. There is no provision for a draw or a tie because the win-lose strategy approaches conflict as a contest, one that cannot be conceived in any other terms.

The second method is the **win-win** or **problem-solving** strategy. What the negotiators strive for here is consensus on how to manage and resolve a mutually acknowledged problem in such a way that both parties can achieve something and gain some satisfaction from their collaborative problem-solving.

Bolton (1979) has suggested six steps in the collaborative problem-solving method of conflict resolution:

1. Define the problem in terms of needs, not solutions. Take the example of two people waiting to use a public telephone. Both want to use the telephone urgently. If they were asked to state the problem in terms of their needs, they would probably say 'I need to use the telephone first'. If we probe further and ask each one: 'Why do you need to use the telephone first?', one might say 'I must ask my supervisor at work to approve a project immediately before our competitors jump the gun'. The other person waiting to use the phone might say 'I need to contact

my solicitor for some urgent legal advice before agreeing to purchase a property. If I don't get this advice now, someone else might buy the property in the meantime'.

Both people are confusing their needs with solutions. One wants to give advice and the other needs advice urgently. The use of the telephone is seen as a solution rather than a need. This conflict could be settled more constructively by both people comparing the relative urgency of their needs rather than quibbling over who should use the telephone first.

2. After defining the problem in terms of needs, the second step is to brainstorm possible solutions. One of the main points of brainstorming is that people aim for quantity, not quality in their generation of solutions to problems. This is not to say that high quality solutions are not required, but the negotiators should try to come up with as many solutions as possible. Hopefully, the best solution will be of high quality.

The brainstorming process is most successful when ideas or solutions are not evaluated prematurely but are fully considered on their merits. This means that each possible solution should be discussed thoroughly before being rejected, and that negotiators should maintain the attitude that there could be several alternative solutions to the conflict. Bolton (1979) notes that 'research findings demonstrate that it is important not to come into a problem-solving session with the attitude that there is only one adequate solution to this conflict. Solution rigidity is responsible for the failure of many problem-solving efforts'(p. 245).

3. Select the solution (or combination of solutions) which will best meet both parties' needs. This is the proper time to clarify any idea or solution that is not understood by either negotiator. However, critical judgment should remain suspended. Since consensus is the optimal goal of the collaborative problem-solving strategy, it is most likely to be achieved when the negotiators ask each other which of the many proposals they are prepared to consider—they can then see which of their selections are mutually acceptable.

4. Choosing a solution, however, does not mean that the problem is solved. The parties involved must now determine who is to do what, and when and where it is to be done. Few strategies work if there is role confusion instead of role clarity. Poor managers fail to delineate areas of responsibility for those they supervise. What often happens in these circumstances is that either more than one person does the same task, or no-one does it. As was mentioned in Chapter 2, role confusion (or conflict) is often strongly identified with the shadow side of organisations.

5. Once it has been decided who is to do the task and where and when it is to be done, it is time to carry out the plan of action developed in Step 4. Many well-intentioned projects fail to get off the ground because the people involved spend inordinate amounts of time on planning. When

the time comes for action, the project may have become less urgent or team members may have simply lost interest. This is not to suggest, however, that planning should be curtailed or dispensed with—poorly planned projects commonly produce something of dubious value. However, *actions speak louder than words*. People believe something is really happening when they can see tangible results. A university faculty introduced a time-off-teaching scheme for academics' scholarly projects. Applicants had to indicate the nature of their proposed project, a timeframe for its completion, and the form it would take (e.g. book, videotape, audio learning materials). After one calendar year most applicants had done little more than slightly embellish their original proposals—they had put their efforts into planning, not their projects.

6. Completing the action on schedule is a very important indication of good faith and commitment. Once the project is finished, it is useful to evaluate how well the problem-solving process has gone. As much as anything, this final step enables negotiators to learn from their experience and decide what they would do differently, what they would do again, and what they would not do at all if they had to face a similar problem again.

The main differences between the win-lose and the problem-solving conflict resolution strategies have been summarised by Johnson and Johnson (1975:182–83) and are presented in Table 7.3.

TABLE 7.3

Win-lose and problem-solving strategies for resolving conflict

Problem-solving strategy	Win-lose strategy
Define the conflict as a mutual problem.	Define the conflict as a win-lose situation.
Pursue goals held in common.	Pursue one's own goals.
Find creative agreements that are satisfying to both parties or present a mutually acceptable compromise.	Force the other party into submission.
Have an accurate personal understanding of one's own needs and show them correctly.	Have an accurate personal understanding of one's own needs, but publicly disguise or misrepresent them.
Try to equalize power by: emphasizing mutual interdepedence; avoiding harm, inconvenience, harassment, embarassment to the other party in order to reduce his fear and defensiveness.	Try to increase one's power over the other party by: emphasizing one's indepedence from the other and the other's dependence upon oneself.
Make sure contacts are on the basis of equal power.	Try to arrange contact where one's own power is the greater.

cont.

Use open, honest, and accurate communication of one's needs, goals, position, and proposals.	Use deceitful, inaccurate and misleading communication of one's needs, goals, position, and proposals.
Accurately state one's needs, goals, and position in the opening offer.	Overemphasize one's needs, goals, and position in the opening offer.
Work to have highest empathy and understanding of other's position, feelings, and frame of reference.	Avoid all empathy and understanding of other's position, feelings, and frame of reference.
Communicate a problem-solving orientation.	Communicate a win-lose orientation.
Avoid threats in order to reduce other's defensiveness.	Use threats to get submission.
Express hostility to get rid of one's feelings that may interfere with future cooperation.	Hostility is expressed to subdue the other.
Communicate flexibility of position to help in creative problem solving.	Communicate highest commitment (rigid adherence) to one's position to force the other to give in.
Behave predictably; though flexible behaviour is appropriate, it is not designed to take other party by surprise.	Behave unpredictably to use the element of surprise.
Change position as soon as possible to help in problem solving.	Concede and change slowly to force concessions from the other.
Promote clarity, predictability, mutual understanding to help in problem solving.	Increase ambiguity and uncertainty in an attempt to use deception and confusion to one's advantage.
Use cooperative behaviours to establish trust and mutual cooperation.	Use cooperative behaviours to grab the chance to exploit other's cooperativeness.
Adopt a consistent posture of being trustworthy toward the other.	Adopt a posture that allows one to exploit the other whenever possible.
Seek third parties to help in problem solving.	Isolate the other to reduce the possibility of his forming a coalition with third parties.
Emphasize exploring both similarities and differences in positions.	Emphasize only differences in positions and the superiority of one's

Source: D.W. Johnson and F.P. Johnson, (1975) *Joining Together: Group Theory and Skills*, Englewood Cliffs: Prentice Hall.

These differences, collectively, are really subsets of one major difference. Whilst the problem-solving strategy emphasises open communication with and an understanding of the other negotiator, the win-lose strategy accepts any type of communication that gains victory. Deceit, threats, ambiguous and unpredictable actions, and a real lack of understanding of other negotiators' needs are typical elements of the win-lose strategy.

In theory, there is a third result: 'lose-lose'. If, for example, both parties are committed to winning at the expense of their opponents (the win-lose strategy), they may fail to resolve their contest of wills, in which case nobody wins anything. Of course, it can also develop into a problem-solving strategy once the parties involved are prepared to negotiate afresh rather than continue to haggle over positions. It is difficult to approach any negotiation with a problem-solving strategy when the other party is determined to play according to win-lose rules. Those preferring a problem-solving strategy are either forced into a win-lose bargaining procedure or must terminate any further negotiations. Both alternatives seriously damage communication and relationships between the parties concerned.

In the second edition of their well-known book *Joining Together*, Johnson and Johnson (1982:283–85) described several conflict resolution strategies in terms of animals and the behaviours most commonly associated with them. For example, the *turtle* strategy involves people withdrawing into their shells and avoiding confrontational issues, partly because they believe that the conflict cannot be settled, and partly because they usually feel helpless in disputes.

Other conflict resolution strategies identified by Johnson and Johnson include the *shark* who exercises forcing behaviour, the *teddy bear* who tries to smooth things over, the *fox* who compromises and looks for middle ground, and the *owl* who see conflicts as opportunities for resolving differences, reducing interpersonal tensions, and improving relationships between two people. To some extent, turtle, shark and teddy-bear strategies resemble the behaviour associated with positional bargaining, whereas the fox's compromising and the owl's confronting strategies are more akin to principled negotiation.

The kind of conflict resolution strategies people choose is also partly determined by the nature of the issue, problem, or disagreement. Many people would argue that in matters of money, opponents play according to win-lose rules more frequently than they play to win-win rules. For example, the major cost centres of any system tend to see the annual budget as a single cake which can be divided into unevenly sized slices. Through devious or even bullying tactics, winners receive larger slices than the losers.

The intention behind either the win-lose or the problem-solving strategy is to terminate the conflict. While the problem-solving strategy is meant to bring the conflict to a conclusion that is acceptable to both negotiating parties, the win-lose strategy usually leads to a resolution favouring one party. Sometimes the win-lose strategy may not even result in a resolution of a conflict but in the escalation of what began as a mild disagreement or dispute.

In the next section we turn our attention to how people can prevent interpersonal conflict. The theme here is that prevention is better than cure. Although the main strategic choices are outlined, you might think of other ways of averting unpleasant or threatening encounters with others.

Strategies for Preventing Conflict 7.5

Although conflict is often unpleasant, it is, as we have already noted, virtually unavoidable. Because it is part of life, we could argue that instead of trying to prevent it, we should learn how to manage it more efficiently. However, not all conflict is inevitable; it can sometimes be headed off before it develops into full-scale war.

Generally speaking, realistic conflicts are easier to control than non-realistic conflicts. Realistic conflicts are characterised by opposing needs, interests, goals, or values, but nonrealistic conflicts stem from 'ignorance, error, historical tradition and prejudice, dysfunctional organizational structure, win/lose types of competition, hostility, or the need for tension release' (Bolton, 1979:210). Nonrealistic conflicts, therefore, may be associated with the shadow side of organisations.

Unrealistic conflict is needless and there are various things we can do to prevent it. We can, for example, try to use fewer roadblocks like threatening, name-calling, giving orders, or offering advice which is neither sought nor needed. Another thing we can do is not expect too much from others. High expectations naturally lead to disappointment when they are not met—it is easy to become angry when someone you have counted on fails to deliver the goods. For example, when people take time off work for tradespeople to make repairs or deliver goods, it is frustrating if the tradespeople are unpunctual. The frustration can develop into hostility, especially if goods delivered are damaged or the wrong merchandise, or if the repairs are not done properly.

Nowadays, with so much emphasis in industry on quality customer service, this kind of frustrating experience should not happen. You can, of course, avoid confrontation with tradespeople by expecting things to go wrong—that way, when things go right, you can consider it a bonus!

When our expectations of another are not met, therefore, the subsequent build-up of frustration can become a catalyst for conflict. Even if there are good reasons why people are let down, the tension caused by disappointment may be directed at someone who is not responsible for things going wrong. This redirection of emotional energy is sometimes called *displaced aggression*. Conflicts that arise when one angry person infuriates another may be difficult to resolve because the emotional energy of each combatant is directed toward the other, not at the problem.

Keeping a check on their emotions and concentrating on issues and problems helps people prevent conflict with others. It is important to raise our level of tolerance of others. Practising tolerance helps us to be less affected emotionally when things go wrong, and to maintain our established relationships.

Nonrealistic conflicts can also be prevented by practising skills like active listening and assertiveness. These skills, however, must be accompanied by our awareness of signs of conflict. As Bolton has suggested:

> . . . observant people can 'read' storm warnings in the sky. Just so, the aware person can look for the signs and patterns in her conduct and

the conduct of her associates which indicate that a storm is brewing. Though there is little that can be done about the weather, these early warning signals in interpersonal relationships can provide both the time and the insights to take effective preventive action. (Bolton, 1979:211)

Some of these signs of impending conflict include a deterioration in a relationship, heightened emotional exchanges between people, and impatience with or intolerance of another. The onset of conflict is also signalled by a noticeable decline in the communication skills and behaviour—for example, poorer listening and aggression rather than assertiveness.

We conclude this section by noting that although it is highly desirable to prevent unnecessary (nonrealistic) conflicts, realistic conflicts are perhaps best left to run their course. If the conflict is mutually acknowledged, solving it may strengthen communication and relationships. In the next section we look at constructive ways of using conflict to solve problems.

7.6 The Constructive Use of Conflict in Problem-solving

When people are involved in emotional conflict they may find that their values or needs are in conflict with those of others. Conflicts of emotions or values are usually difficult to resolve because the issues in dispute are not tangible. On the other hand, if differences over feelings or values can be sorted out, any remaining conflict of needs can be settled with a collaborative problem-solving strategy. The following are examples of conflicting needs.

TABLE 7.4

People's needs can conflict

Need of Person A	Need of Person B
To complete a university term paper	Person A's help with a school mathematics homework problem
To talk to a close friend about a private concern	To take a long-distance call from a physician attending to an ailing relative overseas
To watch the news on TV	To watch *The Addams Family* on TV
To have transport to a sports event	To have transport to a birthday party

When people don't recognise conflicts of needs as opportunities for collaborative problem-solving, they are likely to use less constructive approaches such as denial, avoidance, capitulation, and domination. In the case of Person A and Person B, their competing needs will not be resolved by denying the differences, avoiding the conflict, giving in to the other person, or trying to make the other person yield.

Since interpersonal conflict is bound to occur from time to time, it is unrealistic to run away from conflict just to have peace at all costs. If this was done on a large scale in public life, national and international political, industrial, legal, and commercial agreements would be rare indeed. Some prominent groups and individuals in our society cannot tolerate the needs of others. For example, the sector of the Anglican community supporting the ordination of women is in conflict with the more conservative sector which regards this as a breach of biblical doctrine. Here is a very clear conflict of needs. Women who wish to be ordained claim a need to minister to others; those opposing their ordination claim that the integrity of the Bible's teachings must be preserved.

Perhaps this conflict is really over values: opponents of the ordination of women base their arguments on values derived from their interpretations of the Scriptures, and the supporters adhere to universal values such as equality and justice. Conflicts of this kind are hard to resolve, even if both parties acknowledge their differences in needs and values.

One very important step people can take to prevent unnecessary conflict is to develop the technique of 'issues control', which establishes procedures for handling potential conflicts or disputes before tackling any of the major issues directly. Once people are satisfied with a procedure for managing their dispute, it is more likely to be resolved.

The technique of issues control also entails dealing thoroughly with one point at a time. Flitting too quickly from one matter to the next means that no single point is discussed to its logical conclusion. It is a good idea to break down issues into smaller units so that they can be examined from every angle before the negotiators attempt to reach an agreement.

Another issues control strategy is to deal first with the least contentious issues, since they can be resolved more easily. Early successes in a dispute can encourage both parties to continue productively and amicably.

Many attempts to negotiate start off badly because the parties involved spend too much time skirting around the edges of the real problem. By the time they have argued about various minor points, the major issues might be the straws that break the camel's back. Skilled negotiators will try to steer the discussion back to the important issues.

Finally, disagreements should not degenerate into disputes over the negotiating parties' principles. As far as possible, people should try to find out each other's needs and avoid a contest of ideologies. Effective resolution of interpersonal conflicts occurs when the principles of both negotiating parties are respected. Once individuals have made every effort to eliminate the occurence of unnecessary conflict, the resolution of differences through some form of collaborative problem-solving is likely to be a constructive and useful experience.

As a general rule, people should carefully assess the entire range of potential consequences of a conflict before entering stressful disputes. This is not always easy to do as there are usually some unknown factors in store. For example, negotiators may not be aware of the other party's sensitivity over certain issues. However, every attempt should be made to anticipate the consequences of a lengthy dispute.

7.7 Summary

In this chapter we have considered how conflicts can develop and how people tend to resort to defensive communication to deal with them. The chapter emphasised that skill in negotiating is essential to successfully manage and resolve conflict, and principled negotiation was accordingly distinguished from positional bargaining.

We then compared the win-lose strategy with the problem-solving strategy, which presents the dispute in terms of a mutually acknowledged problem. The problem-solving strategy, as a collaborative exercise, is therefore preferable to the win-lose alternative.

The chapter outlined ways of managing and resolving conflict, and ways of preventing unnecessary (nonrealistic) conflicts. As well, the prevention of unnecessary conflicts and the efficient handling of realistic conflicts can enable negotiators to glean new insights for the management of future conflicts.

To this point, we have examined several important interpersonal communication skills that can greatly enhance communication compe-tence. Effective communication managers need to use these skills appro-priately in a variety of situations. In Chapter 8 we see how these skills can be applied to certain work-related settings.

7.8 Discussion Questions

1. How does negotiating differ from bargaining? Has your perception of this difference been influenced by this chapter? In what way? List some situations where bargaining may be less appropriate than negotiating.

2. Think of a disagreement you had with someone. What was the point of difference between you and the other person? How did you handle the conflict at the time? Now that you have read this chapter, would you have managed this conflict any differently? If so, explain how.

3. Give some examples of how conflicts develop in the workplace and suggest how they could be prevented.

4. When are conflicts nonrealistic or unnecessary? How can you be sure that a potential conflict is nonrealistic? Suggest some strategies for managing nonrealistic conflicts.

5. Suppose you are involved in a non-negotiable conflict—for example, you don't want to sit an examination but you must, to pass a course. How would you act and what would you say to the other person involved in this conflict? Share your thoughts with someone else who has read this book.

6. Why and how do people become defensive when they are in conflict with others? Have you ever used these defensive tactics? How can you avoid being defensive in conflict situations? Discuss your self-analysis with a friend or someone else who has read this book.

7. Are active listening or assertiveness necessary for a negotiator? List some important communication skills for conflict managers.

Activities   7.9

1. Determine your conflict management style. Which of the following statements is most typical of you? Rate each one according to the scale 5-1.

    5 = I always communicate like this in a conflict
    4 = I often communicate like this in a conflict
    3 = I sometimes or occasionally communicate like this in a conflict
    2 = I seldom or rarely communicate like this in a conflict
    1 = I never communicate like this in a conflict

    1.   OK, take it easy! No one is out to get you!   ____
    2.   Like hell I will!   ____
    3.   Sounds like a reasonable idea to me.   ____
    4.   Why don't we just drop the whole thing?   ____
    5.   I'm happy for you to make the decision.   ____
    6.   Let's kiss and make up.   ____
    7.   How about you take half and I take half?   ____
    8.   I give in. Have it your way!   ____
    9.   I'm not giving you something for nothing.   ____
    10. I just want to be friends with you.   ____
    11. Look, I have no quarrel with you.   ____
    12. Why don't you quit while you're ahead?   ____
    13. I'm happy to overlook the special clause.   ____
    14. We can work it out, I'm sure.   ____

15. Who says you're right? ___
16. This is a real problem for us. ___
17. I know you don't mean any harm. ___
18. Try that and just see how far you get! ___
19. We really need to sort this one out. ___
20. Why don't we put in $10 each instead of $20? ___
21. I'd rather not get mixed up in this. ___
22. You want to do it the hard way, do you? ___
23. We can't let this ruin our friendship! ___
24. Here, do what you want. I can live without it. ___

Scoring: The higher the total score for each statement, the more often you use the conflict management style implied by that statement. For example, if you gave yourself 5 for statement 8, 'I give in. Have it your way', you see yourself as typically having a passive conflict avoidance style.

The four conflict management styles and the statements which relate to them are:

Style	Statement
* Passive-avoidance	4, 5, 8, 11, 21, 24
* Aggressive-confrontative	2, 9, 12, 15, 18, 22
* Conciliatory-harmonising	1, 3, 6, 10, 13, 17
* Relationship maintenance -compromising	7, 14, 16, 19, 20, 23

In the spaces provided below, add up your self-rating scores on the six statements representing each style of conflict management. The maximum score for each style is 30. If you score between 24 and 30 for any of the four styles, this is how you see yourself typically managing conflicts.

Self-rating scores

Passive . . .	Aggressive . . .	Conciliatory . . .	Compromising . . .
___ 4	___ 2	___ 1	___ 7
___ 5	___ 9	___ 3	___ 14
___ 8	___ 12	___ 6	___ 16
___ 11	___ 15	___ 10	___ 19
___ 21	___ 18	___ 13	___ 20
___ 24	___ 22	___ 17	___ 23
___ Total	___ Total	___ Total	___ Total

Passive-avoidance style. People who use this style typically do anything to avoid conflict, even to the point of denying their own needs and goals.

Aggressive-confrontative style. Conflict managers using this style see attack as the preferred way of winning a dispute. They are determined to attain their own goals and do not care if their opponents fail to reach theirs.

Conciliatory-harmonising style. Harmonisers are keen to smooth things over with statements like 'Hang on! I'm not against you—I'm on your side'.

Relationship maintenance-compromising style. In this category, people see the point of issue as a shared one with those in conflict. They value relationships and are prepared to give and take so that both parties win a little instead of one party winning everything.

2. Keep a diary of conflicts you have with others, for a month. Describe the strategies and styles you use in these conflicts. Could you have acted or communicated any differently in any of these situations?

Key Terms   7.10

BATNA (best alternative to a negotiated agreement)
Conflict management
Conflict resolution
Defensive communication
Ego-defence mechanisms
Equilibrium (homeostasis)
Positional bargaining
Principled negotiation
Realistic and nonrealistic conflict
Win-win (problem-solving) strategy

Recommended Reading   7.11

Bolton, R. (1979) *People skills: how to assert yourself, listen to others, and resolve conflicts*, New York: Simon & Schuster.
De Bono, E. (1985) *Conflicts: a better way to resolve them*, UK: Penguin.
Donohue, W. A. and Kolt, R. (1992) *Managing interpersonal conflict*, California: Sage.

Fisher, R. and Ury, W. (1986) *Getting to yes: negotiating agreement without giving in*, London: Hutchinson Business.

Jensen, A. D. and Chilberg, J. C. (1991) *Small group communication: theory and application*, California: Wadsworth, ch 7.

Putnam, L. L. and Roloff, M. E. (1992) *Communication and negotiation*, California: Sage.

Ury, W. (1991) *Getting past no*, London: Business Books.

Applications of Communication Skills 8

Everything has been thought of before,but the problem is
to think of it again.

Johann W. von Goethe

There are only two ways of getting on in this world: by
one's own industry, or by the weaknesses of others.

Jean de La Bruyere (1645–1696)

Six essential qualities that are the key to success: sincerity,
personal integrity, humility, courtesy, wisdom, charity.

Dr William Menninger

Working with people is difficult, but not impossible.

Peter Drucker

Now that we have learnt about important interpersonal communication skills like listening, being assertive and negotiating, how do we put it all together as adult communication managers? One thing is sure: we are likely to make occasional mistakes in the way we put it all together but we will try, nevertheless, to make those mistakes only once. This chapter explores how we can synthesise and apply our communication skills where equal employment opportunity practices and intercultural interactions between people are involved, and wherever there is a real danger of technology dehumanising the workplace. We also consider how to develop our oral and written presentation skills. Finally, we consider the importance of plain English and how to keep our written communication free of fallacious thinking.

Learning Objectives

After you have studied the ideas, arguments and suggestions presented in this chapter you should be able to do the following:

- Explain why competent communicators must be able to synthesise their communication skills coherently.

- Develop a set of reasons to support the claim that effective communication managers must be able to learn from their experience and mistakes.

- Demonstrate the importance of an equal opportunity organisational climate for effective communication in the workplace.

- Provide at least two interpretations of what constitutes communication competence in intercultural settings.

- Point out how new technologies can dehumanise the workplace.

- Identify the critical factors that affect oral presentations.

- List some examples of psychological, material and logical fallacies in written communication and presentations.

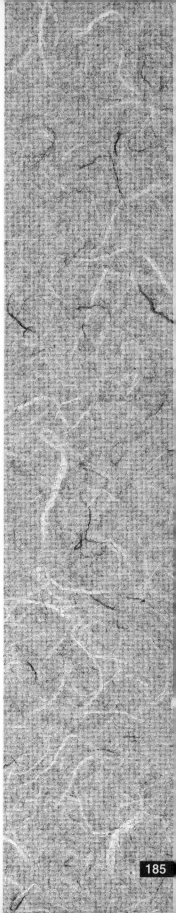

8.1 A Synthesis of Communication Skills

All the human communication skills we have studied so far can enhance the quality of people's lives and relationships. Good listeners and skilful negotiators are appreciated. They are admired for their ability to understand and interpret others' nonverbal cues and for their ability to express clear nonverbal messages themselves. They are also respected for their determination and decisiveness in standing up for themselves.

The most competent communicators are those who can put all these things together. They are sensitive enough to know how to act and communicate appropriately. Most important, they continue to build on their understandings and skills and apply them to each new situation. How well they do this indicates how able and willing they are to learn from each new experience of communicating with others.

Competent communicators, therefore, are also competent learners, particularly when it comes to learning from their own experience and this, in turn, depends greatly on their ability to structure their world in a way that permits constructive reflection. Unstructured reflection, or thinking unsystematically and randomly about people and relationships, is usually unproductive since it often leads to people seeing what they want to see rather than what is actually happening.

Structured reflection helps people learn from their mistakes or their failure to communicate or act appropriately. In this approach, people may systematise their thinking by writing down all the pros and cons of an action or decision they are about to take and weighing them up. Alternatively, they may test out their thinking in a discussion or debate with a colleague or friend. Unstructured reflection differs from structured reflection in that the former lacks a framework for evaluating why some communication or action was appropriate or inappropriate, successful or unsuccessful. Good communicators, like good managers, can allow themselves the luxury of making mistakes once, or in more complex situations, perhaps twice. Any repetition of such mistakes suggests that they have not seized the opportunity to learn from their experience. Although 'to err is human', repetitious mistakes indicate a lack of sensitivity to our own communication and actions and to others' needs.

The extent to which people develop this sensitivity to self and others depends largely on their values. In work settings, it is not uncommon to find some people more concerned with 'getting the job done' than with getting along well with colleagues, and task-oriented people also tend to denigrate any training opportunities that would help them understand how they could become better communicators. They consider that communication training courses do little more than give participants a 'warm inner glow'.

People-oriented communicators, on the other hand, welcome the chance to understand and learn more about communication processes. In particular, they tend to respond positively to training sessions which encourage reflection and discussion on structured learning activities. This is especially true of cross-cultural training where the learning modes usually tend to be interactive and participatory rather than formal (Martin, 1986). This point is resumed later in this chapter.

Competent communicators who have synthesised their communication skills develop their competence even further by learning to apply these skills appropriately in different situations. For example, they know when to crack a joke and when it is appropriate to negotiate, and they are seldom lost for words. They have the knack of saying the right things at the right time, and usually impress others as being open and trustworthy.

Inappropriate jokes signify a lack of communication competence

The following sections present situations where people can apply their communication competence and demonstrate their ability to relate to others. These situations involve equal employment opportunity practices, intercultural relationships, the influence of technology on personal communication, and oral and written presentation skills.

Equal Employment Opportunity 8.2 Practices

Demonstrating communication competence can be difficult in situations where people do not perceive each other as equals. Discrimination against age, gender, ethnicity, or creed create in an organisation a negative, distrustful atmosphere. Although most westernised countries have legislated against discriminatory practices in the workplace, **equal employment opportunity** for certain groups can still be blocked in subtle ways.

Illegal discrimination is often covert; it is part of the 'shadow side' of systems (Egan, 1993). Organisation powerbrokers can divest people of group support, block their career paths, exclude them from attending meetings, or pressure them to resign. Women may be kept from managerial or supervisory positions, older employees may be kept out of new, challenging projects, and people of certain religious persuasions may be totally overlooked for senior positions.

This type of discrimination is usually the result of informal, behind-the-scenes communication among organisation members prejudiced against particular individuals or groups. Such prejudice is seldom expressed in words but indicated by action (or lack of it).

One method of reinforcing EEO principles is to provide 'gender balance' on job selection committees. Approximately equal numbers of male and female interviewers increase the assurance of equal chances for applicants of both sexes. This method assumes that whilst women are unlikely to discriminate against female applicants, men tend to favour male applicants. Gender balanced committees do not, however, guarantee a fair selection of job candidates.

Other breaches of EEO include nepotism and reverse-discrimination. Nepotism in family-owned or controlled oganisations gives family members an advantage over other employees or applicants. Reverse-discrimination is a kind of counter-attack against those thought to be discriminatory. Thus, female interviewers, either individually or as panellists, may tacitly prefer female over male applicants. Note, 'tacitly'—interviewers in such situations are unlikely to admit to private tactics and preferences.

We will return to the processes of interviewing in the following chapter. At this point we simply need to recognise the potential danger of failing to guard against discriminatory attitudes and practices. Many of these attitudes are acquired during our formative years of growth and development, usually before adulthood, and 'unlearning' such discriminatory attitudes can be slow and difficult. However, people can change their thinking and behaviour more easily if their organisation or system discourages discrimination.

8.3 Intercultural Settings

When people have to communicate with others who do not speak the same language, they can often still make themselves understood. How people from different cultures or language groups can do this is a complex question although, of course, people may point to objects, draw diagrams, use gestures, or communicate with facial expressions.

Even without understanding another person's language, people can still construct some meaning from verbal messages by listening actively.

Active listeners not only detect nonverbal emotional messages communicated by facial expressions and voice qualities, but occasionally register the meaning of particular words similar to those in their own language. Many words today are understood universally, even though the spelling varies from one language to another. Thus, 'airport' is like 'aeroporta' and 'musée' resembles 'museum'; English-speaking people may not use the term 'autoroute', but can guess its relation to 'motorway', 'freeway' or even 'tollway'. Recognising such words in a conversation may help to grasp the gist of a message.

Kim (1990, 1988) presents communication competence in intercultural situations as the ability to deal with stress; this ability is essential to the adaptation process of 'cultural strangers', who are likely to be stressed by 'culture shock'. By learning to cope with their stress they can adapt more successfully to the host culture, and enter the final phase of becoming communicatively competent, which Kim (1990) calls the 'growth phase'.

This four-phase sequence of shock-stress-adaptation-growth is the process model for what is called the **general systems theory** of intercultural communication. Central to this theory is the notion of the 'system': 'any entity or whole that consists of interdependent parts' (Kim and Ruben, 1988). The theory also proposes that individuals are systems which function through interactions with the environment and the people who inhabit it. These interactions require 'communication' which involves the processing of information to survive and operate effectively in that environment.

The theory of **uncertainty reduction** is conceptually similar to the general systems theory of intercultural communication; its general principle is that interpersonal communication operates best under conditions of reduced uncertainty (Berger and Bradac, 1982). Reducing uncertainty in interpersonal relationships gives us greater control over our anxiety and a corresponding increase in our confidence to understand and interpret accurately others' communication and actions. Confidence of this kind has been termed 'attributional confidence', which usually increases in proportion to the amount of information available to reduce uncertainty.

When people from different cultures or ethnic backgrounds have to communicate, uncertainties about the others' unfamiliar values or expectations can make them anxious about whether they are communicating and behaving appropriately. For example, they might feel concerned about appropriate salutations (first names or titles), method of greeting (bowing, shaking hands), or whether to begin with small talk.

Such uncertainties have much to do with the values and expectations of people from unfamiliar cultural backgrounds. For example, do they expect formality or informality in initial encounters? Disclosure or concealment? To be treated as equals or deferentially? It is worth obtaining as much information as possible about people from other cultural backgrounds before meeting and talking with them. Brislin, Landis and Brandt (1983) have suggested, in their review of basic approaches to cross-cultural training, that the appreciation of cultural differences in values and expectations is essential to developing mutual understandings and avoiding unintended offence.

general systems theory of intercultural adaptation
Regards people as individual systems that function through interactions with the environment and its inhabitants; usually involves successive stages of culture shock, stress, adaptation, and growth.

uncertainty reduction
This principle states that communication works best when uncertainty about the intent or content of messages is minimal.

The importance of information sharing is also emphasised in the **convergence theory** of intercultural communication. The principle of convergence states: 'if two or more individuals share information with one another, then over time they will tend to converge toward one another, leading to a state of greater uniformity' (Kincaid, 1988:282). Convergence works best when communication between immigrants and members of the host culture is unrestricted.

Regardless of what theory people prefer, one thing is clear: most definitions of intercultural communication competence closely resemble social or interpersonal competence concepts developed in the field of social psychology (Monge et al., 1982). This suggests that interpersonal communication competence is central to all forms and contexts of human communication. In intercultural settings, therefore, good communicators can apply their repertoire of interpersonal skills appropriately when they relate to people of different cultures.

8.4 People Versus Technology

Poor communicators tend to believe, unfortunately, that the technology revolution has obviated the necessity for people to strive for competence in communicating with others. In some modern organisations, certain people can engineer their working lives to the point where very little face-to-face contact with other people is required. Electronic mail via computers, facsimile machines, and teleconference facilities, for example, have made it unnecessary for people to leave their workstations. Some television advertisements for computer workstations promote the advantage of saving time at work by not having to leave our desks to communicate with others.

Apart from the fact that it is not healthy for people to remain glued to their computer screens for long periods, it is undesirable for people to spend a good deal of their time devoid of direct human contact. Neil Postman, Professor of Communication Arts and Sciences at New York University, once referred to speech as 'the primal and indispensable medium'. He went on to say that speech '. . . made us human, keeps us human, and in fact defines what human means' (Postman, 1986:9). Once opportunities for speech are reduced, our humanity is correspondingly reduced and our ability to work with and relate to others suffers.

The substitution of interactive technology for interaction with people has transformed the workplace. Each medium creates its unique metaphor for how users can view their cultures. Personal computers, or PCs, have to a large extent become surrogates for normal colloquial conversations, humour and assurances of rescue for the technologically helpless. Personal computer users can be seduced by the overwhelming supportiveness of the machine and find themselves relying more on their computers, less on other people.

Organisations and systems need not become depersonalised in this way, of course. Wise managers and supervisors make sure that their staff have ample opportunities to meet and confer, both formally and informally. In some systems, such as Australia's unified national system of universities, there has been a groundswell of support for the introduction of 'open learning' which features, amongst other things, distance learning by television. While some of the universities in this system are keen to try it out, many academics still think that it will diminish the quality of learning since it deprives the learner of opportunities to communicate and participate directly in a community of scholars.

There is little doubt, however, that modern technology continues to revolutionise interpersonal communication as well as work practices in many organisations. Whilst the work practices demand occupational health and safety standards (e.g. ergonomic chairs, adequate wordprocessing screens), the quality and patterns of human communication have also changed. Electronic mail and video-conference and tele-conference facilities remove the necessity of personal meetings between people. Some of these electronic processes also deny people a good deal of nonverbal information about the message-senders' feelings—they can tell us what others want us to do or what they want to do for us, but they can't tell us how the senders feel.

The next section looks at how people can apply their understanding of communication processes to make their speech or oral presentations more successful. Such skills include making formal presentations at boardroom meetings, conferences and public lectures. Competent oral presentation requires special skill and appropriate application.

Oral Presentation Skills 8.5

For practical purposes, our definition of a *presentation* is the personal *communication* of information to an *audience* of one or more. 'Presentations' can mean oral or written; in the case of written presentations, of course, the presenter is not seen by the audience, and vice versa. This section of the chapter focuses on oral presentations.

Audience and *presentation* are the main components of our definition. First, it acknowledges presentations as particular forms or facets of interpersonal communication, so the success of presenters depends on how accurately their intentions are interpreted by the audience.

In turn, the accuracy of the audience's interpretation depends partly on the presenters' ability to relate to and communicate with others. Presenters need to know when as well as how to apply their human communication skills. Knowing when to be direct with your audience, when to accommodate their interruptions, when to change tack in response to their reactions, when to increase the tempo, and when to inject variety and humour into the presentation all require appropriate timing. With some audiences, for example, it may be necessary to illustrate the spoken message. Much depends on the nature and complexity of the content of the presentation.

One way to determine the success of the presentation is to monitor audience reactions while it is in progress. Signs of restlessness, for instance, may indicate that the message is abstruse, too technical, complicated, or

Timing.

just plain boring. In such cases, the presentation may need variety, perhaps by introducing audience participation exercises or by using other media. Remember 'one picture is worth a thousand words'.

The key to successful presentation is knowing your audience. This means knowing something about their characteristics, needs and capabilities—for example, age, maturity, experience, gender, and ethnicity. As suggested earlier, people from non-English speaking backgrounds are unlikely to respond to presenters who forget to take into account their cultural background. Poor presenters often fail to distinguish the characteristics of their audience; for example, telling sexist jokes to a mainly female audience, or making racist remarks before a multicultural audience. In such circumstances, the failure to understand one's audience is likely to lead to unsuitable communication tactics such as attempting to captivate listeners with inappropriate remarks.

Understanding audience needs is also important. Some presenters may need to simplify a difficult message. For example, medical specialists addressing community groups may need to substitute everyday language for medical jargon to get their points across. The audience of an after-dinner speaker expects the presentation to be witty and entertaining. Audiences at political rallies and evangelical conventions want presentations that are stirring and uplifting. In the world of work, most audiences want informative messages. The need for information by people in systems is a clear reinforcement of the claim that 'communication is the lifeblood of systems' (Egan, 1988a).

Another essential element is knowing the audience's capabilities. Hearing-impaired audiences, for example, will certainly require the assistance of interpreters or someone who can translate into sign language. An audience of recent immigrants may not understand much of a politician's speech about the nation's economy.

Getting to know your audience is an integral part of the presentation planning process. Good oral presentations, however, involve more than efficient planning, including knowing one's audience. The skilful presenter is able to make the plan work, and putting a plan into practice depends largely on how far presenters develop and synthesise their human communication skills. It is often difficult to know how well these skills have been developed and synthesised into a strategic basis for action and communication, since refined levels of competence are signalled by intangible personal qualities such as sensitivity, eagerness and commitment. However, there are practical ways in which presenters can prepare an oral presentation, and a list of self-check questions follows:

- While I am presenting what will the audience be doing?

- Do I want the audience to keep silent until question time?

- Should I invite the audience to interrupt me so that I can deal with their inquiries on the spot?

- If the audience members become restless have I made any provision for this?

- Should I read from my script or take the risk of ad libbing?

- Are my audio-visual supporting materials well designed?

- What will I do if I forget the point I am trying to make?

- What should I do if I sense I am losing my audience's attention?

- How do I overcome my initial fear of facing an unknown audience?

- Have I ensured that my presentation is free of prejudicial statements?

- What kinds of persuasive appeals have I used (e.g. humour, emotive language, fear)?

- Are these the most appropriate tactics for this type of presentation?

- Have I used plain English wherever possible or is my presentation steeped in jargon?

- Do I really know my audience?

- Is my message tailored to my audience?

- Have I any safeguards in case I get sidetracked by too many pedantic questions from the audience?

- What if the overhead projector doesn't work?

- What if I get tongue-tied?

- What if I lose my notes?

- What if lose my place in my notes?

- How can I be sure that my audience understands my presentation as intended?

- How will I know if my audience accepts my line of reasoning?

- Have my arguments been well constructed? (Am I saying what I mean to say?)

- Are my arguments free from fallacy?

- Should I use a lectern, or move about?

- How should I dress for the presentation?

- Should I speak slowly or quickly?

- Should I speak loudly or softly?

- What other voice qualities should I use? High-pitched or low-pitched? Rising inflection or falling inflection?

- What kind of facial expression should I adopt?

There are other pertinent questions presenters could ask themselves; this list is not exhaustive. Many of these questions, however, do suggest that presenters must give serious attention to developing their expertise in interpreting and expressing nonverbal signals. The necessity of getting to know your audience also suggests that presenters need to listen to what their audience has to say, if this is possible—meeting your audience informally before the presentation is a good idea.

We should also remember that good oral presentations do not require a slavish following of someone else's rules. They involve an element of creative artistry as well as conscientious preparation and thoughtful delivery. Most of us have heard what we would describe as an 'inspired' or 'brilliant' speaker, yet it is often hard to put your finger on what exactly made us think of the speaker that way. Perhaps an inspired speaker has personal qualities that cannot be specified in a set of impersonal rules. However, believing in your message, being enthusiastic about it, and winning over your audience with this conviction and enthusiasm will greatly enhance your presentation.

Now let's turn our attention to how people can present their messages effectively in writing. A great deal of attention has been given to this medium in other texts (e.g. Mohan, McGregor and Strano, 1992), and it is not the intention of this book to give a full explanation of how to become a better writer. The next section identifies some of the key elements of certain kinds of written presentations commonly found in the workplace.

8.6 Written Presentation Skills

Without meetings between people at work, written communication is crucial. Every day while we're on the job, we receive a variety of written messages—memos, policy statements, letters, reports, publicity brochures, just to mention a few. Their presentation has much to do with their reception and acceptance.

Of course, modern technology has helped a lot to make written information look impressive. Word-processing, for example, has enabled people to present written work in a high-quality, professional format. Well set-out word-processed messages create the initial impression, at least, that enough care has been taken to make them worth reading. Poorly presented written messages, on the other hand, can be very off-putting, especially if the intent and structure of the message are not clear.

The theme and structure of a lengthy written message are clarified for the reader when it is divided into sections and given concise headings. It also helps if points are numbered and sentences are short and worded as simply as possible. Many organisations today insist that employees use **plain English** as much as possible. Naturally, in certain technical areas, words that are familiar only to specialists may be unavoidable. Nevertheless, even in some extremely traditional fields such as legal practice, there are strong pressures today to abandon legalese and to rewrite legal documents in plain English.

Plain English could make the following legal jargon comprehensible for the lay person.

plain English
The English language presented directly and simply, without unnecessary words and jargon.

The Mortgagor covenants and agrees with the Bank and it is hereby declared as follows:

1. MONEYS HEREBY SECURED

(1)   Save as, and to the extent, otherwise agreed in writing between the Mortgagor and the Bank, the Mortgagor will pay to the Bank on demand in writing made at any time or from time to time by or on behalf of the bank the whole or such part as is specified in the demand of:

(a)   the amount of all liabilities whether actual, contingent or prospective and whether direct or indirect of the Mortgagor on whatever account to or in favour of the Bank and whether arising on or in respect of any instrument, transaction or circumstance or in contract or tort or otherwise, including, without limitation, the amount of any orders, drafts, cheques, promissory notes, bills of exchange, letters of credit or guarantees and other instruments or engagements (whether negotiable or not) in respect of which the Mortgagor on whatever account is or may become liable and which are drawn accepted endorsed discounted or paid by the Bank or which are or may as a result of any circumstance or transaction entered into by the Bank with or for or on behalf of or at the express or implied request of the Mortgagor on whatever account be held or owned by the Bank whether as a holder in due course or otherwise and whether such orders, drafts, cheques, promissory notes, bills of exchange and letters of credit or guarantees other instruments or engagements have matured or not;

A common justification made for convoluted, legal jargon of this type is that it accounts for any legal loopholes. Many members of the legal profession maintain that plain English gives the client only a general statement of intent that is too open to a range of interpretations. Nevertheless, there are growing numbers in the legal profession today who believe that legal documents can be simplified without loss of specificity or clarity.

Making documents easy to read is an important aspect of good written presentation. The written message must also be based on sound reasoning and free, as far as possible, from fallacies, since these diminish the force of specific points and even the entire argument itself.

There are three main kinds of fallacies: psychological, material and logical.

1. **Psychological fallacies** are 'tricks' of reasoning intended to divert, distract, or confuse people—for example, the ad hominem argument (personal attack), the misuse of authority, the bandwagon effect (impressing by large numbers), pointing to another wrong, and emotive language. Psychological fallacies are fairly easy to find in advertising or in politicians' communication. Some typical psychological fallacies are presented as follows:

TABLE 8.2

*Examples of
psychological fallacies*

Ad hominem argument
Leader of the parliamentary opposition: How could you believe that the 'one nation' package will help to restore Australia's crippled economy when the designer of this package has presided, as the nation's treasurer, over the worst continuing progressive decline in living standards this country has ever witnessed? Can you really put your faith in an economic package put together by someone who has not progressed beyond a high school education and whose only claim to fame is a passion for antique clocks?

Misuse of authority
Mars bars must be nutritious and good for your health because Steve Monaghetti, the nation's top marathon runner, eats Mars bars (as evident in a television commercial repeatedly shown during the 1992 Barcelona Olympics coverage). Many well-known sports champions and other celebrities have appeared in the media to endorse products on which they can hardly be classed as authorities.

Bandwagon effect
We all know that nearly everybody agrees that Australians should devote as much energy and dedication to their jobs as they do to watching sport.

There can be no doubt that the vast majority of its citizens would like Australia to become a republic.

Pointing to another wrong
The real problem with our present hospital system is not the waiting time for urgent surgery but the greed of doctors who object to charging the lowest recommended common fee for consultations.

Use of emotive language
Are you prepared to condemn these refugees to death by not allowing them asylum in this country?

The imposition of this new tax is just another example of how the present government cannot refrain from stealing more from the already heavily plundered pockets of the struggling common worker.

In our everyday lives we are often confronted with written statements to which we are asked to respond in some way. For example, in industrial disputes, employees can expect a barrage of information from their union and their employer. If this information becomes distorted by psychological tricks, employees may become persuaded to act in certain ways without realising that they have been duped or seduced into doing so.

2. **Material fallacies** involve constructing arguments from poor material. Examples include faulty generalisation, false analogy, and the black-or-white fallacy. Faulty generalisation occurs when conclusions are drawn from too few or unrepresentative cases. Here's an example:

Because three major Australian financial organisations competing in international markets have reduced their senior training staff by 40 to 60 per cent, it is clear that staff in successful financial organisations need less training than staff in less successful financial organisations.

This argument is specious. Training staff reductions in three successful organisations do not necessarily justify training staff reductions in any other organisation. You might argue that the three successful companies could be even more successful if they increased rather than decreased their staff training opportunities.

False analogies are also common types of material fallacy. They involve inappropriate comparisons—between 'apples and oranges'. For example:

Special interest activist groups like members of the Greenpeace movement tend to divert the Government's attention from critical national issues like creating employment and improving the economy. Like members of the Greenpeace movement, homosexuals are also members of an activist community. Gays, therefore, are contributing to the financial problems of this country.

Although some might think that Greenpeace activists are disrupting the logging industry, the 'diversion' of gay activists is a false comparison and it does not logically follow that homosexuals are reducing employment opportunities in any way.

The *black-or-white fallacy* is used by people who reason and communicate in either-or terms. Things are either right or wrong, good or bad, suitable or unsuitable, workable or unworkable, and so on: this fallacy assumes that everything can be explained as irreconcilable opposites. There are no shades of grey in between. Let's look at some common examples of black-or-white reasoning:

Either you go to church or you will not be saved from damnation.
Shape up or ship out.
Unless you agree to the union's terms there will be industrial action.
How can people claim to be 'educated' if they haven't read the works of great writers and thinkers like Cicero, Dante, Shakespeare or Thoreau?

TABLE 8.3

Examples of black-or-white reasoning

Each statement relies on the premise that there are only two alternatives, with a particular consequence for each alternative.

Another common form of material fallacy is the manipulation of statistical data to create particular impressions. Graphs, for example, can present information in a variety of ways to suit specific aims. The three graphs in Figure 8.1 show how sales figures for a period of 15 years can be presented differently.

When the same set of data can be graphically presented in such different ways, the written explanation of each graph will appear to be based on sound unbiased evidence.

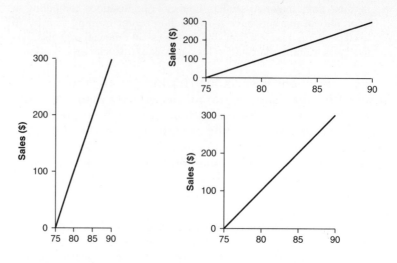

FIGURE 8.1
Three ways of illustrating product sales from 1975–1990

3. **Logical fallacies** are deviations from the rules of *valid* logical reasoning, which date back to the time of the Greek philosophers Plato and Aristotle. In general, these rules concern the balance of terms of reasoning within the premises and conclusion of an argument. Explaining these logical rules is a major undertaking in its own right, so readers are recommended to explore the intricacies of logical fallacies in well-known texts on the subject, such as the one by Fearnside (1980).

Since we seldom subject others' written messages to logical scrutiny, it is easy to overlook a writer's attempts to deceive, mislead or subtly secure our compliance. The logical design of messages, therefore, must be understood if we are to fully understand the message sender's real intentions. Hence, the interpretation of written communication involves more than decoding meanings. Such interpretation requires readers to understand how written language can be subtly twisted to lure them into compliance or agreement.

Apart from resorting to fallacy, there are many practical ways in which people can manipulate written messages to achieve a particular reaction. These practicalities are highlighted in some basic communication texts (e.g. Mohan, McGregor and Strano, 1992). The length of a written message, for example, often determines whether its recipient will actually read it, postpone reading it, or simply throw it away. Readers are often less likely to give priority to a long memo than to a succinct message.

Writers should also think about style. Official correspondence, for example, is typically expressed in a formal style, whereas managers might write informally to staff members when seeking advice. Considerations of style include appropriate salutations and titles (Dr, Prof, The Hon, Justice) for formal communication. How people sign and identify themselves largely depends on the nature of the relationship with those they are writing to. As a general guideline, it is wise to be consistent—one should be formal or informal throughout. Swinging from one style to another may confuse people about your expectations and intentions.

Finally, writers need to consider the purpose of their message. If instructions are not clear, for example, especially in professional settings, it may be interpreted as 'information only', and not acted upon. Instructions in official documents should, for example, include precise deadlines, headings under which information is to be structured, and other general formatting requirements.

Summary 8.7

This chapter considered how the human communication skills discussed in earlier chapters could be appropriately applied, particularly in the workplace. Appropriate application depends much on whether people have integrated their communication skills within a theoretical framework serving as a basis for communication and action. Competent communicators do not apply such skills singly, but 'put them all together'. Good communicators are not simply good listeners, or good negotiators, or good speakers; they are good at all these things.

The chapter then explored how human communication skills could be synthesised for appropriate application to a range of situations including equal employment opportunity practices, intercultural settings, and organisational settings where technology may depersonalise workers' interactions and communication. When people are required to communicate with others orally or in writing their presentations need to be carefully planned. This includes finding out as much as possible about the audience before communicating the message. It is also important that the message is clear, concise and free of faulty reasoning.

In the next chapter we consider more closely how to apply what we have discussed so far to communication management roles in systems. In particular we consider how they relate to interviewing, conducting meetings, and managing arationality (the shadow side of organisations).

Discussion Questions 8.8

1. How does the failure to observe equal employment opportunity principles detract from competence in adult communication management? Suggest some specific ways in which your communication skills could reinforce your commitment to equal employment opportunity principles and practices. Share your views with a friend.

2. Indicate how your communication skills are useful if you work with people from different ethnic backgrounds. In particular, how could these skills reduce the possibility of being misunderstood? Discuss these questions with a friend or someone from a different ethnic background.

3. If speech makes us human, suggest some examples of how modern technology can dehumanise workplace communication. How can we prevent dehumanising effects? Share your thoughts on these questions with someone else who has read this chapter.

4. What makes people nervous about making an oral presentation to an unfamiliar audience? What can these people do to overcome their apprehension?

5. Why is it important to know how fallacies can undermine arguments? Think of some examples of psychological and material fallacies which can weaken the credibility of an argument. Remove the fallacious statements and reconstruct the argument. Discuss this exercise with someone else who has read this chapter.

6. Explain how the ability to think critically is related to competence in adult communication management. Share your explanation with a friend or colleague.

8.9 Activities

1. Write a brief argument (one or two pages) about some issue or contemporary development in our society about which you feel strongly. Suggest a target audience. Now write an argument from the opposite point of view. Examine both arguments carefully for any fallacies. Can you improve these arguments?

2. Make a brief (3 to 5 minute) oral presentation to a colleague or group of colleagues. How successful was your presentation? What would you do differently if you gave it again? Why?

8.9 Key Terms

Convergence theory
Equal employment opportunity (EEO)
Fallacies
General systems theory
Plain English
Presentation
Uncertainty reduction

Berger, C. R. and Bradac, J. J. (1982) *Language and social knowledge*, London: Edward Arnold.

Fearnside, W. W. (1980) *About thinking*, Englewood Cliffs, New Jersey: Prentice Hall.

Gudykunst, W. B., Ting-Toomey, S. and Chua, E. (1988) *Culture and interpersonal communication*, California: Sage.

Kim, Y. Y. and Gudykunst, W. B. (eds) (1988) *Cross-cultural adaptation: current approaches*, California: Sage.

Monge, P. R., Backman, S. G., Dillard, J. P. and Eisenberg, E. M. (1982) 'Communicator competence in the workplace: model testing and scale development', in *Communication Yearbook 5: An Annual Review*, International Communication Association, Burgoon, M. (ed.), New Jersey: Transaction Books.

Postman, N. (1986) *Amusing ourselves to death*, London: Heinemann.

PART III

Applications of Communication Management

Managerial Applications

9

The leaders's goal is not mere explanation or clarification
but the creation of meaning.
Warren Bennis

To rule is easy, to govern difficult.
Johann W. von Goethe (1749–1832)

When the President says 'Jump!' they only ask 'How high?'
John Ehrlichman

I must follow the people. Am I not their leader?
Benjamin Disraeli (1804–1881)

All people in human systems or organisations are potentially communication managers. This observation is the theme of this chapter. It proposes that communication managers must see themselves as team members in their organisations, and highlights the importance of people working together and helping each other. It then presents five different kinds of roles which communication managers in organisations may be expected to perform, and the necessity for open communication in their systems. Next, we look at how these roles can apply in workplace practices such as interviewing and meetings, and how communication managers must understand the shadow side and politics of their organisations. Finally, we will study what communication managers need to know and do to prevent communication failure in their systems and how this involves their contribution to the building of a positive organisation climate.

Learning Objectives

After you have studied the ideas, arguments and suggestions presented in this chapter you should be able to do the following:

- Explain why communication managers need to be good team members.

- Define the term 'interdependence' and indicate why the interdependence of an organisation's members is vital for its successful operation.

- Identify five roles which communication managers can perform in their systems.

- Demonstrate how these roles can be performed in interviews and meetings.

- Discuss why it is important for communication managers to understand and manage the politics and shadow side of their organisations.

- Give two reasons why communication can fail and suggest two strategies communication managers can use to prevent such failure.

- Suggest how communication managers can contribute to a positive organisation climate.

9.1 Effective and Ineffective Communication Managers

To distinguish effective communication managers from ineffective ones, we need to review the meaning of 'communication manager'. In my work on adult communication management, I propose that all individuals in systems exercise some form of communication management, albeit in varying degrees of intensity, opportunity, or skill (Kaye, 1994b:7). Some people in systems have more reason or opportunity to interact and communicate with fellow workers than others do, sometimes because their job requires close collaboration with others.

The idea that all individuals in systems are communication managers is further reinforced by a study by Kaye and McArthur (1993) which, over a period of three months, examined a large number of job advertisements stipulating 'good communication skills' or equivalent criteria such as 'the ability to communicate well with others', 'sound interpersonal communication skills', or 'applicants must enjoy dealing with people'. This study showed, among other things, that:

> . . . in general, employers today place high value on the criterion of good communication skills. Although the meaning of this criterion varies from one kind of job to another, applicants who can demonstrate communicative competence appear to be favourably regarded... the study highlights the present trend for modern organisations to emphasise the importance of employees having communication skills. (Kaye and McArthur, 1993)

Since most people in systems need to be able to communicate well with others, they have some kind of communication management role or function to perform. Because of the type of work they do, some people do not need to meet regularly with colleagues from other departments or sections in their organisations, yet they are still potentially 'communication managers'. This is a bit like saying that all people in a system are potentially leaders, especially if their system allows worker participation in corporate decision-making. On this point it has been suggested that 'anyone who contributes in any way to the accomplishment of the goals of the system participates in system-oriented individual leadership' (Egan, 1985:195). Thus, communication management within systems resembles participative leadership, since it involves the *interdependence* of all members of the system.

Effective communication managers are therefore team members. They see themselves as parts of a body which cannot function properly unless every part of it is healthy and operating in harmony with all the other parts. Hence, the really capable communication managers are those who genuinely understand the meaning of interdependence and who can act and work interdependently with others.

By contrast, ineffective communication managers tend to prefer to operate alone. These people are *the lone wolves*. They find it difficult to see themselves as team members, often because they mistrust others' abilities and believe that the only work that will be done to their satisfaction will be the work they do themselves. Whilst there is some virtue in self-reliance, it can also be a millstone around one's neck because at some stage everyone in a system needs help with their tasks. The lone wolves can only operate in isolation for a limited period. Sooner or later, because of their independent rather than interdependent approach to their jobs, the lone wolves may find themselves becoming increasingly out of step with the needs and goals of their systems. This effect of being out of step is magnified when senior managers and superiors fail to maintain close liaison with their peers and subordinates.

Effective communication management, therefore, is based on knowing what others are doing and ensuring that one's own work fits in with and contributes to the entire system. Competent communication managers are alert to any danger of getting out of step and to any necessity to change their approach to their work. Flexibility, the management of change in one's self, the ability to size up a situation and then to make resolute decisions or take appropriate action are all characteristics of effective communication managers.

Decisive, action-oriented people are able to take initiatives and capitalise on opportunities as they occur. They are not merely rule-bound, nor do they depend on instructions from their superiors. Theirs is a creative approach: they constantly reflect on their practices, actions, and communication; they devise better ways of achieving their goals by monitoring and refining their communication and relationships with others.

Roles and Skills of Effective Communication Managers 9.2

There is probably a very long list of specific skills that could be associated with various communication management roles. We will therefore focus on some of the more general roles and skills—those that extend across traditional job descriptions, classifications and boundaries. The roles and skills of communication managers are essentially generic and apply to all people in systems. How well developed they are is some indication of the position of the person performing the communication management role. We might assume that as people continue to rise in their system hierarchies, their competence as communication managers should increase as a matter of both expectation and necessity.

It is important to distinguish this view of communication management from the more traditional notion held by scholars like Farace, Monge and Russell (1979) and revived more recently by Ticehurst, Walker and Johnston (1991). The traditional notion is that the communication manager should be located at the centre of the 'message flow' in the organisation, and that 'communication managers' can be identified as those who control the flow of information in their organisations.

Assuming, perhaps, that only some people in systems are really communication managers, Ticehurst, Walker and Johnston (1991) seem to promote the idea that communication managers occupy certain kinds of positions, usually associated with human resource development/ management or public relations/marketing types of functions. They conclude that 'position titles for people filling communication management roles were varied. Data from all phases [of their study] suggested that responsibility for communication management is often shared between Human Resource Management/Development and Marketing/ Public Affairs departments' (p. 94).

The fundamental flaw in this selective view of communication managers is the assumption that human resource managers/developers and marketing/public relations officers are the major controllers of information flow. It is true, of course, that human resource management and public relations personnel do exact some control over specific kinds of information flow. Nevertheless, it would be ridiculous to suggest that people in other departments cannot be regarded as communication managers. People in sales or production departments, for example, have significant control over sales and production information flow; staff in customer service roles are also managers of the communication process.

Taking the broader view proposed here, we can identify a set of different kinds of roles from those implied in particular position descriptions. Keeping in mind that they apply to all people in systems, we can expect every individual to perform the following roles, admittedly with varying degrees of intensity, opportunity or skill:

1. Information sharer.
2. Helper/supporter/counsellor/creator of opportunities.
3. Quality controller/organiser of self.
4. Mentor/role model.
5. Leader/climate setter.

information sharer role
Involves giving and receiving of information, the reciprocal construction of meaning, clarification, sharing interpretations, self-disclosure, mutual disclosure, and the development of mutually acceptable strategies for further communication and action.

Let's look at each one of these roles more closely. The **information sharer** role eschews the traditional notion of 'control'. In the sense intended here, 'control' of information is jointly owned by those involved in sharing or exchanging information. Thus, the information sharer role of communication managers concerns giving and receiving information, the reciprocal construction of meaning, clarification, sharing interpretations, self-disclosure and mutual disclosure, and the consequent development of mutually agreed upon strategies for further communication and action.

Note that the sharing of information ought not to be a selective process. All information, whether it is likely to be well received or not, must be shared. As Egan (1985) has argued, information sharing involves feedback, and feedback, whether confirmatory or corrective, is necessary for the development of a strong, positive, overt organisational culture. The concealment of information, especially negative or 'corrective' information, strengthens the covert culture (the shadow side) of an organisation by creating a climate of uncertainty and unpredictability (Egan, 1988a, 1991, 1993).

A typical example of corrective feedback being withheld is the case of a supervisor's unfavourable perception of a staff member's level of performance. If the supervisor suppresses this unfavourable impression, the staff member will not be aware of failing to live up to expectations. Without corrective feedback from supervisors, staff members are likely to continue performing poorly.

Unfortunately, a further problem can arise from withholding corrective feedback. If underperformers hear of their supervisors' negative impression from other workers, the relationship between superior and staff member may deteriorate into mistrust, resentment, and a desire to get even. Communication between them will probably become adversarial and deceitful.

Communication managers may also have a **helping role** within their systems, to create opportunities for others to achieve their goals or perform their duties in a supportive environment. Ineffective managers are often oblivious of the volume of work they delegate and of the unrealistic expectations they have of their staff members, so that they not only fail to create opportunities for them but also put obstacles in their way. Warren Bennis, in discussing what he termed 'basic truisms about leadership', formulated **Bennis' First Law of Academic Pseudodynamics** which states: 'routine work drives out nonroutine work and smothers to death all creative planning, all fundamental change in the university—or any institution' (Bennis, 1991:15). Bennis' First Law is a good example of how managers can fail to support their staff by reducing their opportunities to think, act and communicate creatively.

As helpers, effective communication managers are considered approachable and able to counsel others when necessary. Counselling is not restricted to superiors—subordinates can counsel superiors, depending on the nature of the organisation, since the helping role is not the sole prerogative of those who supervise others. Effective communication managers, therefore, are open to receiving as well as providing advice or help when appropriate. Ineffective communication managers do not want to be helped since they believe that any request from them for help could be construed as a symptom of professional weakness.

The **quality controller** (or organiser) role of communication managers is closely associated with their helper role. Effective communication managers should be able to monitor and if necessary improve the quality of their communication with others. Monitoring the quality of communication requires a special kind of mental alertness. Apart from sensitivity and the ability to change one's pattern of behaviour and communication, the ability to be self-organised is integral to the quality controller role of communication managers. People who are self-organised are not nonplussed by any unexpected failure in communication with others. They are able to analyse their interpersonal encounters relatively quickly and determine alternative, more appropriate strategies for any future communication. Sensitivity, self-monitoring and self-organisation, therefore, are important communication management skills required by the quality controller role, and are essential to the ability to learn from experience.

A fourth communication management role is that of **mentor** or role model. In this sense, managers are exemplars of the art of maintaining

helping role
Creation of opportunities for others in their systems to achieve their goals, or to support their efforts to perform their duties.

Bennis' First Law of Academic Pseudodynamics
Routine work drives out nonroutine work and smothers to death all creative planning and fundamental change in any institution.

quality controller (organiser) role
Involves their ability to monitor and, if necessary, improve the quality of their communication with others.

good communication and give others a basis for social learning and self-change. Managers who fail in this role tend to spend little or no time in reflection on their communication and relationships with others—they take the communication process for granted.

The rationale for taking the communication process for granted may be explained by drawing an analogy between communicating and other developmentally acquired abilities like walking or skimming stones on a flat surface of water. When people have learned to walk, they no longer think about how to walk because it happens naturally and without conscious effort. In the same way, poor role models of communication management see communication as a natural and automatic activity. To them, communication is like walking: once you can do it, you don't need to think about it any more. It is not difficult to appreciate that the flaw in this analogy is the failure to acknowledge that human communication is more complex than the simple act of walking. Since people communicate from the time they are born, one might well ask at what point of people's lives does the ability to communicate become 'natural'? Clearly, this is a meaningless question.

The **leadership role** of communication managers, like the role of quality controller, involves ensuring as far as possible that communication occurs under the most favourable or desirable conditions. Managers performing this role realise that good morale indicates a favourable organisational climate. One sure way of maintaining it is to maximise all workers' opportunities for open communication and participative decision-making.

Open communication means ready access, for all workers, to any information that can affect their system. Naturally, in any system, certain items of information have to be kept confidential; for example, referees' reports on job applicants, personal information about employees (e.g. salary details), and security matters. For the most part, however, open communication makes most information available to all.

In systems dominated by closed communication, only superficial information is readily accessible, so that a few people attempt to control the amount and kind of information available to the rest. This control over what others can and should know is a form of power often exercised by autocratic managers who believe that information sharing leads to a loss of control over their staff members. Closed communication systems often have a flourishing shadow side. Not knowing exactly what is going on in parts of the organisation, its members begin to speculate and draw up scenarios to fit their particular suspicions and misgivings.

Regardless of which role communication managers are performing at any given time, they need a repertoire of communication skills. They must also understand why those skills are essential to their communication management functions, and when and how to apply them—for example, when it is time to listen or to counsel, when to be assertive, when to negotiate or concede. Communication managers also need to be sensitive to what they say and how they are saying it. Their verbal and nonverbal communication with others must therefore be constantly self-monitored.

We turn now to some specific contexts in which communication managers typically perform these roles. Two major areas of activity are interviewing and meetings. Then we explore strategies by which people can manage the shadow side of their organisations, including ways of preventing communication failure and of building positive organisational climates.

Interviewing 9.3

First, it is important to distinguish between the terms 'interview'and 'interviewing'. The term 'interviewing' refers to a particular kind of structured communication process where at least one person asks questions of another or others. In essence, interviewing is a structured type of interpersonal communication. On the other hand, 'interview' refers to the structure of the process. For each kind of interview the process of interviewing is structured differently. We will look at some of these structures and consider some of their implications for enhancing communication in interviews.

There are several common kinds of interviews conducted in professional practice. For example, in *selection interviews* competing job applicants are examined for their suitability. Where there is more than one applicant, the shortlisted interviewees are usually ranked in order of merit. Some organisations now contract human resource development consultants to oversee the entire recruitment process. These consultants advise the appropriate authorities about the applicants' suitability.

In social service agencies the recruitment of high quality volunteers requires a reliable selection procedure. Traditional interviews, the most commonly used procedures in the corporate world (McComb and Jablin, 1984), are inadequate for predicting an applicant's success in job performance because they are often unreliable (Arvey and Campion, 1982; Latham and Saari, 1984). Recently it has been argued that *structured interviews* predict job performance much more reliably (Hollwitz and Wilson, 1993). These interviews have three distinctive features: a series of job-related questions, rating scales for evaluating applicants' answers, and consistent administration to all applicants. In Australia, this practice is common in organisations that follow equal employment opportunity (EEO) principles.

The success of selection interviews, however, depends not only on the ability of interviewers to structure interviews by asking standard questions and following consistent procedures; the effect of the interviewing process on the applicants also has a profound influence. A recent study of interviewing for campus positions concluded that applicants' satisfaction with the quality of communication in the interview correlated closely with their intention to accept second interview offers (Ralston, 1993).

People are also interviewed when they resign from positions. In *exit interviews* they are questioned about their reasons for leaving their organisations. The reasons vary from securing a better position elsewhere to dissatisfaction over lack of management support or inadequate leadership.

Of course, people also leave for personal reasons such as family commitments, chronic illness, or change of lifestyle.

When employees fail to carry out their duties satisfactorily they are likely to be warned or reprimanded by their superiors. Such encounters are known as *discipline interviews*. Because of the sensitivity of the matters and issues raised in such interviews, it is very important that interviewers have all their facts straight. Unsubstantiated accusations can lead to union counteraction if an employee experiences unjustified disciplinary action.

One of the most important kinds of interview in organisations is the **performance appraisal** (or review), which has tended to focus on employees' performance to determine their career prospects. For example, job promotions or financial bonuses could be the outcome of appraisals of successful performance. A negative performance appraisal, however, can mean that an employee is given a warning to improve their performance or have their employment terminated, so traditional performance appraisals are potentially adversarial and can be likened to some kind of contest between the appraiser and the appraised.

performance appraisal (review)
An interviewing process that periodically or regularly evaluates someone's work performance.

Performance appraisals are sometimes like contests

There is a tendency now to view the performance appraisal less as an evaluative exercise and more as a developmental opportunity. This involves creating opportunities for employees within the context of the organisation's mission, goals and business plan, so that the performance appraisal is transformational rather than punitive. The essential aim of the **transformational performance appraisal** is progress towards the strategic intent of an organisation.

This means that the process is very much a team effort. The appraiser assumes the role of transformational leader, helping the appraised to share and interpret the system's mission. On the other hand, the role of the appraised is that of:

transformational performance appraisal
A special form of appraisal that aims to develop performance and potential in line with the organisation's mission and goals.

> a self-managed associate, who uses the information to develop understanding, to realign the support system, to leverage his/her contribution, and to commit to new behaviours and greater responsibility. The new insights, alignments, behaviours and

commitments, in the final analysis, come from the employee, and he/she assumes the role of problem identifier and joint problem solver to ensure that it happens. (Twomey and Twomey, 1992:30–31)

For any interview, the quality of communication between the interviewer(s) and interviewee(s) is critical to its success or failure. For example, in selection interviews it is important to use questions that verify the accuracy of information supplied by the interviewee's letter of application and resume. By not asking the right questions, interviewers might assess an applicant's suitability from insufficient data. Anecdotes abound on the appointment of people with bogus qualifications, alleged achievements that are difficult to check, and dubious records of professional experience.

In exit interviews, obtaining the real reason why someone leaves an organisation is also important since the reason could indicate that the organisation needs to change in some way. Interviewees may feel diffident about expressing their true reasons for resigning if they need the support of former superiors as referees for job applications elsewhere, or in case there is a future opportunity to apply for a more senior position in the same organisation.

A high level of communication competence is also required in discipline interviews. Interviewers can, through heated emotional exchanges with interviewees, convert the interview into a theatre of conflict. Experienced interviewers realise the necessity to generate statements or questions based on fact rather than on generalisations. For example, it is relatively simple to point out, from the office's time register, that over the past two months the interviewee was half an hour late on 20 mornings, and on six occasions left work 18 minutes before normal closing time. Such evidence is preferable to statements like 'you're invariably late for work' or 'you haven't done a full day's work for quite some time'. Further examples are given in Table 9.1.

TABLE 9.1

Examples of what to say and what not to say in interviews

What to say	What not to say
Your section of the annual report is behind schedule	You work too slowly
The agenda papers were not ready in time for the board meeting	You are a slack secretary
Your strategic plan does not include performance indicators as required in the guidelines	Your strategic plan is incomplete
Here are five written complaints from customers about lack of service from the floor	Your shop assistants are lazy
You have parked in the sales manager's car space every day this week	Can't you read signs?

As already suggested, interviewing is a specialised process of inter-personal communication. It is distinguished from other communication activities by its goal-orientation, its expectations, and its outcomes. For example, the goal of selection interviewing is to identify the best applicant; its expectation is that the best applicant will satisfy all the essential (and, if possible, desirable) selection criteria; its outcome is making a suitable appointment.

By thinking in terms of 'interviewing' rather than of 'interviews', we are in a better position to consider how the communication management roles of information-sharer, helper, quality controller, mentor, and leader apply to these special contexts. Vital to the performance of any of these roles in the interviewing process is the type of relationship interviewers wish to have with those they are interviewing. Depending upon the goals and the type of interview, the relationship may be formal or informal. Furthermore, the extent of disclosure varies according to the kind of relationship that develops between interviewers and interviewees and according to mutual assurances of confidentiality.

Regardless of the relationship between the interviewer and interviewee, interviewing is significantly improved when an appropriate level and form of rapport is developed between them. Jorgenson (1992) has suggested that this issue of rapport has been researched relatively little. Whilst this claim relates specifically to interviewing as a research procedure, it does lead one to broaden the consideration of rapport to interviewing in general. Indeed, it is difficult to imagine how any kind of interviewing could be successfully conducted without serious thought about the development of appropriate rapport between interviewers and interviewees.

There are today some highly 'people-focused' professions where significant improvements could be made to communication in interviewing. Some solicitors, for example, see legal interviewing solely in term of 'legal matters': solicitors and lawyers exist to give expert legal advice, first and foremost. Whilst this is true, giving this advice would be a smoother communication process if more solicitors took a moment to listen to their clients' related emotional concerns. After all, clients often tend to experience their legal problems not just in logical or rational ways but also through worry, anxiety, fear and uncertainty. The issue of the importance of communicating under conditions of reduced uncertainty has been re-emphasised (Berger, 1987). When these emotions are also recognised by solicitors interacting with their clients, rapport is often improved and the consequent giving of advice becomes an easier task.

Lawyers are not the only professionals who would benefit by considering the type of relationship and rapport they need to have with their clients. For example, ministers of religion, in their capacity as spiritual leaders, often find that they are required to give comfort to the bereaved, and medical practitioners often have to inform patients and their families about terminal diseases. In such situations, professionals may strive to be clinically detached, but it is difficult not to see clients, patients, parishioners, or customers as people with real feelings.

Whatever communication management role professional interviewers occupy, they soon discover that listening, questioning, assertiveness, the judicious use of language, and the reception and expression of nonverbal cues are vital skills. This holds true for any type of interviewing and many other personal encounters. Such competence benefits others besides professional 'carers' (e.g. social workers, welfare counsellors, therapists, nurses); people typically seen as 'task-oriented' (e.g. public accountants, financial managers, actuaries, conveyancers) also need to be communicatively competent.

Listening is the most essential communication skill needed by interviewers of any kind. It ensures that the communication between them and the interviewees is genuinely reciprocal and they gain the information they need to assess those being interviewed. Good listening is apparent when interviewers' questions logically build upon what the interviewees have just said. When interviewers repeat or paraphrase accurately what the interviewees have expressed, it is clear, also, that they have been listening attentively. Experienced interviewers also check and clarify their interpretations of the interviewee's remarks, to ensure that their recollection of them is, as far as possible, free from bias.

Another important aspect of communication competence in interviewing is questioning, which may be defined as any solicitation to speak—it includes statements like 'Tell me all about the time when . . .' or 'Describe all you can remember about the accident'. Good interviewers know when to use open or closed questions. Open questions invite an extensive answer; for example 'How can I help you?' or 'Tell me in detail why this machine is still not working properly'.

Closed questions, on the other hand, require brief answers—often just 'yes' or 'no'. Court witnesses are generally required to answer yes or no to closed questions like 'Were you at home between the hours of 8 and 10 p.m. last night?' Other examples of closed questions are 'How fast were you travelling at the time of the collision?', 'What is the name of your employer?', 'Which is the nearest cross-street?', 'Have you ever suffered from diphtheria?' or 'How much money do I still owe you?'

The judicious use of open or closed questions usually depends on the interviewer's objectives. Open questions are generally used to get the interviewee talking. Lawyers and medical practitioners use them early in their consultations for diagnosis. Later they may switch to closed questions when more specific information is required.

The relationship between interviewers and interviewees is also affected by nonverbal behaviour and cues. How people dress and present themselves at interviews often influences the outcome of the interview. Inappropriately dressed job applicants, for example, may create the impression that they are gauche, poorly prepared for the interview or unconcerned about making a good impression on their prospective employers.

Besides clothing and appearance, people's facial expressions, voice qualities, use of space, and gestures can obviously help or hinder communication between the parties concerned. For instance, simple unintentional actions like gazing out the window or absent-mindedly doodling on a notepad while someone is speaking can be very disconcerting for them. Similarly, speaking in a flat monotone may suggest that the speaker is bored, unconcerned or even impatient.

When interviewing is conducted in opulent surroundings like oak-panelled boardrooms or executive meeting-rooms, the experience can be very intimidating. Interviewees may feel even less at ease if they are separated from the interviewers by a long boardroom table or an expansive desk and have to raise their voices to be heard.

The intention in this chapter is not to provide an exhaustive analysis of interviewing but to make the point that communication competence in critical processes like listening and questioning is vital to good interviewing.

The next section considers how communication management skills apply to the conduct of meetings and attempts to distinguish well-run meetings from those that participants regard as a waste of time. Most important, we will try to identify the elements of communication competence that contribute to the success of presiding members or chairpersons at meetings.

9.4 Conducting Meetings

People in supervisory or managerial positions spend a good deal of their time in meetings. Some meetings are formal in structure and governed by rules of procedure and debate. They are generally chaired by the chief executive officer of an organisation, although in some instances the responsibility of presiding at meetings is shared by the group's members. Formal meetings usually also entrust a secretary or executive officer to record the minutes, prepare agenda papers, and issue the action sheets that delineate particular task responsibilities. Formal meetings include regular board and committee meetings, annual general meetings, stockholders' quarterly meetings, professional conferences and seminars.

Quite often at work people find it necessary to meet colleagues informally. Such meetings may be scheduled but frequently occur spontaneously or as the need arises. Some scheduled regular meetings are 'catch-up' or 'feedback' sessions where colleagues share information about recent developments in their particular spheres of activity. Catch-up meetings are very useful, therefore, because they make regular opportunities for people to communicate and provide feedback on current events in the system. A lack of catch-up meetings may force people to use informal networks such as the organisation grapevine, and run the risk of mixing information with hearsay and rumour.

Regardless of whether the meeting is formal or informal, several things can be done to ensure that a meeting is productive. In the first place, all those who meet should be prepared for the event so that they do not waste time reviewing material that was available beforehand. For this reason, it is advisable to circulate agenda papers in advance of meetings whenever possible. When this is not possible, people will find it helpful to have at their meeting a summary of highlighted points accompanying any detailed document.

Secondly, it is a good idea for presiders at meetings to deal with high priority agenda items as early in the meeting as possible. People become frustrated when the discussion of trivial matters occupies so much time that the meeting is concluded before urgent or important items are presented. Placing agenda items in some order of priority is a particularly important aspect of planning meetings. Some presiders, however, deliberately spend inordinate amounts of time on comparatively insignificant matters so that important items have to be dealt with outside meetings, usually through autocratic executive action. Such ploys tend to build up the shadow side of systems.

A third essential for successful meetings is that chairpersons must know how and when to control communication and maintain order. Unless they can maintain this firmly, no amount of planning will prevent chaos. Good chairpersons always make sure that attendants know the time limits and that people's comments and contributions must be kept brief. As well, they indicate when any further questions or debate should cease. Sometimes, in formal meetings, other members can also help move things along by recommending that a motion be put.

The best run meetings, therefore, are those where all members perform communication management roles. For example, the leadership role may pass from member to member depending upon the expertise required for particular agenda items. Members can also exercise the helper role by encouraging others to contribute, where appropriate, and by resisting the temptation to use the meeting as a forum for self-aggrandisement. When meetings are hijacked by people demanding attention, the enthusiasm and commitment of other members can be seriously impaired. Capable chairpersons nip such attempts in the bud.

Another communication management role which is critical in some kinds of meetings is the information sharer role. In some instances, it is important that all attendants have the chance to express their views or make suggestions. Good presiders sometimes arrange this by using approaches like the Nominal Group Technique (NGT) (Fox, 1989; Delbecq, Van de Ven and Gustafson, 1975). This method is based on the principle that the most creative ideas from people emerge from sessions where everyone's thoughts are listed and clarified before being assessed against group problems or goals.

The information sharer role of managers in meetings also requires team facilitation skills, an understanding of the group's or work team's dynamics, and ways of using authority and power to best effect. According to Katzenbach and Smith (1993:112), teams and working groups in organisations can be distinguished as follows:

> . . . a working group's performance is a function of what its members do as individuals. A team's performance includes both individual results and . . . 'collective work products'. A collective work-product is what two or more members must work on together, such as interviews, surveys or experiments. Whatever it is, a collective work-product reflects the joint, real contribution of team members.

To develop their teams, managers need to create as many opportunities as possible for team members to share information, have group discussions and debate issues. Ultimately, managers may authorise teams to make decisions about their own and their organisation's development. This process is known as **empowerment**. Good managers see themselves as team members and not as dictators. Their job is to help the team make the best decisions. The ability to provide this help depends on how well managers understand the way each team member relates to others in the team—thus the selection and building of teams of compatible workers is an important skill for successful managers.

People who are skilled and experienced in chairing meetings can serve as role models for future presiders. Such ability is not simply learned from textbooks; much of it is acquired by learning from the communication and actions of other chairpersons. If people are exposed to poor models, they may emulate undesirable speech and behaviour habits.

empowerment
The delegation of authority by managers to staff to make decisions about their own and their organisation's development.

The ability to chair meetings efficiently is not simply learned from textbooks

The debilitating effects of the arational—the shadow side of communication in systems has already been alluded to. We now direct our attention more closely to how communication managers can deal with arational forces in their organisations, and to understanding the shadow side of communication.

9.5 Managing Arationality in Organisations

Scholars have paid comparatively little attention to the shadow side of systems. This is partly understandable since it is fairly difficult to study, and people tend to think that systems can be analysed in fairly simple ways. Linear models of systems and organisational flow charts often reinforce this impression. However, most systems can be severely 'messed up' by a powerful shadow side, which Egan (1985) has also equated with the term *arationality*. Essentially, arationality refers to occurrences, in systems, which are neither rational nor irrational. Arational developments are usually unpredictable and undiscussable. They may be associated with the unwritten rules by which some people act and communicate. Unwritten rules form part of a covert organisational culture and serve to establish hidden agendas that promote personal goals. Arational behaviour is therefore often calculated, consciously deceptive and symptomatic of power play and office politics.

Here is an example of arationality. An organisation's chief executive officer (CEO) has to allocate budgets to each of the organisation's department heads. One department head whom the CEO does not particularly like is making an important presentation at an international forum which coincides with the next budget meeting, so the absent head will be represented at the meeting by an acting head who is not very experienced in financial matters.

At the budget meeting a funding formula, which favours all departments except the one whose head is absent, is debated and approved. The absent department head would never have agreed to this formula, as the CEO very well knows. Nevertheless, the CEO has seized this unexpected chance to undermine a subordinate. On returning from the international forum, the substantive department head is advised by the CEO that the replacement acting head approved the new funding formula. It is too late to change the formula since funds have already been allocated. In this case, the immediate effect of the CEO's arational method of allocating budgets is to disenfranchise a senior member of staff. The long-term effect has been to put that department head on guard for any future important decisions that need the CEO's approval.

Another example of arationality is when people take on projects without conferring with their superiors or peers. Things begin to happen, but those who will be accountable are not aware of them. In one organisation a series of advertising promotions was released to the newspapers without the awareness or approval of the senior officer who would eventually be required to cover their costs. Those who lodged the advertisements acted this way because they were not confident that their superior officer would have approved funding at the time.

A feature of the shadow side of communication in systems, therefore, is the withholding of information from people who are unsympathetic with the goals and intentions of those acting covertly. Withholding information is the antithesis of the communication manager's information-sharing role because things are done by someone going behind others' backs. When things happen in an organisation without consultation, people's future communication with the perpetrators of the deceit is likely to be highly defensive, adversarial, and less frequent.

Withholding information is a symptom of intraorganisational politics. Egan (1993:111) notes that 'while some systems are less political than others, all systems have some kind of politics. This includes large conglomerates such as General Motors, institutions such as correctional facilities, and community systems such as churches and families'. For the most part, people in systems engage in political behaviour and communication to gain advantage over others. Thus, politics in systems are about competition for resources, power, territory, and ideology.

However, the motives behind political communication in systems are not invariably bad or counterproductive. It is important to distinguish between the politics of self-interest and the politics of institutional enhancement. The politics of self-interest usually result in constraints upon productivity or quality of life in systems. Thus, promoting personal favourites to key positions in preference to more capable people is a prime example of the politics of self-interest at work. Another instance is where members of different parts of a system struggle for control over limited resources, especially financial resources. When money is scarce, it may be less practical to dole it out evenly to each department than to close down certain departments. Drastic measures such as this can seriously damage organisation morale.

By contrast, the politics of institutional enhancement can influence positively the productivity of a system and its members' quality of life. Behind the politics of institutional enhancement is the motive of service for the good of the system. Local council aldermen are sometimes held up as exemplars of community leadership intent on ensuring the welfare of their constituents. Of course, such community leaders can be corrupted by powerful individuals or groups engaging in the politics of self-interest. When this happens, the motive of service is replaced by the motive of putting self before others.

To perform their communication management roles competently, people in systems must be aware of others' political manoeuvres. Whilst it is not always easy to know when political knives are being thrown, astute people make sure that their network of informal communication is maintained by loyal, reliable supporters. Knowing in advance about an opponent's intended moves gives communication managers an advantage because appropriate countermoves can be planned.

Just as the development of awareness is the first step for managing the politics of systems, 'the starting-point for positive politics is an institution-enhancing agenda' (Egan, 1993:115). Idealistic individuals with vision and commitment are often those who have developed institution-enhancing agendas. Even without the support of conservative superiors or peers, dedicated visionaries strive to turn their vision into reality since their motives are characteristically focused on service to others rather than to self.

Naturally, even visionaries have their breaking-points. It is difficult to stay committed when those whose lot can be vastly improved fail to share one's vision and resist any potential changes for the better. For this reason, leaders with vision often work better when they can create a new department from the ground up rather than by inheriting a long-established group of people who have become used to doing things the same way over many years.

Nevertheless, visionaries can set institution-enhancing agendas by concentrating on the strengths rather than the deficiencies of staff. This may mean basing their agendas on realistic stages of individual and organisational change rather than on programs of radical reform to communication practices in the workplace. As older staff retire, new appointees offer more expertise to help realise executives' visions. Realistic agendas like these need not be concealed or part of a system's covert culture. Because they are forward-thinking, these enhancing agendas are often reflected in the system's strategic and business plans.

In addition to developing awareness of and skill in managing the politics of systems, communication managers confronted with self-defeating or system-defeating forms of arationality should continue to strive for further excellence in their communication with other people. This ability, or competence, has been discussed at some length here and in previous chapters. Egan (1993:103–5) has suggested that the communication skills most useful for managers and leaders are listening skills, listening-based responding (or empathy), challenging skills, innovation-focused dialogue, and negotiation skills.

Whilst listening and empathy have been considered in some detail in Chapter 6, the concept of 'challenging skills' relates to the adult communication manager's role of helper, and particularly to learning in the workplace. Leaders and managers challenge others to examine critically the assumptions, value systems, beliefs, attitudes, and norms which make up the corporate culture and which may jeopardise opportunities for individual and organisational development.

Very often, challenges are issued in the form of either confirmatory or corrective feedback. Feedback from one individual to another helps to maintain high standards in systems; it is also challenging when it is intended to tap people's strengths rather than their weaknesses. This kind of challenge is not as commonly used by managers as it should be, but it works well in their capacity as role-models. By showing others that they themselves are prepared to accept challenges, managers are effectively inviting others to take up their own challenges. In such instances, it is important to stress that challenging and feedback are more likely to succeed when they are not construed as personal attacks on anyone's deficiencies.

Finally, innovation-focused dialogue is a communication skill not usually found in traditional listings of interpersonal skills. In the sense intended by Egan (1993), it means more than simply dealing with problems at work, and entails identifying creative alternatives to conventional means of tackling recurrent problems. For example, unresolved personal conflicts may be handled better by formalising differences than by striving to find common ground. For example, when two ideologically opposed groups of university academics found it intolerable to work in the same department, the problem was resolved by creating two departments for that discipline. This resolution was clearly innovative as it did more than attempt to establish a common ground for people who preferred to differ.

Undoubtedly, there is room for a good deal more study of the shadow side of communication and management. As communication managers begin to accept the importance of developing competence in this area, there will probably be greater pressure on scholars and researchers to provide fresh insights on arationality in systems, and how to combat it. Bearing this in mind, some ways of preventing communication failure, especially when it is due to the influence of arationality, are suggested in the next section.

9.6 Preventing Communication Failure

In everyday speech we often hear expressions such as 'there's been a breakdown in communication'. Why does communication between people break down? How can it be restored? What can people do to prevent communication failure? These questions tax all of us at one time or another, for several reasons.

One reason why people find it difficult to explain communication failure is their ego-involvement in the process. Many people are very aware of others' behaviour and communication but blind to their own, often because they believe they are infallible. When people maintain that they have not contributed to communication failure, they imply that someone else has, and deny that successful or unsuccessful communication management depends on both communicating parties. It takes two (or more) to tango!

Rule 1 for preventing communication failure, therefore, is to recognise one's own part in communication and relationships. This paves the way for self-examination and, where necessary, appropriate change in our behaviour. When both parties are prepared to recognise their potential to contribute to a breakdown, there is a good chance that they will proceed to share their thoughts about it. As some separated couples have discovered, the chances of getting back together increase in proportion to the amount of dialogue which takes place. The more people talk to each other, the more chance there is that differences will be understood and perhaps resolved.

Another thing people tend to do is to blame communication failure on 'barriers'. The concept of 'communication barrier' was proposed as the logical opposite of 'communication gateway' by Rogers and Roethlisberger (1952). Some people have used broad terms like 'noise' or 'interference' to refer to situational (usually external) elements that inhibit communication—for example, electric power drills or jackhammers, loud music, rattling train carriages, or peak-hour traffic.

The concept of noise or interference is only a simplistic basis for explaining what communication barriers are. People's internal filters can also become barriers to communication with others. For instance, when people hold stereotyped images of others, their actions and communication are influenced by these images.

There is usually some truth in stereotypes or generalisations. The point is that when people form stereotypes of particular professional, social, ethnic, religious or other groups of people, they tend not to vary their communication and behaviour with different individuals from those groups. If, for example, they think that all clergy are naive and unworldly, they might be patronising to any individual church leader they meet. When people see groups primarily in terms of 'all', they tend to communicate consistently with the entire collection of individuals who make up the 'all'.

Stereotyping often occurs when we have strong feelings, beliefs, attitudes, values, rules of conduct, and standards. All these constitute our 'personal cultures' which govern how we act and communicate. If we hold people in high esteem, we treat them with respect, and the reverse applies. Thus, our personal cultures can become internal barriers to communicating and relating with others.

Some people argue that other personal and physical characteristics or qualities are potential barriers to communication—for example, gender, ethnic origins, weight, disability or socioeconomic status. This view ignores the fact that such personal characteristics are realities, and only become barriers when people allow their prejudices to judge and stereotype others.

A cynical view is that regardless of what people do to prevent communication from failing, more often than not it will fail anyway. For example, Osmo Wiio (1979) developed a set of laws of communication. The first law is that 'communication fails—except by chance'. Wiio then added four corollaries to his first law: (a) 'if communication can fail—it will; (b) if communication cannot fail—it usually fails; (c) if communication seems to succeed in the way which was intended, it must be in a way which was not intended; and (d) if you are satisfied that your communication is bound to succeed, then the communication is bound to fail'. Wiio admits these assertions are exaggerated and at times paradoxical, but they reflect his own frustrating experiences of communication in organisations.

Communication between people, however, need not fail if it is characterised by openness, honest disclosure and trust—attributes closely associated with source credibility. On the other hand, breakdowns in communication are often the result of shadow-side effects. Whilst good interpersonal relationships are based on trust, honesty and open communication, they are weakened when the people involved act and communicate predominantly in deceptive, secretive and untrustworthy ways.

To ensure that people communicate openly and trust each other, it is important for communication managers to concentrate their efforts on building a positive organisational climate. How this can best be achieved is the subject of the next section. It also considers the concept of 'organisational climate' and the factors that contribute to a positive organisational climate.

Building a Positive Organisational Climate 9.7

The term 'organisational climate' is drawn from the meteorological term for weather. When we say such things as 'What's the climate like in California?', we probably mean 'How cold does it get in winter?' or 'Is there more rain than sunshine in summer?' So, just as Chicago is known as the 'windy city', or Queensland as the 'sunshine state', organisations may be described in terms of their climates or weather conditions. However, the rainfall, temperature or humidity in any part of the world can be measured fairly accurately by standard instruments and gauges, but an organisation's climate is somewhat more difficult to measure, partly because the assessment is subjective.

Timm and Peterson (1982) describe 'organisational climate' as 'the ways in which organisation managers define (and the objectives that reveal those definitions) the plans and objectives of the organisation (what we have referred to as policies), (2) how they believe an organisation should be managed, and (3) how they regard the people working in the organisation' (p. 301). Their definition suggests that an organisational climate is primarily influenced by its planning, its managerial philosophies, and the personal perceptions of its leaders.

An alternative way of conceptualising an organisational climate is to see it as the synthesis of the perceptions of all its individual members. These perceptions would concern issues such as working conditions or 'atmosphere', the system's mission and goals, and management style and philosophy. This understanding of 'organisational climate' differs from that of Timm and Peterson (1982) in its separation of the organisation's management practices and policies from its members' perceptions of them.

Redding (1972) suggests that organisational climate is influenced by five interdependent factors: (1) the extent to which management supports the efforts of subordinates; (2) the amount of participative decision-making in the system; (3) the degree to which employees trust management; (4) the freedom to communicate openly; and (5) the organisation's emphasis on high performance goals. Ideally, therefore, strong organisational climates are characterised by high levels of trust, confidence, and credibility, participative decision-making, supportiveness, openness in communication, and by a genuine commitment to achieving high performance goals. There appears to be some consensus that the single most important ingredient of good organisational climate is trust among organisational members (Timm and Peterson, 1982:105).

Freedom to communicate openly is also very important for the establishment and maintenance of good organisational climate. In this connection, there are two highly recommended working principles. First, wherever possible, there should be openness in **downward communication.** This means that except for security reasons, employees should have ready access to any information relating to their immediate tasks or to the work of others in the system. Lack of access creates a climate of uncertainty and mistrust. The second working principle for the freedom to communicate openly is that listening should occur in **upward communication.** In simple terms, managers should listen to those they supervise. Staff members' ideas and suggestions about organisational problems and issues are often useful, and when managers listen to their staff members they are in a better position to understand their needs and motivations. Managers who are good listeners invariably score winning points with their staff members.

downward communication
The practice of superiors initiating communication with staff members.

upward communication
Opportunities for staff members to communicate freely with their superiors.

Competent managers are good listeners

The freedom to communicate openly discourages reliance on grapevines, rumours, informal networks, or shadow-side communication tactics. It cannot be emphasised enough that both the sharing of information and the sharing of individuals' reactions to information are critical to the development of mutual understanding and reciprocity between people in systems. Ultimately, mutual understanding provides a sound basis for people trusting and supporting each other.

Summary 9.8

In this chapter we revisited the concept of 'communication manager'. We noted that communication managers in systems are effective when they can perform key roles such as information-sharer, helper, quality controller, mentor, and leader. These roles, moreover, are especially apparent in specific kinds of applied managerial contexts such as interviewing or the conduct of meetings.

This chapter also examined understanding and managing arationality in the shadow side of organisational communication. Since arationality can cause failure in communication, we considered ways of preventing this, and ways of building a positive organisational climate, and noted the paramount importance of developing trust and openness in organisational communication.

Chapter 10 focuses on how we, as individual members of human systems, can develop into competent self-managers who continue to learn, develop and refine our communication skills and understandings. Ideally, this learning is characterised by the ability to operate autonomously and by the desire to understand the bases for developing and improving our relationships and communication with others at work and elsewhere.

9.9 Discussion Questions

1. Think of any experience you have had as an interviewee. Was the interviewing process effective or ineffective? Why? Could anything have been done differently?

2. Recall a meeting you have attended—for example, a meeting of your body corporate, the district progress association, your local PTA meeting or a council meeting. What kinds of communication management roles were performed at that meeting? What effect did they have on the meeting?

3. Name some 'positive politics' communication managers can identify and practise to promote 'institution-enhancing agendas'. Could you apply any of these positive politics to any work or social system you are associated with?

4. What previous assumptions about communication management competence would you 'challenge' now that you have read this chapter? Why is it important to keep challenging your own assumptions about the ways in which you communicate with others?

5. Why does communication between people fail? List as many reasons as you can. Suggest some positive ways communication managers could prevent communication breakdown.

6. Can managers be effective without developing communication competence? Support your answer and then discuss it with someone else who has studied the chapter.

9.10 Activities

1. Make a personal action plan for how you could continue to improve your effectiveness as a communication manager in your place of work or in some voluntary organisation role. Focus on specific goals and evaluate these later when you have had a chance to put your plan into

practice. For example, you might concentrate on developing your skill in what Egan terms 'innovation-focused dialogue'. When you have carried out your plan, evaluate it with a trusted colleague or friend who may be able to give you other useful suggestions for your personal and professional development as a communication manager.

2. Negotiate with your supervisor (or a colleague whom you respect) an opportunity for you to experience a transformational performance appraisal. This could be an 'unofficial' appraisal of you by your colleague, and it should be kept confidential. Compare this appraisal with any formal performance appraisal required of you as part of your normal work. What differences, if any, were there between the official and the unofficial performance reviews? Are there any lessons to be learned for making official performance appraisals more worthwhile and productive?

Key Terms 9.11

Arationality

Bennis's First Law of Academic Pseudodynamics

Communication failure

Downward communication

Empowerment

Helping role of communication managers

Information sharer role of communication managers

Interdependence

Interviewing

Leadership role of communication managers

Mentor role of communication managers

Quality controller or organiser role of communication managers

Transformational performance appraisal

Upward communication

Recommended Reading 9.12

Downs, C. W., Smeyak, G.P. and Martin, E. (1980) *Professional interviewing*, New York: Harper & Row.

Egan, G. (1993) *Adding value: a systematic guide to business-driven management and leadership*, San Francisco: Jossey-Bass.

Stewart, C. J. and Cash, W. B. Jr. (1988) *Interviewing principles and practices*, 5th edn, Iowa: William C. Brown.

Timm, P. R. (1987) *Successful self-management: a psychologically sound approach to personal effectiveness*, California: Crisp.

Timm, P. R. and Peterson, B. D. (1982) *People at work: human relations in organizations*, St. Paul: West.

Personal Effectiveness in Communication 10

Let us permit nature to have her way: she understands her business better than we do.

Michel de Montaigne (1533–1592)

People have one thing in common: they are all different.

Robert Zend

The purpose of learning is growth, and our minds, unlike our bodies,can continue growing as long as we live.

Mortimer Adler

Life can only be understood backwards; but it must be lived forwards.

Soren Kierkegaard (1813–1855)

How important are our needs for personal development in communication competence? What do we need to be able to do when we confront critical points in our lifetimes? Is 'mid-life crisis' too difficult to cope with? All of us, at some stage or other in our lives, will be asking ourselves these questions. As we think about these things, we will remind ourselves that we are not simply creatures of work. We are also 'complete beings' who need to adjust our communication with others when we try to resolve our life crises. This chapter concerns these issues and the nature of human relationships. It deals with how we can become better communicators in our continually evolving and expanding range of interpersonal relationships as we grow and develop. It reflects on how our social and personal cultures influence the ways we develop personally in the human systems to which we belong. It explores how the concepts of 'psychosocial crisis', 'developmental task' and 'self-actualisation' relate to our personal development needs as communicators. The chapter concludes with some practical suggestions on how our personal development in communication can be enhanced.

Learning Objectives

After you have studied the ideas, arguments and suggestions presented in this chapter, you should be able to do the following:

- Provide at least two examples of how people's personal development and needs complement their professional development and needs.

- State three practical considerations we should keep in mind for developing and maintaining good relationships with others.

- Give two or three examples of how our personal and social cultures can influence our development of communication competence.

- Define the terms 'psychosocial crisis', 'developmental task' and 'self-actualisation', and provide an example for each.

- Identify one specific psychosocial crisis and one developmental task each of us must deal with during our lifetime and suggest how these challenges influence the way we communicate with others .

- Describe two practical lifelong learning strategies that can enhance our personal development as communicators .

10.1 The Nature of Human Relationships and Needs

Human relationships differ according to the settings in which they form and develop. Although many people become friends as a result of frequent, close contact in their organisations, most professional or working relationships are to some degree formal. This formality appears to become more pronounced as people move up in their organisational hierarchies. Those who reach the upper echelons spend much of their working time relating to others in formal board or committee meetings.

Depending on the culture and climate of their organisation, people's relationships vary in terms of the amount of trust and honesty they share. Organisations that promote such values as diligence, commitment, quality service, and fairness do much to help people realise career and job satisfaction. Corporate values like these are also usually expressed by practices which indicate that individual members are valued and should be rewarded for their contributions. Such practices may include career-path planning and development opportunities, recognition of initiative and of creative output and innovation, and the provision of continuous challenges to conscientious, energetic workers.

In positive organisational climates people's relationships tend to reflect the high value accorded to co-operation. This is not invariably the case, however, as some people are driven by personal ambition so that colleagues are seen as potential rivals. When climbing the corporate ladder becomes the main aim of people in systems, their behaviour toward their workmates may become adversarial, even deceitful. For example, they may refrain from saying what they really mean for fear of having this used to someone else's advantage.

People sometimes come up with new, exciting ideas that are given a lukewarm reception by superiors who subsequently claim them as their own. Another adversarial communication practice in organisations with large pyramidal bureaucracies is for immediate superiors to insist that subordinates have no formal contact with other senior staff—for example, all correspondence with senior staff must be cleared and forwarded by their line manager. When this happens, rank-and-file staff members are rarely brought to the attention of senior employing staff because any new ideas seem to come from section heads.

It is evident, therefore, that while people are at work, personal effectiveness in communication may be judged by how people succeed in their relationships with others. Part of this success depends on their ability to manage the shadow side of the communication of superiors and colleagues whose actions are often covert and governed by self-interest. Thus, in one sense, effective communication may mean being able to outsmart or hoodwink one's boss; for example when staff members make unrealistic demands of their superiors and then make the smaller demands which they intended in the first place, so that it seems unreasonable for the superiors to refuse.

However, people's competence in communicating does not depend on deception, which ultimately damages relationships. Deceivers are seldom concerned when relationships with those whom they are deceiving break down because they see relationships in terms of conflict. They satisfy personal goals at the expense of those they deceive.

The need to develop, maintain and strengthen both personal and professional relationships arises from other kinds of needs. These range from the physiological—sexual desire, hunger or thirst—to the desire to be liked or to be with someone we like, the need to create, the urge to communicate our creativity, and the need to be recognised for our achievements. Maslow (1970) suggested a hierarchy of needs in which lower-order needs like the need for food are called 'prepotent'. Until prepotent needs are satisfied, other needs in the hierarchy are not important. For example, someone who is craving sleep does not want to be aesthetic or creatively expressive.

People need others for a variety of reasons, depending on circumstances. At the most basic level, they depend on others for their livelihood. Employers provide employees with the means of sustaining themselves and their families. People also want to develop close, even intimate relationships with others they associate with daily. To this extent, the workplace is a potential source of both personal and professional need fulfilment. How well people communicate with others is a good indicator of whether intrapersonal and interpersonal needs are being met.

Whilst it is difficult to imagine anyone who is in no way dependent on others, some people give the impression that others matter very little to them. Usually, people who give this impression have trouble in establishing anything more than superficial acquaintanceships with fellow workers or neighbours. Their conversation is usually task-oriented and seldom candid.

The next section looks at how people can develop good personal relationships, particularly at their places of work. It also considers what practical part we can play in developing our own communication competence to enhance our relationships with others. This practical analysis should provide a basis for sound, mature reflection on our present relationships with others.

Developing Personal Relationships 10.2

Perhaps the most important determinant of personal relationships is the extent to which we care about our association with others. This applies to all kinds of relationships: intimate, personal, professional, formal, informal, long-term or short-term. Often this attribute of 'caring' derives from a more general value: that people are worth caring about. People who treat all others with respect are generally the kind who form good relationships of all kinds.

In their book *The One Minute Manager*, Kenneth Blanchard and Spencer Johnson (1984) suggested that the best minute managers can spend is the one minute they invest in people. One thing managers can do to make more time for the people they manage is to delegate more work. By freeing themselves of their war with paper, they can devote more time to developing good working relationships with their staff. However, some managers prefer not to take the risk of delegating important tasks. When this happens, employees may perceive them as remote and task-oriented rather than person-oriented.

As we noted earlier, person-oriented managers tend to spend a lot of their time in managing by walking about (MBWA), and are better informed about how each of their staff thinks and feels. If there is a powerful shadow side in their systems, MBWA managers are likely to learn how to counteract its effects. They can increase their understanding of the shadow side by spending time with colleagues in lunchrooms, staff lounges, coffee shops and other recreational places.

Spending time with fellow workers, therefore, indicates that people care about their relationships with others at work. A caring attitude, however, must be complemented by other qualities. For example, they must know what kind of relationships they should develop with professional colleagues, peers, subordinates or superiors. Furthermore, good professional relationships permit people to feel comfortable in their dialogue. When they know what level and type of relationship to have with others, people are less uncertain about protocol and the correct way to conduct themselves.

Sometimes organisations undergoing change do not have a clearly defined culture. In such circumstances, their members are not always sure of appropriate ways to act and communicate. For example, in Australia, when new universities were formed through the amalgamation of former teachers' colleges and other advanced education institutions, many lecturers seemed to have no idea of how to address the senior staff. Junior staff from the new faculties addressed even the vice-chancellors (the chief executive officers) by their first names when they met for the first time.

One reason for this may be the difference between the culture of universities and the culture of former colleges of advanced education. Most of the pre-amalgamated institutions like teachers' colleges had an egalitarian culture in which a senior member of staff was considered first among equals, so it was quite proper to call senior executive staff by their first name. Some kept up this practice in the new university culture even though titles like 'Vice-Chancellor', 'Professor' or 'Doctor' are expected in most university circles. Perhaps this is more typical of Australia than of other Westernised countries. In America, for instance, senior university staff are usually addressed as 'Dean', 'President' and so on.

The use or neglect of titles for very senior staff affects professional relationships. Clearly, when people communicate on a first-name basis, their relationship is less formal. As a general rule, it is wise to use titles with superiors until one is invited to do otherwise; the initiative should come from the senior person.

Another factor in developing effective interpersonal relationships is knowing how much of oneself to disclose. In one sense, all human relationships may be classified in terms of their degree of mutual disclosure; the more there is, the more intimate the relationship becomes. When a professional relationship becomes intimate, as in an affair, complications can develop. If one of the lovers wishes to end the affair, maintaining a workable professional relationship can be difficult.

When professional relationships become too intimate, complications may occur

When self-disclosure in a relationship is not mutual but one-sided, revelations by one may be used by the other for political advantage; for example it may be leaked to those in authority and power. Such professional relationships are, in a sense, adversarial. In such cases it would appear that the self-disclosing individual is naive, and unaware that words spoken in confidence are being used to the other person's benefit and advantage. It is important, therefore, to know how trustworthy a listener is, and when *not* to be candid.

A final point about developing personal relationships is that people must want to get on well with others. Whilst this may seem obvious, some organisation leaders seem to believe that life at the top should be lonely and that efforts to understand their staff members are not only unnecessary, but may be construed as weakness and an inability to command. Those who give little thought to relating well to their staff will probably take little trouble to do so. Conversely, those who value getting on well with others usually work hard at their professional relationships.

In the next section we turn to how 'culture' can affect our ability to communicate well with others. Here the distinction between individual and corporate or organisational culture is significant. The implications for developing communicator competence are also considered, especially as our individual cultures greatly influence our communication with others and our control over our social environments.

10.3 The Culture of Individuals and Society

The concept of 'culture' is not clear-cut. For example, some people equate culture with urbanity and refined behaviour and manners—they refer to others who are polite, well educated and generally sophisticated as 'cultured'. This popular view of the 'cultured person', however, is a stereotype and fails to take into account cross-cultural differences; a person perceived as 'cultured' in one society may be regarded as boorish in another.

Different greeting rituals are a good example. The French exchange kisses on both cheeks; eskimos rub noses; Orientals bow to each other, and English-speaking people usually shake hands. Whilst people from one society may acknowledge cultural differences in greetings, they are less likely to tolerate others of their own culture not conforming to the social norms of communicating and behaving.

Traditionally, 'culture' has referred to the attitudes, beliefs, values, norms, rules, principles, ideals, taboos and mores which govern the way people as individuals or in groups communicate and act. This means that 'culture' can be thought of as belonging to individuals or to groups or communities. Individuals sometimes have certain values, principles and ideals, for example, which differ from those of the collective majority. If an individual's values are at extreme variance with those generally held by the group or community, he or she may be labelled a 'radical', 'rebel', 'iconoclast' or 'rugged individualist' by the rest of their group.

Of course, in any community, there may be several cultural subgroups with different value systems and rules of behaviour. For example, in Australia defiance of parental authority is more often tolerated by Anglo communities than by Asian, Greek or Italian groups. Similarly, the extent to which religion, education, family life, women's rights, or socioeconomic status is valued varies considerably from one cultural group to another. When people operating from different, even opposing, cultural frameworks work closely together as professionals, their amicability at work depends on their ability to understand and tolerate cultural differences, and their willingness to learn from others and, if necessary, to modify their ways of thinking and feeling.

Some societies have an indeterminate sense of cultural identity. In Australia, for example, it would be difficult to list a set of common cultural values. Although most Australian citizens would probably espouse broad values such as 'justice', there may well be subcultural differences over values such as 'the right to work', for example.

Since many successful organisations today owe their success to the interdependence of their members, it seems reasonable to assume that these organisations encourage members to share certain values. Often this is done by creating a strong mission statement. In many Japanese companies 'total quality control' has shifted from special quality control departments to all staff (Goldman, 1992). This shift contrasts with traditional Western work practices and has been summed up in the following way:

> . . . while Japanese group behaviour, and the deeply ingrained principle of *amae* or mutual dependency (or interdependency) is in harmony with the shared responsibility for quality, Western principles of individuality, specialization, territoriality and proxemics, and fragmentation were almost insurmountable obstacles to TQC management theory . . . quality was no longer a staff function, it was delegated as a line function. (Goldman, 1992: 18)

By contrast, organisations whose staff hold opposing values are less likely to develop such interdependence. Within any system, therefore, a sense of cultural identity is often seen in the way individuals communicate with and relate to each other. When people in systems begin to operate as a team, they usually enhance quality (Deming, 1982). Fairhurst (1993) has suggested, however, that repeated references to 'quality' and 'total quality management' have reduced the term to a popular buzzword. When 'quality' becomes taken for granted, moreover, genuine gaps in quality control or assurance may be overlooked (Fairhurst and Wendt, 1993).

Two types of culture can exist within organisations: overt and covert. The overt culture is generally observable. For example, it is relatively easy to conclude whether the culture of a city department store places high value on customer service. Are customers being courteously attended to by staff? Do the customers look satisfied while browsing through merchandise? Or do they seem frustrated because they cannot find help and advice?

There are other ways by which people can size up the overt culture of an organisation. For example, do its members seem happy with what they are doing? Do they treat one another courteously? Do they show pride and care in their work? Do they enjoy spending their recreation time at work in the company of others or do they prefer to spend this time alone? When a staff member needs help, are colleagues quick to rally around and offer practical support? No doubt, there are many other similar questions to ask.

The covert culture of an organisation is more difficult to identify. Here things tend to happen behind the scenes, without everyone being aware of what is being said or going on. Moreover, the communication and activities contributing to the covert culture or shadow side are often unpredictable. Many industrial conflicts have resulted in plant shutdowns, mass walkouts and strikes. Such direct action takes place often because a group of union or employee representatives and management have failed to negotiate a satisfactory agreement. Most of the people who are affected by a decision to strike or close down operations have been kept ignorant of negotiations. When there has been no concerted attempt by shadow-side operators to consult workers, such negotiations effectively form part of the organisation's covert culture. It is from this covert culture that organisational change or resistance to it may result.

The covert culture or shadow side of an organisation includes informal aspects of communication and activity amongst certain members. Here, personal communication effectiveness involves understanding and dealing with the shadow side. Effective communicators in organisations know what is going on and even what is about to or likely to happen. They are effective because they are in a position to make strategic choices about how to behave towards and communicate with others. In other words, the basis of their actions and communication is very much informed, and they develop communication strategies based on reality, not idealised or wished-for scenarios.

It may be argued that some human systems or organisations, like schools, are microcosms of society because they are concerned with the development of the 'whole person'. If this is true, we would expect them to reflect and apply the social values of their society. We might also assume that people in those systems communicate there much as they do in society generally.

In reality, however, few systems are microcosms of the wider community or society; most are specialised societies with their own peculiar organisational cultures. Prisons, for example, are totally unlike the outside world. Hospitals are concerned with the healing and rehabilitation of the sick, and the specialised communication between doctors, nurses and patients cannot by any stretch of the imagination be seen as typical of communication in general. Thus, the culture of a particular system greatly determines the type of communication that takes place among its members.

The concept of 'culture', like 'climate', provides a context for explaining why people communicate as they do in certain kinds of organisations. Personal effectiveness in communication, therefore, presupposes the necessity for people to understand fully the subtleties of the organisational context or environment in which they act and communicate. As emphasised earlier, effective communicators appreciate that communication must be appropriate to their particular situation. Understanding the situation, therefore, helps people to make sure their communication with others is appropriate.

The next section considers some of the critical times in our lives when our communication with others may be seriously affected for personal reasons. To an extent, these critical times represent stages in our development from childhood through adulthood, and we will concentrate on the critical stages adults face in the course of their working lives.

10.4 Psychosocial Crises in Human Development

For most people, critical events during their adult years include courtship and marriage, the birth of children, purchasing a home, and career promotions. When these events occur successfully (i.e. the outcome is the desired one) people are usually regarded as being 'well balanced' or 'adjusted', but when things go wrong their ability to cope is brought into question. Personal effectiveness in communication depends to some degree on our ability to adjust when things don't happen the way we would like them to.

Most of us can think of times when we felt that our world was 'caving in'. We thought we were in love with someone only to find that our love was no longer reciprocated. Our marriage, which started so promisingly, turned sour and became something tantamount to torture or incarceration. Some of us have grieved when loved ones or close friends have died or suffered. At some time or another we have experienced the disappointment of missing out on a job we applied for, or of being passed over for promotion. In all these situations we have had to adjust in order to be able to continue to communicate effectively with and act suitably toward others.

Of the various kinds of crises people face in their lifetimes, among the more significant are what the noted psychologist Eric Erikson (1969) termed 'psychosocial crises'. He also suggested that these periods of crisis could be thought of as the 'eight ages of man [sic]'. The crises relate to a person's development and image of self. They are called 'psychosocial' crises because they affect not only how we see ourselves but also how we see ourselves in relation to others. These images of self, in turn, influence how we perceive and communicate with others at the critical time. Our images of self, moreover, are at the very core of our potential to be good adult communication managers.

Among the popular ways of describing one of the most common psychosocial crises is the term 'identity crisis'. It has a close link with the familiar 'mid-life crisis' since most people take stock of their achievements and failures about the time they turn 40. Erikson has suggested that at this mid-life point we tend to assess ourselves in terms of the dichotomy between 'ego-integrity' and 'despair'. 'Integrated' people have 'got their acts together'. They have acccomplished what they set out to do, in terms of tasks and career goals and especially in terms of personal goals and development. They can look back on their lives without regret or longing for new opportunities to achieve what they would have liked to achieve. On the other hand, some people continue to search for an image of the kind of person they would like to have been; for some reason or other they have failed to live up to some ideal image of self. For such people 'the time is now short, too short for the attempt to start another life and to try out alternate roads to integrity' (Erikson, 1969: 260).

The temptation to feel sorry for oneself can be fairly strong when, at relevant psychosocial crisis points, people reflect on their failure to achieve their goals. Effective communicators resist lapsing into self-pity by reminding themselves that not all personal goals are attainable with - out support from others with power or authority. In nepotistic organisations, for example, opportunities for recognition and reward are often rarer than in organisations that abide by equal opportunity principles. The omission of the names of talented individuals from succession plans may not be any fault of theirs, but due to myopic, misguided, biased superiors. Hence their failure to achieve what they have aspired to may in no way reflect on their potential to succeed.

Resisting the temptation to self-pity and helplessness is only part of what effective communicators may do at crisis points in their life. Another tactic is to subject one's private and professional goals to some form of reality-testing. By this means we may discover that our expectations of ourselves were too tough. This process enables people to re-examine their goals and aspirations so that new, more attainable targets are set for the future. Note that the reality-testing process begins in childhood. Throughout their school years, children often experience inner conflict—between the motive to succeed and the motive to avoid failure. An example is the high school student who must decide between an advanced stream subject, thus running the risk of failure, and a lower-level subject with a higher chance of success.

People who remain 'altogether' in times of disappointment or disillusionment are those who do not let personal crises destroy their sense of self-worth. Effective communicators can rise above adverse circumstances and continue to communicate with dignity and self-control. People who are unable to adapt or accept the need for inner change tend to develop a poor image of themselves which can affect their relationships with others, especially those who seem successful at achieving their personal goals.

Sometimes specific events can trigger off a crisis episode—for example, the reunion of a high school graduating class of 25 years ago. Although people are ostensibly pleased with the opportunity to find out what former classmates have been doing over the 25 years, there is still the temptation to ask oneself 'Have I done as well as the rest ?' When people force themselves into comparisons with others, they run the risk of feeling inadequate. It is healthier to assess our progress toward our own goals than to compare it with others' achievements. Effective communicators are those who remain true to themselves instead of trying to keep up with the achievements of others.

Closely associated with our ability to handle personal crisis points is our ability to take on the challenges and tasks of each stage of our development. The next section examines some of those tasks and various stages, and suggests that the successful undertaking of these tasks results in a sense of fulfilment and satisfaction.

10.5 Developmental Tasks and Self-actualisation

As people progress through life, they are confronted with certain 'human development tasks'. If they carry out these tasks successfully, they are likely to find their lives satisfying and rewarding, but if they fail they usually feel frustrated and inadequate. Robert Havighurst, the noted social scientist who coined the term 'developmental task', believed that at every stage of human development people had to become 'competent' in certain tasks to achieve happiness. Thus, a developmental task 'arises at or about a certain point in the life of the individual, successful achievement of which leads to his happiness and success with later tasks, while failure leads to unhappiness in the individual, disapproval by society, and difficulty with later tasks' (Havighurst, 1953:2).

Havighurst's notion of developmental task probably applies best to adolescence since the list of tasks for this stage of human development appears to be more fully articulated than for other stages. Some of the tasks for adolescents overlap with early adulthood. For example, 'preparing for marriage and family life' and 'selecting and preparing for an occupation' apply to many young adults of today, especially since the latter may extend to years of postgraduate study.

The notion of 'stages of human development' is a little imprecise, partly because the beginning and final limits of each stage are arbitrary and partly because human development is more of a lifelong process than a set of discrete stages. Nevertheless, it is a useful way to mark the critical times of challenge and change in people's lifetimes. For this reason, we could also argue that the notion of developmental tasks may be usefully linked with challenges arising from the advent of psychosocial crises.

One of the problems with associating tasks with stages of human development is that the categorisation of tasks inevitably reflects contemporary values that are not necessarily relevant to people's future roles and expectations. For example, several decades ago it was a social expectation in some circles that women would not need to be income earners once they were married, certainly not once they became parents. In general, men were expected to pursue careers while women maintained the households. The developmental tasks for women 50 years ago, therefore, were different from those of women of today.

Over the years, major changes have occurred within families as human systems. One trend is for men to take paternity leave and look after young children while women return to the workforce; another is for unmarried people to live together; another is to marry but not have children. Again, the greater tolerance of homosexuality by contemporary society has led to a set of totally different expectations about lifestyles and personal relationships. The tasks associated with these changes vary significantly from one person to another depending upon the kind of lives they want to lead.

Drawing on the collective wisdom of several scholars on human development, Cross (1983:174–75) described the 'life-cycle phases' of adults from the time they leave home (ages 18–22) to the time they look back over their lives (65+). At each phase, certain 'psychic tasks' were related to 'marker events'. Examples of psychic tasks are 'establish autonomy and independence from family', 'develop capacity for intimacy' and 'confront mortality'. Marker events in adulthood include leaving home, selecting a mate, establishing children in school, separation, divorce, death of spouse, retirement and physical decline. Summary descriptions of the life-cycle phases of adults are provided in Table 10.1.

TABLE 10.1 *The life-cycle phases of adults*

Phase and age	Marker events	Psychic tasks	Characteristic stance
Leaving home 18–22	Leave home Establish new living arrangements Enter college Start first full-time job Select mate	Establish autonomy and independence from family Define identity Define sex role Establish new peer alliances	A balance between 'being in' and 'moving out' of the family
Moving into adult world 23–28	Marry Establish home Become parent Get hired/fired/quit job Enter into community activities	Regard self as adult Develop capacity for intimacy Fashion initial life structure Build the dream Find a mentor	'Doing what one should' Living and building for the future Launched as an adult
Search for stability 29–34	Establish children in school Progress in career or consider change Possible separation, divorce, remarriage Possible return to school	Reappraise relationships Reexamine life structure and present commitments Strive for success Search for stability, security, control	'What is this life all about now that I am doing what I am supposed to?' Concern for order and stability and with 'making it' Desire to set long-range goals and meet them
Becoming one's own person 37–42	Crucial promotion Break with mentor Responsibility for three-generation family; i.e. growing children and ageing parents For women: empty nest; enter career and education	Face reality Confront mortality; sense of ageing Prune dependent ties to boss, spouse, mentor Reassess marriage Reassess personal priorities and values	Suspended animation More nurturing stance for men; more assertive stance for women 'Have I done the right thing? Is there time to change?'
Settling down 45–55	Cap career Become mentor Launch children; become grandparents New interests and hobbies Physical limitations; menopause Active participation in community events	Increase feelings of self-awareness and competence Re-establish family relationships Enjoy one's choices and lifestyle Reexamine the fit between life structure and self	'It is perhaps late, but there are things I would like to do in the last half of my life' Best time of life
The mellowing 57–64	Possible loss of mate Health problems Preparation for retirement	Accomplish goals in the time left to live Accept and adjust to ageing process	Mellowing of feelings and relationships Spouse increasingly important Greater comfort with self
Life review 65 +	Retirement Physical decline Change in finances New living arrangements Death of friends/spouse Major shift in daily routine	Search for integrity versus despair Acceptance of self Disengagement Rehearsal for death of spouse	Review of accomplishments Eagerness to share everyday human joys and sorrows Family is important Death is a new presence

Source: Cross, K. P. (1983) *Adults as Learners: Increasing Participation and Facilitating Learning*, San Francisco: Jossey-Bass, pp. 174–75. Reprinted by permission.

With the reappraisal of individual value-systems at each life-cycle phase, people will undoubtedly change their perceptions of their social and professional worlds. These new perceptions will, in turn, change how they communicate with and relate to others. Effective communicators are those who address psychic tasks constructively so that they learn and 'grow' from the experience and develop greater expertise in communicating personally. Those who cannot come to terms with marker events and related psychic tasks are likely to continue to communicate as though no significant changes are taking place. Ineffective communicators, therefore, through their inability or unwillingness to address the challenges of adulthood, are often described as 'not having grown up'.

Adults who have 'grown up' at each critical point in their development can be said to have *self-actualised*, a term used by Maslow (1970) to denote the highest level on the hierarchy of human needs. It suggests that people have achieved what they set out to achieve and become what they set out to become. Self-actualised people are complete, 'integrated' human beings. They are at one with themselves and they have come to understand and control their worlds, including their interpersonal worlds. In short, they have developed, at succeeding stages of their development, increasing levels of 'communicator competence' (Parks, 1985).

As people reach critical stages in their adult lifetimes, their experience in dealing with their emotions and their self-appraisals should be, ideally, a valuable form of learning. With each learning experience, adults should become wiser and all the more able to manage and learn from new crises. Thus, self-actualisation depends, among other things, on our capacity and enthusiasm for 'learning to learn'. When faced with critical moments, competent communication managers learn from their present experiences how to communicate better in future. Good communication management, therefore, rests on the assumption that those who are sensitive to their own strengths and weaknesses in relating to others can improve their communication by putting their present abilities to the test in times of personal crisis.

The following section considers some practical strategies people can use to enhance their ability in communication. Some of these strategies have been briefly alluded to in earlier sections. The emphasis now is on how people can take the initiative in changing themselves so that they can communicate more appropriately with others in a greater range of human systems.

Strategies for Personal Development   10.6

So far we have considered, in relation to influences on personal development in adulthood, some specific strategies for improving communication effectiveness. It is now the time to review in broad terms practical ways to refine our competence in communication management. By becoming more competent in managing their communication with others, people can contribute significantly to their personal development and growth in adulthood.

Since communication, like breathing, is an inevitable part of being alive, the first step in developing a strategy for effective personal development is to ensure that any human activity involving one's self and its relationship to others is conceptualised from an adult communication management perspective. This applied theoretical perspective is a synthesis of the constructivist, the people-in-systems, and the competence contributing perspectives (Kaye, 1994). Some of the key questions to ask at any significant point in one's life, to assess the effectiveness of one's communication, are: 'Am I understanding others in the ways they intend me to understand them?', 'Am I being understood by others in the ways I intend them to understand me?' and 'Are these the appropriate ways for me to communicate with and relate to others in these kinds of specific situations?'

In some respects, these three questions subsume other, more specific, questions people might ask themselves when appraising their effectiveness as communicators. One such specific question might be: 'If I am not handling my present crisis too well, is it affecting my communication and relationship with significant people in my life?' Assuming the answer is 'yes', we could then ask: 'What can I do to restore the good communication I had with those who are important to me?'

One of the great stumbling-blocks to effective personal development as an adult communication manager is the tendency for those with considerable professional responsibilities to become workaholics. These people become excessively task-oriented, often to the cost of their development as integrated human beings. Sometimes becoming a workaholic is due to being poorly organised, especially with time management; such workaholics have to work long hours to meet deadlines. In any event, the neglect of their personal development is usually evident in the deterioration of their physical fitness, emotional stability, and growth in spirituality. There is, instead, an intense concentration on mental activity or time-consuming routine work.

Integrated people have balanced lives; their spiritual, mental and physical selves are in harmony. This harmony and balance is reflected in integrated, balanced communication. In other words, the communication of integrated people is a balanced blend of thinking, feeling, action and awareness; they can communicate emotionally, rationally, or nonverbally, and are less likely to have frequent emotional outbursts or operate in a seemingly unfeeling fashion. Balanced people can operate with feelings, reasoning or action as the occasion requires.

What are some practical ways of maintaining balanced communication? One thing which people can do before communicating with others is to ask themselves: 'How will my future communication and relationship with this person be affected if I proceed to communicate as I intend to now?' This question could be simplified: 'Think before you speak' or 'Look before you leap'. People communicate, however, not only through speech but through action. In general terms, therefore, people should not commit themselves to any speech or action that could damage a relationship without first weighing up the consequences.

A second practical suggestion is to learn from one's mistakes in communicating with another, and thus avoid repeating them. It is important to think back on how well or how poorly we managed communication with someone else. Ineffective communicators not only blunder in ways they later regret but continue to blunder because they have not learned from experience to control themselves and their social environments.

Personal effectiveness in communicating is not developed only from our own efforts and resources. Sensitive and perceptive people can learn a good deal by observing highly competent role models. Such observation reinforces and complements what we can learn from reading about ways of communicating effectively with others.

The final practical suggestion concerns attitudes people should cultivate to refine their expertise in communication. Personally effective communicators always leave room to learn more, and never assume that there is nothing else for them to know or demonstrate. Since learning is a lifelong process, keeping open to new ideas and being willing to build upon existing strengths goes a long way toward helping people grow in their ability to be effective adult communication managers. Lifelong learners of this kind eventually become role models of good communication practice.

Summary 10.7

In this chapter we have considered how people can become more proficient in their communication and relationships with others. Such proficiency requires us to understand which factors, within and beyond ourselves, can profoundly affect our actions and communication management. These factors include the nature of the culture that permeates different kinds of human systems, the 'personal culture' of individuals, and the social values that influence organisational culture and communication practices.

Attention has also been given to internal factors such as psychosocial crises in human development and the developmental tasks confronting adults at critical points in their lives. It was suggested that addressing these tasks successfully would enable adults to experience self-actualisation, thus providing a basis for further growth and development. Finally, the chapter offered practical suggestions for refining our ability in adult communication management.

The next and final chapter looks to the future, and tries to balance a vision of what men and women of the next decade will be like as communicators, with a vision of some of the changes that are taking place and will occur in the next few years. It emphasises the need to understand, manage and forecast change. It concludes that constant striving to develop competence in adult communication management is something our society should strongly support. This effort will acquire greater depth and meaning once we acknowledge that the tip of the information iceberg reveals very little about the people with whom we want to communicate and relate to effectively.

10.8 Discussion Questions

1. Is it possible for us to be too informal or familiar with others in the workplace? If so, what are some of the likely consequences? How can we guard against giving others the impression that we are overly familiar?

2. List some examples from your own experience where your workplace satisfied your professional and personal needs. As you reflect on your list, ask yourself how human systems can help their members to fulfil their professional and personal needs.

3. In what ways can the culture of an organisation or system influence the productivity and quality of life of its members? Share your thoughts with a colleague at work or with someone who has also read this chapter.

4. How does the culture of an organisation or system relate to the effectiveness of communication among its members? Does this relationship have any bearing on their motivation to be productive and take initiatives?

5. Suggest some ways in which the interdependence of staff can be encouraged in organisations. When an organisation makes little or no effort to encourage its members' interdependence, what tends to happen? In particular, how does this affect their personal development?

6. How can people's inability to confront and resolve psychosocial crises affect their work performance and motivation? Discuss with a colleague or friend some approaches people could take to resolve those crises satisfactorily.

10.9 Activities

1. Construct an argument to support the claim that 'effective communicators are able to rise above negative circumstances and continue to communicate with dignity and self-control'. Now construct a counter-argument refuting this claim. Present both arguments to a non-involved person or group and ask them which argument is more persuasive. What reasons do they give for their choice?

2. Keep a record of all the people you communicate with over a week. From an adult communication management perspective, where was your communication most successful? Explain why. Now write down

how you could have improved your communication in other situations where you were not as effective as you think you could have been. Share your thoughts with a friend and solicit any other ideas you could build into your personal development plan for improving yourself as a communication manager.

Key Terms 10.10

Amae

Covert culture

Culture

Developmental task

Life-cycle phases of adults

Marker events

Overt culture

Personal development

Psychosocial crisis

Self-actualisation

Self-disclosure

Total quality control (TQC)

Workaholic

Recommended Reading 10.11

Cross, K. P. (1983) *Adults as learners: increasing participation and facilitating learning*, San Francisco: Jossey-Bass.

Glass, L. (1993) *He says, she says: closing the communication gap between the sexes*, Sydney: Bantam Books.

Plant, R. (1987) *Managing change and making it stick*, London: Fontana/Collins.

Timm, P. R. (1987) *Successful self-management: a psychologically sound approach to personal effectiveness*, California: Crisp.

PART IV

Future Development in Adult Communication Management

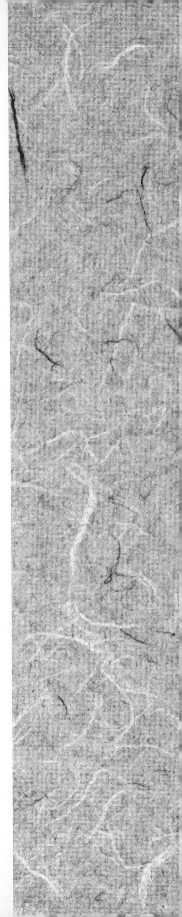

Adult Communication Management: Future Directions

Change is the new metaphysics of our age. Everything is in motion now.

Warren Bennis

The art of progress is to preserve order amid change
and to preserve change amid order.

Alfred North Whitehead

The philosophers have only interpreted the world:
the thing, however, is to change it.

Karl Marx (1818–1883)

The evolution of a culture is in fact a gigantic exercise in self-control.

B. F. Skinner

*C*an you imagine what the world will be like in a few years? Will people be any different? What lessons will they have learned from their predecessors? What skills will they need to cope with a changing world? The theme of this chapter is 'change'. It considers the argument that understanding the process of change and having the ability to manage it are critical to adult communication management competence. We will also come to appreciate the need for effective change agents to develop the capacity to forecast change, and realise that competent communication managers are people who can think strategically. Parallelling this ability to think strategically is the growing need for capable communication managers to find new and more profound ways of understanding the nature and intentions of the people they interact with. This chapter does not provide foolproof answers to such a complex question but highlights the need for more research to be done on how people can develop greater competence in person perception. It concludes with the message that despite the technological revolution of the workplace, competence in interpersonal communication is the very essence of effective adult communication management practice.

Learning Objectives

After you have studied the ideas, arguments and suggestions presented in this chapter you should be able to do the following:

- Construct an argument to support the claim that communication competence will continue to be important for people in the future to cultivate and develop.

- Suggest one or two ways in which the world in 2001AD may have changed and discuss how these changes might affect the practice of effective communication in the workplace.

- Indicate why it is important for facilitators of change not only to understand and manage the process of change but also to cultivate the ability to forecast the nature and direction of change.

- Explain why it will be important for communication managers of the future to develop more accurate and sensitive ways of interpreting the personalities and intentions of others.

- Defend the claim that regardless of the effects of new technologies on workplace communication and practices, 'people will still need people'.

11.1 Homo/Femina Sapiens: 2001 AD

Over the years, a few writers have tried to imagine what people of the future would be like. Aldous Huxley (1932) saw a 'brave new world' where men and women became dependent on the drug 'soma' and craved perpetual entertainment. George Orwell (1949) in his book *Nineteen Eighty-Four*, envisaged a world partitioned into three superpowers. The women and men of that world ceased to have any personal identity, living their lives in total subservience to the dictates of the state. Kurt Vonnegut (1969), in his classic work *Slaughterhouse-five or the children's crusade: a duty-dance with death*, foresaw the demise of civilisation as we have come to understand it, with the destruction of any literature considered subversive. The behaviourist psychologist B. F. Skinner argued that people could strive to become 'autonomous' but would inevitably fail because ultimately they would become slaves to environments or worlds of their own making (Skinner, 1973). Ayn Rand, a novelist and philosopher, saw a danger in people of the future renouncing reason and preferring a world where the thinking of intellectuals would no longer be valued (Rand, 1970).

These writers, in their individual ways, have presented somewhat pessimistic pictures of the future world of men and women. People were seen as marionettes, without minds of their own, manipulated by political and bureaucratic forces. Communication occurred through officially approved languages like 'doublespeak'. The very nature and form of communication, moreover, was shaped by social value systems and human emotions that discouraged personal growth and integration. In *1984*, for example, people lived in fear of running foul of the state. Social values were clearly spelt out in slogans such as 'ignorance is strength'.

It is perhaps easier to depict women and men of the future in these rather pessimistic ways. After all, how much have people of today learned from the mistakes of their forebears? There are still wars, other forms of violence, and crime. In many cities of the world it is unsafe to roam the streets. Intolerance toward and persecution of people of different ethnic or racial backgrounds are still prevalent. Gaps between the cultures of one generation and the next are deepening. Drugs have created a new set of values for some and a new approach to communication with others.

Amongst the most disillusioning examples are those of politicians and other leading public figures. Formerly heroes in our society, they are now perceived by many as fallen idols. Promises glibly made at election time are now seldom expected to be honoured during terms of office. To some, there appears to be one rule for citizens, and another for politicians and others from privileged sectors of society. For example, it seems that whilst most workers need to fight hard to maintain adequate salary levels, politicians, doctors and members of the legal profession can determine, within their own ranks, their own levels of remuneration.

Public figures and prominent identities who are found wanting in their actions and communication are undesirable role models for youth. The almost daily examples of greed, corruption, fraud, and sex scandals are rapidly becoming the norm. Evangelistic preachers with their rhetoric of love and hope continue to charm and captivate large unsuspecting audiences whilst accumulating vast financial empires and mind-bending power bases. Entrepreneurs and tycoons have squandered shareholders' money and betrayed their trust before going bankrupt. Bureaucrats and politicians have used taxpayers' money on extravagant lifestyles, with free first-class travel and luxury accommodation, chauffeured limousines, and generous retirement packages.

It may be useful, therefore, to present a vision not so much of what society in 2001 AD will be like, but rather of what it could be like if it took advantage of its accumulated wisdom, its lessons from history and experience, and its present and likely future resources. In 1970, Alvin Toffler took the world by storm with his book *Future Shock*. Toffler said that as a consequence of the industrial and technological revolutions, people were being confronted with an increasing diversity of lifestyles. In times of 'identity crisis', people could simply decide to change their patterns of existence. Thus, the unsuccessful business professional could opt to get out of the commercial world altogether and become a 'hippie'.

Although written over 20 years ago, *Future Shock* sought to provide a long-range insight into how people might live in the future. In essence, they would face the dilemma of 'overchoice'. As an example, Toffler suggests that the current system of higher or university education with its emphasis on standard courses, majors and degrees would disappear by the year 2000 AD. This claim was followed with the confident assertion that 'no two students will move along exactly the same educational track' (Toffler, 1970:249). Remember, this prediction is over 20 years old! Yet as we draw closer to the turn of the century, this trend is only just beginning. Although new fields of study continue to be explored, the standard course offerings are still very much in demand by contemporary students.

No doubt times will change, perhaps even in the direction predicted by Toffler, but the changes will come more slowly than first thought. This is particularly true of people, their values and the ways they communicate. One of the most compelling visions of what people of the future will be like has been that of Neil Postman in his powerful book *Amusing Ourselves to Death*. According to his vision, there are two ways by which 'the spirit of a culture may be shriveled. In the first—the Orwellian—culture becomes a prison. In the second—the Huxleyan—culture becomes a burlesque' (Postman, 1986:155).

Events of recent years have shown us that Orwell's vision of the future world as a prison has not eventuated. On the other hand, Huxley's prophecy that people of the future will want to learn and communicate in a world of amusement and entertainment appears to be coming true. Postman comments:

> Huxley teaches . . . that in the age of advanced technology, spiritual devastation is more likely to come from an enemy with a smiling face than from one whose countenance exudes suspicion and hate. In the Huxleyan prophecy, Big Brother does not watch us, by his choice. We watch him, by ours. There is no need for wardens or gates or Ministries of Truth. When a population becomes distracted by trivia,

when cultural life is redefined as a perpetual round of entertainments, when serious public conversation becomes a form of baby-talk, when, in short, a people become an audience and their public business a vaudeville act, then a nation finds itself at risk; culture-death is a clear possibility. (Postman, 1986: 155–56)

The men and women of tomorrow, therefore, will have their learning, thinking and communication shaped by 'technological distractions made possible by the electric plug' (Postman, 1986:156). Schoolchildren of today are, from an early age, exposed to a new language, a new culture, and a new ideology shaped by computers and television. As they grow up, much of what these children think, say and do is being shaped by those who control these new visual modes of public conversation. Part of the new ideology is premised on the belief that to every problem there is a solution and that solution can be found in the visual library of amusement.

One implication of Huxley's warning to us is that the men and women of tomorrow may become less resourceful than their counterparts of the past. By relying more on technology than on other people for information, guidance and advice, they may be in danger of undervaluing the importance of interpersonal relationships and communication as a source of learning for personal growth and development. The very character and identity of people of the future, therefore, may be formed through depersonalised ways of learning and knowing the world.

In part, the technologising of the human spirit and culture may be simply an outcome of economic necessity. The current trend to replace face-to-face learning in classrooms with high technology open learning is an example, since the cost of providing and funding additional places in colleges and universities far exceeds that of creating opportunities for learning by non-traditional means such as correspondence courses and interactive media, including electronic mail and facsimile machines. In this way, the community of scholars will become a 'mediated' community. The indirectness of learning from and communication with others will thus be an inevitable by-product of the new age of super-technology. Moreover, as it has been suggested, our mediated relationships with others will be set in the context of a 'global village' or 'global network' (McLuhan, 1987).

We can take this thinking a step further. The mediation of learning from and communicating with others could mean at one extreme that some people may not need to leave their homes to accomplish their daily work. Information can be readily transmitted from home to the office or vice versa. When this happens, the home becomes a sort of prison and working from home can be seen as a form of detention. This is very much like the experience of criminals sentenced to periods of home detention (Aungles, 1991). At work, meetings in person may be unnecessary with the time-saving possibilities of tele-conferencing and video-conferencing. In short, the new age of super-technology may bring with it a depersonalisation of the social order and the despiritual-isation of the person. According to one Australian writer, most technological discoveries have an equal capacity for the enhancement and degradation of life, depending on how those technologies are understood and used (Jones, 1983). This paradoxical facet of technology has been labelled **Jones' Law No. 8**.

There is nothing inherently good or bad in the new media. In fact, the potential for improving learning, communication and personal growth is vast. It is only when people insist that new technologies must render older forms of media obsolete that we risk losing something truly valuable. I can recall someone saying to me that the time would come when all books would be available on computer disks. All we would need to do would be to take our microcomputers and disks to wherever we were heading and still be able to enjoy our moments of leisure. It does still seem odd, however, to think that reading a book from a computer screen would be any more convenient than reading a paperback in a plane, on a beach, or anywhere away from our normal workstations or offices.

Another vision of women and men of tomorrow is that they will be stronger emotionally, rationally, spiritually and physically than their counterparts of today. Of course, it is very difficult to generalise about such matters. Undoubtedly, there will always be those who abuse their minds and bodies despite warnings from experts. Drugs will continue to be available and used by some. Others will still need the support of psychoanalysts and psychiatrists. These, however, may not constitute the majority.

Between the 1950s and the 1990s men and women have gone through radical changes in their roles and lifestyles. Roberts, a contemporary journalist, noted in her investigations:

> . . . in the fifties, women were housewives; if they worked, they earned 'pin' money. By the eighties, women have become much more visible outside the home . . . Women have moved into senior positions in industry, local government, trade unions, and now run organisations unique to females such as the GLC's Women's Committee, with a budget in 1983/84 of six million pounds. Also established are Women's Studies, women's refuges, women's history, women's theatre, the list goes on. (Roberts, 1984:7–8)

Men too have changed over the years. As husbands, they now often witness the birth of their children. Their chauvinism at home has also diminished. Today, men share with their partners household tasks which were once considered to be women's work, such as childcare and household chores. In our permissive, more tolerant society men and women do not invariably limit their choice of partner to members of the opposite sex. Changes of such magnitude must in the long run affect how we project ourselves and communicate with others.

The signs of changing patterns of communication are already evident. Men no longer give up their seats for women on buses or trains; nor do women expect this to happen. Not all women expect men to open doors for them, although in certain circles this practice is still customary. No doubt there are other examples we could think of. The point is that as such changes occur and are reinforced by society, other changes in the ways people communicate and form interpersonal relationships begin to take place. For one thing, partly due to policies like EEO, there now seems to be

Jones' Law No. 8
The paradoxical facet of technology—the potential for technology to enhance or degrade life.

fewer instances of preferential treatment for one sex over the other in a great variety of social and workplace settings.

It is probably a utopian dream to envisage a future world of nations embracing a common set of values. Nevertheless, this dream is something which idealists, visionaries and dissidents such as Martin Luther King, Germaine Greer, Alexander Solzhenitsin and Bryce Courtenay have spoken out about. Their message of hope for a world free of tyranny, prejudice, and hatred has reached many in the present world. It is not an entirely original message. Almost a millenium ago, Paul the Apostle wrote of a society in which there was no discrimination between Greeks and Jews, males and females, or slaves and free people. In this new world order, all people would be 'one in Christ Jesus'.

Events in some countries, South Africa for example, suggest that the momentum for the realisation of this dream is gradually increasing, although it will take some time before old ways and values change. One could argue that the present world is entering a period of awakening and learning rather than one of rapid action and change. It will be some time before universal principles like equality and justice are accepted throughout the entire world. The 1990s, therefore, will see men and women in a time of transition when social, national and international values are translated into genuinely new patterns of behaviour and communication.

If there is something firm to hold on to in believing that a better future world is possible it is this: people no longer believe that progress, knowledge and personal development occur naturally or as a matter of course. They need to work hard to increase their knowledge and understanding of themselves, of others in their world and of how to adapt to and manage changing social circumstances. In intimate sexual relationships, for example, orgasm does not happen automatically or without an understanding of one's partner's needs and responses. In multicultural communities people may not realise that they are hurting or distressing others unless there is enough open dialogue for direct and informative feedback to occur.

If the world of tomorrow does become a better place, it will be because people will talk to each other more. In a better future world, people will communicate whenever opportunities arise so that their understandings of others who are different improve their interpersonal relationships. The effective communication managers will be those who learn from their experiences, where their information source is Life itself. It would be fair to suggest, therefore, that while in ten years time people will still differ in the depth of their sensitivity to others, those who have worked at improving their knowledge and understanding of human communication processes may well be even better communication managers than their present counterparts.

In the next section we focus on ways in which people can develop such understandings of others. This involves the ability to identify change and to explain the processes by which such change occurred. In turn, this ability, as we shall see, becomes vital to managing and adapting to change processes and also vital to the even greater challenge of forecasting change.

Change is usually manifest in some difference in the way people act or communicate or in the way things happen. When people change, they go through a learning experience. As a result of that learning experience, their actions, their communication, their beliefs, their attitudes or their understandings may change. In some cases, changes in people may be relatively easy to bring about. Acquiring new information, for example, is relatively straightforward. On the other hand, accepting and believing that new information requires a radical shift in attitude is more difficult for many people. If current attitudes are powerful influences on our communication and behaviour, changing our thinking habits may take some time.

In human systems, changes can occur at two levels. At the intrapersonal level, people can bring about changes within themselves. Often such changes come about from necessity. For example, executive warnings like 'Shape up or ship out!' or 'Get your act together!' may be enough to make us change our patterns of behaviour and communication and improve performance at work. On other occasions, however, intrapersonal changes may be self-initiated. Generally speaking, such changes may be regarded as the tangible outcomes of one's soul-searching or realisation that some kind of change is needed for better communication with and under-standing of others.

The second kind of change may occur at interpersonal or system-wide levels. These changes affect more than one person at a time in an organisation. For example, there may be changes wrought by policy or new technology. External changes of this kind may force individuals and groups of people to change their ways of acting and communicating. When people refuse to change themselves, new policies may become difficult to reinforce without penalties. Many of us have become familiar with such warnings as 'Littering is an offence. Penalty $200' or 'Warning. Penalty for fare evasion $100'.

Note that some changes may be dramatic, swift and orchestrated on a large scale while others are less obvious, gradual, and on a relatively small scale. When changes are introduced gradually, we usually find it easier to adjust to new ways of doing things. However, when changes in organisations are introduced with little notice and when they cast a cloud over the future of their members, the acceptance of these changes may be grudging and made with trepidation.

In some systems, large-scale changes involving internal restructuring can have devastating effects. For example, positions may become redundant, and people may find themselves demoted or even without jobs. One of the disconcerting things that can happen here is that people may find that they have to report to others who were formerly their subordinates. Extreme cases of organisational restructuring have involved successive waves of change in a short space of time. In such instances, each new wave of change may cancel out previous changes. For example, workers may be elevated in the system's hierarchy during the first wave of change only to find shortly afterwards that they are without portfolio or seniority because of a new restructuring. In recent years, extreme changes of this kind and their shattering effects were felt in such Australian systems as the higher education and the technical and further education (TAFE) sectors.

People resist change in their systems or organisations for various reasons. A group of friends who have played tennis once a week over many years may resist a casual suggestion that they introduce a 13th game tie-breaker at the expense of playing out two-game advantage sets. In this case, the players are resisting change because of practices which have become customary. Tie-breakers would disrupt their tradition.

One common reason for resisting change is people's fear either of failing to make the change successfully or of losing something valuable as a consequence. In other words, when something new is introduced, it may be at the expense of the old. Sometimes even the most persuasive, reasonable arguments do not convince people of the need to change. For instance, there is little point in explaining the benefits of converting some recreational space into office workstations if staff feel they are being deprived of a cherished meeting-place, even if these workers have been putting up with inadequate work space. People are also apprehensive when they need to acquire new knowledge or skills because their existing expertise is inappropriate or out-of-date.

Another example of the fear of loss is the introduction of technology that can render certain people redundant. Word-processors, for instance, have, to a large extent, replaced typists. In some organisations this has led to industrial action over the issue of continuing employment for staff in the typing pool. The acceptance of innovation is sometimes at odds with the fear of losing something or someone valued.

The other kind of fear, in times of change, is the fear of not being able to make the change successfully. This can happen when people are required to take on new roles and drop others. In some communities, for example, schoolteachers have extended their traditional roles to become community resource persons in their area of expertise; trained nurses, similarly, have taken on public relations roles in an effort to alert community members to the need for healthier lifestyles. When the people concerned find it difficult to make the transition from one kind of role to another, they may succumb to the temptation to avoid changing and to rationalise their reason for doing so.

Sometimes people remain unchanged because of their apathy towards organisational and personal improvement. They may not consciously or actively resist change, but watch it taking place, apparently unaffected by it. Let's take an example. In recent years, staff of former teachers' colleges became academic staff in universities, largely because various tertiary institutions were amalgamated as part of the rationalisation of the higher education sector in Australia. Some of the former teachers' college lecturers expected that, as university lecturers, they would now engage in more scholarly activity and research than previously. At face value, this seems a reasonable expectation and the lecturers seemed to accept this change of role. Many of them, however, made no apparent change in their work patterns or professional commitments—their working lives remained static. Faculty annual reports indicated no scholarly achievements by these people. In addition, they spoke the same way and related the same way to colleagues and students as they had in their previous employment. Clearly, they did not consider the expectation to become scholars as either relevant or important to their work. The sad part of it was that they lost an opportunity to develop and grow professionally.

Convention, fear and apathy, therefore, are three obstacles to change in people and systems. A fourth reason why people fail to change is simply their lack of ability to assume a new role and carry out the related duties. In part, this can be explained by the Peter Principle which states that sooner or later all individuals in an organisational hierarchy are promoted or translated to positions where they perform incompetently (Peter and Hull, 1975: 22). The teachers' college lecturers who were eventually required to become university scholars simply did not have what it takes to be effective academics.

It seems reasonable to conclude, therefore, that effective communication managers are able to conquer natural tendencies to be afraid, to stick with convention, to be apathetic, or to think that they are incapable when confronted with the need to change. Rather than ignore the need to change, they are prepared to treat it as an exciting challenge. Just how they go about meeting this challenge is the subject of the next section.

Managing Change 11.3

In view of the many major changes to modern workplace practices it is no wonder that the topic of managing change has attracted so much interest from applied scholars, professional consultants, and practising managers. One important question is how changes in systems and organisations concur with changes in people's behaviour and communication. Similarly, how significant or big do organisational changes have to be before their members feel the need to change themselves?

When changes in organisations are perceived by members to be bureaucratic, trivial, or unpalatable, they are 'managed' by being ignored. It seems almost ironic that prohibition signs like 'no smoking' or 'keep your feet off the seats' frequently invite defiance. Merely posting a warning does little to induce people to change. A notice condemning racist graffiti is just as likely to provoke more graffiti as to reduce it.

The commissioners of change may choose to manage change in ways ranging from total worker participation to coercion. Most would prefer, however, to include as many people involved as possible since their participation would probably also lead to greater commitment. Neglecting to involve as many staff as possible may be perceived by those excluded as some form of dictatorial exercise and they might seek industrial action.

Not every employee may want to become involved in the change process. However, all members of an organisation will want the *opportunity* to participate even if they have no firm intention of contributing to it constructively. When meetings of all members take place because change agents feel it desirable that all members feel free to contribute, the change process can become quite drawn out. More often than not, a handful of energetic individuals will be the key contributors.

Total worker participation in organisational change is perhaps more ideal than practical. For example, I have pointed out elsewhere that total worker participation in the revision and reaccreditation of degree courses in university schools or departments significantly slows down the change process (Kaye, 1994a). In the long run, it seems the documentation for the reaccreditation of a course is the product of a few individuals' collaborative efforts.

Sometimes change managers lose patience with participating workers because original deadlines later seem to be too tight and unrealistic. When this happens, the change managers may decide to move things along by appointing a few people with drive and initiative to see the change process reach a satisfactory conclusion. Such changes in strategy require change managers also to be competent communication managers as they will need to maintain their credibility, their communication and their relationships with others.

Managing communication with people who are undergoing change is bound to be a sensitive task. Some of the qualities of good communication managers have already been discussed in general terms earlier in this book. Here we need to identify what qualities communication managers need when they assume the role of change facilitator. We can assume that effective change managers are skilled in listening, assertiveness, negotiating, persuasion and conflict resolution. It is also to their advantage if they have acute person perception ability, including skill in interpreting nonverbal cues. Clearly, managing change also means managing people; and managing people involves managing one's communication and relationships with them. Hence the competent facilitator of change is also a competent communication manager.

In addition to skill in managing change, a competent change manager needs the ability to forecast change or the need for it. The next section focuses on this. The concept of 'vision', therefore, is central to the theme of this next section.

11.4 Forecasting Change

For some people, the idea of predicting future change is a bit like crystal-ball gazing. It could be argued that people should live in the present and let the future look after itself. The truth is, however, that just as the present plays a part in shaping the future, a vision of the future can also shape the form and nature of the present. People who look beyond the immediate time and try to imagine the shape of things to come are often referred to as 'strategic thinkers'.

Those who try to forecast change are special kinds of strategic thinkers. Some base their visions of the future on present trends and the extent to which these present trends are likely to escalate. For example, if the present trend of an organisation is to reduce annual expenditure on full-time staff by 5 per cent, there would probably be little or no opportunity for creating new positions to attract young talent. Another present trend might be to 'multiskill' current staff, despite the cautionary warning that 'changing the organisation of work is not merely a matter of multiskilling the workforce' (Williams, 1991:25). Thus, a prediction for five years ahead might be that all staff will have developed sufficient competence to function satisfactorily in at least three areas or sections.

A second basis for forecasting change is to identify current deficits or needs. For example, if the organisation lacks leadership in strategic management and development, astute change managers will be quick to point out the need to recruit experts. Non-visionaries, on the other hand, tend to think only in terms of the present. If someone retires from an organisation, they want to replace that person with someone with similar or identical attributes. In other words, non-visionaries do not see the retirement as an opportunity to do some creative strategic planning.

Regardless of how visionary change managers forecast change or the need for it, they will have to convince others that it is necessary and/or beneficial. It is clear, therefore, that strategic change managers will need all their communication management skills to secure others' constructive contributions. In this connection, both person perception and self-presentation skills will be needed.

Communication management ability at convincing others to accept change also involves some seemingly paradoxical qualities. For example, strategic change agents need to know when to be tough and resolute and when to compromise. They need to know when to stand their ground or when to yield. Skill in diplomacy should be complemented by presentation of a strong self-image. Active listening should be counterbalanced by knowing when there is nothing further to listen to as arguments become circular. Regardless of which communication skill is brought into play, strategic change managers need to know how and when to apply specific communication management skills.

Right at the start of this book it was suggested that we tend to base our communication with others on 'surface information' which we receive through our senses. In the next section we begin to consider the possibility of obtaining deeper understandings of those with whom we communicate, to enhance our ability to communicate accurately and purposefully.

A Subliminal Perspective of 11.5
Communication Management

The search for deeper meaning and insight into human behaviour and communication has prompted a good deal of speculation on ways of tapping into subconscious levels of awareness. Aldous Huxley, in his book

The Doors of Perception: and, Heaven and Hell described individual human perceptions of the immediate environment. These perceptions were induced by the drug mescaline which is derived from the root of peyote. Under the influence of this drug, people saw inanimate objects come to life and acquire personal identities, and were even able to relate to and communicate with inanimate household furniture.

During the past three decades many people have experimented with drugs of different kinds. Among the various reasons for such experimentation was undoubtedly the curiosity of seeing the world with differently tinted spectacles. A good deal of the imagery in the Beatles' films, for example, depicted the world and its inhabitants in bizarre ways. It is commonly assumed that much of this was meant to be a recreation of drug-induced experiences. Judging by the words of some songs written by popular musical groups like the Beatles, the desire to see the world differently stemmed from a sense of disillusionment with the present world. Phrases like 'a new world for you and for me' or statements such as 'and the world will be a better place' imply a hope for a better environment. This new world would be characterised by love, not hate, by peace instead of war, and by fun instead of tedium and drudgery. Flowers, not weapons, were the symbols of the new world.

In some ways, the mechanism for this vision of a better world was a defensive one. Ego-defence mechanisms such as repression and denial were perhaps typical of disillusioned youth coping with their current lot. During the 1960s and 1970s social values were seriously challenged by generations of young adults. For example, work was becoming to be seen as a means to an end, the fun of beaches and parties became more desirable than the satisfaction of getting a job done well. Dedicated professionals and workers were caricatured as pompous, boring and pedantic fuddy-duddies.

The new visions and perceptions of youth and young adults of the 60s and 70s appeared to be inspired by psychedelic models. There seemed to be an emphasis on creating fantasy images, apparent in new styles of clothing in bright colours and floral designs. There was also a touch of surrealism in the world of young people during that period.

With its emphasis on peace, harmony and love, people in the new world would understand each other better and therefore communicate better with each other. There would be less racial tension and conflict, as the words of Stevie Wonder and Paul McCartney suggest 'ebony and ivory live together in perfect harmony'. As love would dominate interpersonal relationships, people would learn to understand and communicate with each other in more profound, intimate ways.

In our world of tomorrow, if there could be one outstanding development, it would be that people would acquire ways of tapping into below-the-surface information about people with whom they were communicating and forming relationships. This probably means that a better new world would be characterised by trust, and a genuine desire to understand others. When the trust between people deepens, the willingness to disclose information about oneself is also likely to increase. In tomorrow's world, we require more than catchy slogans about loving each other and being nice to each other.

In interpersonal relationships where trust has deepened to the point of mutual self-disclosure (i.e. both people share private information about themselves), communication management is destined to be better, mainly because the data which forms the basis for strategic communication will be more complete and accurate. How much information people disclose will be determined by the extent to which confidants encourage their private feelings, beliefs, values and attitudes to surface, along with their wisdom, their capacity to reason, and their stores of knowledge.

This forecast of a better world where we would understand and communicate with each other more competently might seem far-fetched and remote from the realities of the workplace. A future world of better communicators, however, need not be restricted to people's private lives, where disclosure in intimate relationships is likely to happen. In professional spheres, we still need to communicate with and relate to other people. As all members of systems carry their own cultures with them, knowing something of their beliefs and value systems helps us to know what kind and level of relationships will be workable. In other words, effective communication managers of the future will know how deep and intense their relationships and communication should be from one case to another.

It is difficult to predict whether people in the future will develop alternative means of becoming more adept in their communication with and sensitivity to others. During wartime, it has been claimed, some people developed a sixth sense and communicated with distant comrades-in-arms telepathically. Australian Aborigines, some say, have refined their powers of telepathic communication to a fine art. Japanese Ninja warriors of the past were supposed to be able to detect the presence of others without relying on their five basic senses.

Perhaps, as in most martial arts, where advanced levels of mastery involve significant degrees of spiritual as well as mental and physical development, future generations of people will develop a sixth sense. Whilst such a claim is purely conjectural at this stage, it represents a compelling and complex challenge to people in our society who have already developed powers of introspection and the ability to reflect systematically. A sixth sense, of course, may be nothing more than intuition. Nevertheless, intuitive people have been known to assess with some accuracy the character and intentions of other persons.

A clinical method which has been used to tap into the subconscious levels of people's minds is hypnosis. Under hypnosis, some people reveal information about themselves which they cannot always disclose in their normal waking state. Whilst the art and science of hypnosis and hypnotherapy is very much in the province of psychiatric practice, it is not inconceivable that people could learn certain hypnotic techniques to enhance their communication management.

One such technique is auto-suggestion which has to be learned from experts in hypnosis. It has been used to overcome pain, stress or apprehension or to gain confidence to cope with uncertainty or anxiety. By putting oneself into a hypnotic state for a brief period (e.g. 10 seconds), people can wake refreshed with a more positive approach to the immediate future. Repeated practice in auto-suggestion has been known to help break habits like smoking or nail-biting. Other intrapersonal problems like diffidence in being assertive could perhaps be resolved by auto-suggestion.

Until people experiment with and find new ways to gain deeper understandings of others, they will continue to rely on their basic senses for information to guide their communication. There is nothing really wrong with this as it is natural to communicate with our sensory faculties. Nevertheless, any new development in the communication management abilities of future generations is unlikely to emanate from what is already known and understood about human communication processes. The discovery and cultivation of inner powers such as intuition, telepathy or a sixth sense, therefore, is more likely than anything else to advance human skill in managing communication processes.

If, however, the state of the art of communicating in ten years time is much the same as it is now, what lesson above all can we learn from the present to ensure that best communication practices are being maintained? In the next section we attempt to answer this important question and by doing this are reminded never to take good communication practices for granted.

11.6 People Still Need People

In recent years interest in good communication practice has become a major preoccupation and concern with many progressive organisations. High quality customer service, for example, has been understood to depend on those who serve possessing highly developed communication skills. Good salespeople give the impression that they have refined person perception skills when they have to diagnose a customer's needs. Thus, customer service has come a long way since salespeople were trained to utter perfunctory statements like 'Have a nice day!', 'You're welcome!' or 'Enjoy!'.

Several good communication practices have been developed in recent years; some have been dealt with in this book. For example, people have learned the value of acting assertively to protect their rights without infringing those of others. Conflict has been studied extensively and now that the process is well understood a variety of effective methods have been devised to deal with it. Those who have studied communication have learned the importance of being good listeners and negotiators in a range of situations.

When we think of all these good communication practices collectively, however, we find the answer to our question about the greatest lesson to be learned from today: people are at the heart and meaning of life, the point of existence, and the challenge to continue to learn and discover. People make the world go round. True, we need other things like money to survive. But whatever our various needs are, without communicating and relating to other people, our lives would be barren indeed. In the words of a well known song, 'people who need people are the luckiest people in the world'.

Human systems, regardless of whether they are small like nuclear families or large organisations, work best when their members act interdependently. We have seen that many successful Japanese companies of today have this quality which they call *amae*. The interaction of and communication between people are vital for human systems to operate in a co-ordinated and smooth fashion. With this kind of effort the left hand will always know what the right hand is doing. In short, for the smooth running of human systems, people still need people. Professionally, they need people for support, guidance, advice, help or simply information. Personally, they need people in order to develop and mature as fully integrated beings.

There will always be the few who need people only to manipulate them before discarding them once they have outlived their usefulness. Manipulators, in the long run, must be pitied. Their gains have been self-serving; their goals have not enhanced their personal or social growth. If our major lesson to be learned from the present is heeded, it would be reasonable to hope that fewer people will need to be pitied in years to come.

The fact that people need people no matter what kind of human system they happen to be in suggests that competence in communicating with others is absolutely necessary for people's needs to be met. As we noted much earlier, communication is inevitable. The need to communicate is as natural as breathing. This theme has recurred, implicitly or explicitly, throughout this book. Hopefully, by becoming role models of good communication practice and by gaining ever deeper understandings of communication management processes, readers will be able to help others to develop competence in interpersonal communication.

Summary 11.7

In this chapter we have explored the possibilities of the future. Ten years from now men and women could be even more able as communication managers if they heed the major lesson of today: to value people, to learn from other people and, in sum, to need other people. However, it is not just enough to need people. Individuals of tomorrow should consider new, alternative ways of gaining deeper understandings and insights into human communication and behaviour. Additionally, they will need to develop these understandings in times of change. Developing skill in understanding, managing and forecasting change will assist people greatly in their quest for personal growth and development as effective communication managers.

11.8 Discussion Questions

1. In the light of what has been said in this chapter, what kind of competencies do you need to develop to become an effective communication manager at work? How do these competencies resemble or differ from those described in this book? Share your thoughts with a friend or colleague whom you respect and trust.

2. In your opinion, how will your life and world in 2000 AD resemble or differ from your life and world at present? Will people's values change as well as the circumstances which surround them? Why or why not? What lessons from our present reflections can we learn and pass on to future generations facing their future worlds?

3. How are our current ways of communicating with each other likely to be affected by the rapidly increasing development of new technologies? In your view, what will change and what will stay much the same? Share your thoughts with someone else who has read this chapter.

4. Who are today's role models for the people of tomorrow? Think of some individuals you know or have read about whose lives and achievements you believe exemplify an ideal world that is productive, constructive, purposeful and satisfying. In particular, what communication management qualities distinguish these individuals from other people.

5. Why do many people resist or fail to accept the inevitability of change in their lives and in their worlds? What are some of the changes we are going to have to come to terms with in our lifetime? How can we best prepare for those changes? Think of one or two examples (e.g. growing older, retirement). Discuss your thoughts with a friend or close colleague.

6. How can the lifelong development of adult communication management competence help people bridge what is popularly termed 'the generation gap'? Which abilities in particular will help individuals from different generations to reciprocate and share the meanings they create about their private and professional worlds? Can these abilities be developed by people who seem to lack them? How? Exchange your ideas with someone else.

11.9 Activities

1. If you had the chance to make this world a better place, list all the things you would change and all the things you would keep the same. Then write down what you would have to be able to do to bring about

those changes. Put an asterisk next to any ability associated with communication competence. How many asterisks do you have? What conclusions can you draw about the relationship between communication competence and the management of change?

2. Some changes we would certainly like to prevent from escalating. For example, we would like to see violence, crime, poverty, and illiteracy diminish. Suggest some strategies that we could adopt to prevent the acceleration of undesirable trends in our society. Then identify the types of communication competencies we need to make those strategies work.

Recommended Reading 11.10

Aungles, S. (ed.) (1991) *Information technology in Australia: transforming organisational structure and culture*, Sydney: University of New South Wales Press.

Glass, L. (1993) *He says, she says: closing the communication gap between the sexes*, Sydney: Bantam.

McLuhan, M. (1987) *Understanding media: the extensions of man* [sic], London: Ark Paperbacks.

Postman, N. (1986) *Amusing ourselves to death*, London: Heinemann.

Roberts, Y. (1984) *Man enough: men of 35 speak out*, London: Chatto & Windus, The Hogarth Press.

Skinner, B. F. (1973) *Beyond freedom and dignity*, UK: Penguin.

Toffler, A. (1970) *Future shock*, London: Pan.

Glossary

Active listening. The ability to restate or paraphrase what a speaker has just said. The three essential ingredients of active listening are being non-judgmental, reflecting the feelings of the speaker, and giving the speaker feedback.

Adaptation. An intercultural communication theory term: the process by which strangers to a new culture cope with the stress of culture shock. Adaptation to the new culture leads to growth within that culture.

Ad hominem. A form of argumentation and reasoning involving a personal verbal attack on a message source.

Adult communication management. The processes by which people competently manage their communication in various systems.

Affect. A noun and synonym for *feelings* or *emotions*.

Amae. A Japanese term for mutual dependency or interdependency within organisations.

Ambushing (strategic ambushing). A selective listening process where people listen for information to trap the speaker.

Anxiety reduction. An intercultural communication theoretical principle which holds that communication between strangers and members of a host culture improves when the anxiety of strangers is reduced.

Arationality. The unpredictable and undiscussable communication and interpersonal behaviour that characterises the shadow side of organisations and systems. Often associated with organisational politics.

Assertiveness (assertion). The ability to stand up for one's rights without infringing on the rights of others.

Attitude. A tendency or predisposition to act toward a particular group of people, objects, events, or other phenomena in highly specific ways.

Attribution of meaning. Explaining or suggesting reasons why people behave or communicate as they do.

Attribution theory. A body of theoretical and research literature which holds that when we perceive the behaviour and communication of others we attempt to explain what we perceive by attributing external or internal causes to it.

Attributional confidence. Confidence in interpreting others' intentions, behaviour, personality and communication.

Bandwagon effect. A psychological fallacy (also known as *impressing by large numbers*); the false argument that since many people believe something is true, it must be true.

Bennis' First Law of Academic Pseudodynamics. Routine work drives out nonroutine work and smothers to death all creative planning and fundamental change in any institution.

BATNA. A negotiation and conflict resolution strategy that determines the best alternative to a negotiated agreement.

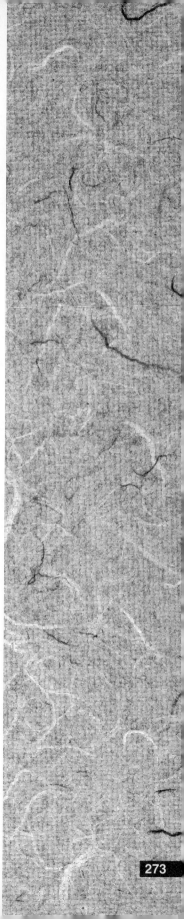

Black-or-white fallacy. A material fallacy that presents arguments in all-or-nothing terms, particularly when there are other alternative solutions to a problem.

Body language. Popular term to describe how people communicate non-verbally.

Cerebrotonic. A person whose personality is characterised by introversion and intellectual pursuits.

Change agent. One who helps others to learn or to bring about change within themselves or their interpersonal systems.

Climate-setting role. See **leadership role**.

Closed communication. Occurs in a system where only superficial information is readily accessible to its members.

Closed questions. Soliciting a restricted answer; e.g. 'yes' or 'no'.

Cognitive complexity. The number of interpersonal constructs we use to form an image or impression of someone. The greater the number of constructs, the more cognitively complex that user is considered to be.

Communication. The reciprocal construction, co-ordination and clarification of meaning by interacting people; essentially involves the interpretation of relationships and interactions between self and others.

Communication barrier. Sometimes called *communication roadblock*, *interference* or *noise*. Any external factor or influence that interferes with communication between people.

Communication breakdown. See **communication failure**.

Communication competence (also referred to as **communicator** or **communicative competence). **The extent to which people can control their interpersonal or social environments, including uncertainty or anxiety.

Communication failure. Also called communication *breakdown*. A popular term for when two or more people no longer share common meanings about people, events or phenomena.

Communication management. The process people engage in when communicating; i.e. constructing, co-ordinating and clarifying meanings.

Communication roadblock. See **communication barrier**.

Competence. Also called *expertise*, *authoritativeness* or *qualification*; people's ability to discern truth, or to know what is right or correct; vital to source credibility.

Compliance-gaining. Producing messages intended to influence others' attitudes, behaviour and communication.

Compliance-resisting. People's approaches to resisting or combating the influence of compliance-gaining messages directed at them.

Confirmatory feedback. Messages from one person to another indicating that work performance or communication has been favourably viewed.

Conflict. Events or situations in which people's needs, goals or interests differ from each other's to the point of interference.

Conflict management. The ability of people in disagreement to explore mutually acceptable ways to resolve conflict without damaging their personal or professional relationship.

Conflict resolution. Achieving mutually acceptable settlements of disputes. Personal, inner conflict is resolved when a person consciously chooses their direction of communication or action.

Connotation. Concepts and ideas one indirectly associates with specific people, objects, events or phenomena.

Construct. Bipolar terms like 'attractive-unattractive' used when we construct images of others. May be psychological (e.g. 'friendly-unfriendly') or physical (e.g. 'tall-short').

Constructivism. Theory of communication as the reciprocal construction of meaning; it views communication as an interpretive process in interpersonal relationships.

Convergence theory of intercultural communication. If two or more people share information they eventually converge toward one another, to a state of greater harmony.

Conversion disorder. Also called *hysteria*. A psychological disorder producing physical symptoms such as paralysis or illness without organic cause.

Corrective feedback. A message from superior to staff member indicating unsatisfactory performance, communication or behaviour.

Covert culture. The imperceptible aspects of an organisation's culture, including unwritten rules, hidden agendas, secret political manoeuvres etc.; closely linked with the *shadow side* of human systems.

Credibility (source credibility). Attitude of a receiver toward a message source; made up of factors such as competence (expertise), trustworthiness and dynamism.

Critical listening. Evaluating the logic and validity of what a speaker just said.

Culture. A complex synthesis of attitudes, beliefs, values, norms, rules, mores and taboos espoused by individuals or groups.

Culture shock. The initial experience of a stranger settling in a new country or land.

Deception. An act of purposefully conveying to others information the deceiver believes to be false, and which is intended to benefit the deceiver.

Decoding. Interpreting sensorily received information.

Defensive communication. Justifying oneself, usually by applying psychological ego-defence mechanisms. One form of defensive communication is defensive listening.

Defensive listening. Listening with the expectation of being attacked by the speaker.

Denotation. The literal definition of objects or phenomena according to commonly understood and agreed terms.

Despair. The developmental psychologist Erik Erikson's term for the negative, final stage of the 'eight stages of man'; the last psychosocial crisis experienced by those who look back on their lives and achievements with self-pity or regret. The opposite of despair is *ego-integrity*.

Developmental tasks. Challenges facing us at different stages of our lives. Meeting them successfully leads to a satisfactory, balanced lifestyle.

Discipline interview. Occurs when a superior reprimands a staff member for failure to perform duties satisfactorily. The consequences might be an official warning, being placed on probation, demotion or dismissal.

Double-bind message. Also called *incongruent message*. An ambiguous message where verbal cues appear to contradict nonverbal cues.

Downward communication. The practice of superiors initiating communication with staff members.

Dynamism. The enthusiasm and energy speakers give to their subject. A source credibility factor that complements trustworthiness and competence.

Ectomorph. A person with a slight or slender body build.

Egocentrism. Also called *egocentric thought* or *egocentricity*; coined by Jean Piaget to describe perceiving things solely from one's own point of view. Claimed to be more typical of children than of adults.

Ego-defence mechanisms. A psychological term to describe how people alter their thinking and perceptions of unpleasant realities so that they are easier to confront.

Ego-integrity. Erik Erikson's term for the positive aspect of the last psychosocial crisis in the 'eight stages of man'; the ability to look back on life without self-pity or regret. The opposite is *despair*.

Emotive language. A device whereby connotations of words, rhythm, and dramatic arrangement of phrases and sentences are used to persuade.

Empathy. The ability to understand other's feelings and to express that understanding without censure.

Empowerment. The delegation of authority by managers to staff to make decisions about their own and their organisation's development.

Encoding. Constructing a message.

Endomorph. A person whose build is round or fat.

Equal employment opportunity (EEO). Employment practice free from discrimination against age, gender, sexual preference, ethnic background, religious affiliation etc.; based on the principle of employing the most meritorious applicant for a job.

Equilibrium. See **homeostasis**.

Equilibrium Theory. Gaze involves two competing forces: looking at someone; avoiding looking. The equilibrium or balance of gaze between two people is proportional to the amount of liking and attraction they have for each other.

Etiquette. Conventional requirements or expectations for acceptable social or professional behaviour in particular circumstances or community sectors. Also involves protocol, e.g. in law courts, professional ceremonies.

Exit interview. Conducted when people leave organisations, to determine why they are leaving.

Eye contact. Mutual gaze between two people.

Facial expression. Emotional signals due to muscular activity in the face.

Facilitator. One who helps others learn and change. A term for 'teacher' used in some adult education contexts.

Fallacies. Faulty arguments; errors in reasoning; may be psychological, material or logical.

False analogy. A material fallacy that makes inappropriate comparisons, e.g. between apples and oranges.

Faulty generalisation. A material fallacy, sometimes due to hasty generalisations based on too few cases or drawn from cases that are not typical of the data sampled.

Feedback. The effect on each person of information they share, whether confirmatory (positive) or corrective (negative), immediate or delayed. It either comes directly from the person affected, or indirectly from a second-hand source.

Gaze. One person's visual attention fixed on another.

Gender balance. Normally associated with EEO; the practice of placing approximately equal numbers of men and women on work committees and other decision-making bodies.

General systems theory of intercultural adaptation. Regards people as individual systems that function through interactions with the environment and its inhabitants; usually involves successive stages of culture shock, stress, adaptation, and growth.

Gestures. Body movements that communicate information.

Hard negotiation. The process where negotiators see the situation as a contest of wills and are therefore not prepared to yield any ground.

Hearing. The physical act of receiving sound.

Helping role. The creation of opportunities for others in their systems to achieve their goals, or to support their efforts to perform their duties.

Homeostasis. Also called *equilibrium*. The regulation of physiological factors like blood pressure or body temperature to maintain their optimum level.

Human systems. Networks of communicating people that range from units as small as nuclear families to large organisations, communities and neighbourhoods.

Hysteria. See **conversion disorder**.

Id. A Freudian term for the subconscious repository of our urges and basic impulses. The id is one of the three divisions of the human mind (along with *ego* and *superego*).

Immediacy. The degree of liking or disliking for a person or task.

Impression formation. The image we form of another during interaction or as a result of meeting; includes judgments about another's actions and intentions.

Impression management. The sum total of people's plans, ideas, skills and motivations that influences their communication with others.

Incongruent messages. See **double bind messages**.

Information sharer role. Involves giving and receiving of information, the reciprocal construction of meaning, clarification, sharing interpretations, self-disclosure, mutual disclosure, and the development of mutually acceptable strategies for further communication and action.

Integrity (of managers). Their belief in and commitment to what their organisation or system stands for.

Interdependence. The extent to which members of a human system need each other to achieve, as a team, group and individual goals.

Interference. See **communication barrier**.

Interpersonal attitude. A person's nonverbal way of signalling like or dislike, or dominance or submissiveness toward another.

Interpersonal communication. The verbal and nonverbal exchange and sharing of information.

Interpersonal conflict. Conflicts or disagreements between people with different needs or goals.

Interpersonal construct system. A person's set of constructs to form an image or impression of another person.

Interpersonal distance. A concept used by scholars of proxemics to denote spatial relationships between communicating people.

Interpersonal relationships. Affiliations between persons; may be intimate (personal) or impersonal; private or professional.

Interview. The structure of the communication process of interviewing.

Interviewing. A structured form of communication where one or more people are questioned by one or more others.

Intrapersonal communication. Communication (thinking and feeling) within oneself. Sometimes called *self-talk*.

Intrapersonal conflict. Personal, inner conflict caused by the need to make choices between competing needs or motives.

James–Lange Theory of Emotion. Behaviour and physiological responses are prompted by situations and, in turn, feelings and emotions result from these behaviours and responses.

Jones' Law No. 8. The paradoxical facet of technology—the potential for technology to enhance or degrade life.

Kineme. The smallest unit of body movement or action.

Kinesics. The systematic scientific study of body movements and their role in multichannel communication.

Leadership (climate setting) role. Requires communication managers to ensure that communication with others occurs under the most favourable or desirable conditions.

Learner. A self-agent of change who can demonstrate some gain in knowledge, thinking, feeling, or acting.

Learning. A change in a person, resulting from training or experience.

Libido. A Freudian term for *life energy*—the driving force in our lives.

Life-cycle phases of adults. Critical stages in adults' lifetimes.

Linguistic-relativity hypothesis. (Also known as the *Whorf-Sapir* or the *Whorfian Hypothesis*.) The structure of a culture's language determines its behaviour and thinking habits.

Listening. Interpreting and attaching meaning to what we have heard.

Logical fallacies. Errors in reasoning or argument due to the infringement of established rules of logical argument.

Manager. Someone who helps others perform organisation tasks and fulfil organisation goals.

Marker events. Specific events that mark a change from one life-cycle phase to the next.

Material fallacies. Errors in reasoning or arguments due to the use of poor materials.

MBWA. Managing by wandering around.

Meaning. The entire set of reactions that people assign to a symbol.

Mentor role of communication managers. Also called *role* model; involves being an exemplar of the art of maintaining good communication with others.

Mesomorph. A person whose body build is athletic and muscular.

Metacommunication. The hidden 'communication' behind the overt message; communication about communication.

Miscommunication. The receiver's interpretation of a message is inconsistent with the sender's intentions.

Mission statement. A broad statement indicating all that an organisation stands for; sometimes reflected in an organisation's motto.

Misuse of authority. A psychological fallacy where expertise in one area is used to promote or justify expertise in another, unrelated field.

Multi-message gestures. Gestures which may be interpreted in more than one way.

Mutual gaze. Two people maintaining eye contact with each other.

Noise. See **communication barrier**.

Nonevaluative listening. Suspending judgment about a speaker's remarks.

Nonrealistic conflict. Preventable and therefore unnecessary conflict, usually characterised by roadblocks such as giving orders, name-calling, issuing threats, patronising communication, or gratuitous advice.

Nonverbal communication. The sharing, between two or more people, of facial, vocal, and body signals and gestures, including spatial (proxemic) signals.

Nonverbal cues. Body signals and vocal accompaniments of speech.

Open communication. Access for all members of a system to any information that affects its functioning.

Open listening. The process where listeners try to forget their own concerns and biases so that their response to what is being said is as intelligent and sympathetic as possible.

Open questions. Questions that require unrestricted answers.

Organisational climate. An organisation's 'weather' or atmosphere, including personal and professional relationships, corporate philosophy, work practices, attitudes and goals.

Organisational culture. The values, beliefs, rules, taboos and norms espoused by members of an organisation.

Organiser role of communication managers. See **quality controller role**.

Overt culture. An organisation's perceptible culture, including its openly stated or commonly known rules, standards, mission, values, taboos etc.

Paralanguage. Vocal cues that signify a person's emotional state and other attributes (e.g. age, gender).

People-in-systems. Egan and Cowan's term for a theoretical perspective on relationships in human systems.

Performance appraisal (review). An interviewing process that periodically or regularly evaluates someone's work performance.

Personal control over the interpersonal environment. Achieving personal goals through interpersonal relationships; an integral component of communication competence.

Personal culture. Also called *individual culture*. A person's set of values, beliefs, attitudes, norms, standards, rules, and taboos.

Personal development. Aspects of a person's development that do not concern task performance or professional competence.

Persuasion. A deliberate attempt to change a person's or group's attitude, beliefs or behaviour; the appeal may rely on reasoned argument or emotive language.

Peter Principle. In any organisation hierarchy, people rise to positions where they cease to function competently.

Phatic communication. Aims to build and maintain social relationships rather than transmit information.

Plain English. The English language presented directly and simply, without unnecessary words and jargon.

Pointing to another wrong. A psychological fallacy in which one wrong is claimed to justify another.

Politically correct language. Language acceptable to all groups in a human system. 'Political correctness' has been traditionally associated with radical leftist movements, e.g. in feminist scholarship.

Positional bargaining. A contest in which each disputing party tries to force the other to change its position.

Power dressing. A way of dressing to create an 'executive' or 'person in power' image.

Presentation. The oral or written communication of information (or message) by one person or more to an audience of at least one.

Principled negotiation. Deciding issues on their merits rather than haggling over them.

Problem-solving (win-win) strategy of conflict resolution. A co-operative strategy by which conflicting negotiators recognise each other's interests and/or needs and search for a mutually acceptable solution.

Projection. An ego-defence mechanism by which people deny their unacceptable urges or drives and attribute them to others.

Proxemics. The study of how we use physical and interpersonal space and territory, and how this influences the communication of information and construction of meanings.

Psychological fallacies. Tricks of reasoning intended to divert, distract, or confuse others.

Psychosocial crisis. A critical phase in a person's life; their success or failure to deal with it greatly affects their development and their satisfaction with the rest of their life.

Quality controller (organiser) role. Involves their ability to monitor and, if necessary, improve the quality of their communication with others.

Questioning. Any solicitation to speak or respond.

Racism. Communication or behaviour that discriminates against or disparages anyone of a particular race or ethnic background.

Racist language. Speech or writing offending or deriding a particular ethnic or cultural group, or individuals.

Rationalisation. A Freudian ego-defence mechanism used to establish acceptable reasons for unacceptable urges, behaviour or communication.

Reaction formation. A Freudian ego-defence mechanism by which a person 'substitutes' one emotion for another; e.g. feeling disgusted about pornographic material which the person actually finds exciting.

Realistic conflict. An unavoidable and usually rational conflict, free of the emotional roadblocks typical of nonrealistic conflicts.

Reciprocity. The ability to understand and appreciate two viewpoints simultaneously, usually your own and another's. In relation to Equilibrium Theory, 'reciprocity' refers to the tendency for two people who are attracted to each other to intensify their mutual gaze and move closer together.

Reference. Our thought or mental image of an object before we give it a label or sign.

Referent. An external object or entity to which a word, sign or linguistic expression refers (e.g. the referent of the *word* 'chair' is the *object* 'chair'.

Referential triangle. The process by which we associate signs with objects by constructing mental images of them.

Relationship clarity. Convergence of people's expectations about the integration and distribution of work.

Repression. A Freudian ego-defence mechanism for preventing unpleasant or harmful knowledge from surfacing to the conscious mind.

Roadblocks. In conflict resolution, roadblocks include shadow-side features such as ignorance, error, tradition and prejudice, dysfunctional organisational structure, win-lose competition, hostility, and tension.

Role. Expectations and/or performances associated with positions in human systems. In simple terms, a 'hat' one wears for a specific occasion or circumstance.

Role ambiguity. Occurs when we are unsure about the limits and scope of our duties or spheres of responsibility; can result in duplicating others' work or failing to carry out tasks we thought were assigned to someone else.

Role clarity. Occurs when interdependent individuals understand how their particular duties or spheres of responsibility complement or are distinct from those of others.

Role model. See **mentor role**.

Role overload. Occurs when people assume or are given more roles and responsibilities than they can manage.

Selection (recruitment) interview. Competing applicants are examined for their suitability for a job.

Selective listening. The tendency to listen to parts of a message rather than the whole message.

Self-actualisation. A term coined by Abraham Maslow for the highest level of needs that motivate people; the need to maximise one's potential.

Self-concept. Our own view of ourself.

Self-disclosure. Revealing significant, sometimes intimate, aspects of oneself to another or others.

Self-esteem. The value or importance we place on our images of ourselves.

Self-image. The impressions or images we have of ourselves.

Self-knowledge. Awareness and understanding of one's emotions, needs and intentions; knowing one's personal culture.

Self-monitoring. Our tendency to look to others for cues for appropriate behaviour in personal situations.

Self-presentation. Our communication based on how we see ourselves and how we would like others to see us.

Sexism. Any communication or behaviour that discriminates against or disparages either females or males; more usually applied to females.

Sexist language. Speech or writing deriding females or males; usually derogates or discriminates against females.

Shadow side. Also called the *arational* side of human systems; characterised by uncertainty, unpredictability; is 'undiscussable', covert and usually informal.

Social influence. A research and theory perspective of communication between people that focuses on concepts of persuasion, credibility, compliance-gaining and compliance-resisting.

Sociofugal-sociopetal orientation (SPF axis). A concept used by scholars of proxemics to denote a measure of how directly people face each other.

Soft negotiation. Avoids conflicts with others at all costs; soft negotiators tend to give in rather than strive for better deals.

Solution rigidity. The firm belief that there is only one adequate way of resolving a conflict.

Somatotonic. A personality characterised by mental toughness and aggressiveness.

Somatotype. A description of a person that relates body build with personality type.

Source credibility. The receiver's perception of and attitude toward a message source. The three major dimensions are competence (or expertise), trustworthiness and dynamism.

Stereotyping. Labelling and categorising people according to fixed, general impressions of the groups they are associated with.

Straw person fallacy. Selecting a portion of an argument and then making out a case against it to destroy the entire argument.

Sublimation. An ego-defence mechanism for diverting one's psychic energy from a socially or morally unacceptable drive to an acceptable one.

Territoriality. A person's preference for areas and objects; usually the area where most of the interactions between that person and others take place. Similar to *personal space*.

Territorial marker. Frequently used object (e.g. a favourite desk or seat) by which we signal our occupancy of a space.

Territory. Any area possessed or controlled by people.

Token. Group members who stand out because of their visible differences from the rest of the group.

Total quality control (TQC). Coined by W. E. Deming; also called *total quality management (TQM)*, *total quality assurance (TQA)* or just *total quality (TQ)*. An approach to management that aims to improve product or service quality and increase customer satisfaction mainly by strong leadership, the more efficient use of resources, participation in team structures, and the statistical monitoring of work processes.

Transformational (transformative) leaders. These leaders create a new vision for the future of their organisations, communicate it to the public, stakeholders and the organisation's members, and carry out the vision throughout the organisation.

Transformational performance appraisal. A special form of appraisal that aims to develop performance and potential in line with the organisation's mission and goals.

Trustworthiness. Also called *character*, *personal integrity* or *safety*; generally relates to people's honesty with others; vital to source credibility.

Uncertainty reduction. This principle states that communication works best when uncertainty about the intent or content of messages is minimal.

Upward communication. Opportunities for staff members to communicate freely with their superiors.

Visceratonic. A personality that is extroverted, easy-going, and pleasure-seeking.

Vision. When applied to organisation leadership the term refers to leaders' ability to develop a future-oriented view of their organisations' goals and strategic directions.

Win-lose conflict resolution strategy. A competitive approach to conflict that assumes that the other party is hostile and intends to defeat its opponent. The parties in conflict consider only their own positions, needs and interests.

Win-win conflict resolution strategy. See **problem-solving conflict resolution strategy**.

Workaholic. A popular term for those who are totally obsessed with and consumed by their work.

Yin-yang. Natural polarities or opposites which complement each other: night-day, male-female, hot-cold.

References

Adler, R.B., Rosenfeld, L.B., and Towne, N. (1983) *Interplay: the process of interpersonal communication*, 2nd edn, New York: Holt, Rinehart & Winston.

Altman, I. and Haythorn, W. W. (1967) 'The ecology of isolated groups', in *Behavioral Science*, 12, 169–82.

Argyle, M. (1976) *Bodily communication*, London: Methuen.

Argyle, M. and Cook, M. (1976) *Gaze and mutual gaze*, London: Cambridge University Press.

Argyle, M. and Dean, J. (1965) 'Eye-contact, distance and affiliation', in *Sociometry*, 28, 289–304.

Arvey, R. D. and Campion, J. E. (1982) 'The employment interview: a summary and review of recent research', in *Personnel Psychology*, 35, 281–322.

Asante, M. K. (1992) 'The escape into hyperbole: communication and political correctness', in *Journal of Communication*, 42, 141–47.

Athanasou, J. A., Pithers, R. T. and Cornford, I. R. (1993) *Describing occupations: development of occupational descriptors for the Australian standard classification of occupations*, Canberra: Australian Government Publishing Service.

Aungles, A. (1991) 'Electronic surveillance and organisational boundaries: the home as the prison', in *Information technology in Australia: transforming organisational structure and culture*, Aungles, S. (ed.), Sydney: University of New South Wales Press, ch. 10, 195–209.

Aungles, S. (ed.) (1991) *Information technology in Australia: transforming organisational structure and culture*, Sydney: University of New South Wales Press.

Barker, L. L. (1984) *Communication*, 3rd edn, Englewood Cliffs, New Jersey: Prentice Hall.

Barker, L. L., Edwards, R., Gains, C., Gladney, K. and Holley, F. (1980) 'An investigation of proportional time spent in communication activities by college students', in *Journal of Applied Communication Research*, 8, 101–9.

Barroso, F. and Feld, J. K. (1986) 'Self-touching and attentional processes: the role of task difficulty, selection stage, and sex differences', in *Journal of Nonverbal Behavior*, 10, 51–64.

Beardsley, M. C. (1979) *Thinking straight: principles of reasoning for readers and writers*, 4th edn, Englewood Cliffs, New Jersey: Prentice Hall.

Bennis, W. (1991) *Why leaders can't lead: the unconscious conspiracy continues*, San Francisco: Jossey-Bass.

Berger, C. R. (1987) 'Communicating under uncertainty', in *Interpersonal processes: new directions in communication research*, Roloff, M. E. and Miller, G. R. (eds), Newbury Park, California: Sage, 39–62.

Berger, C. R. and Bradac, J. J. (1982) *Language and social knowledge*, London: Edward Arnold.

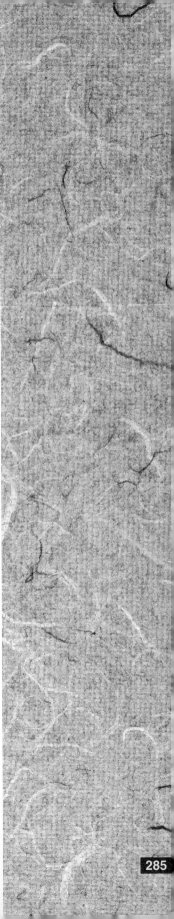

Berlo, D. K. (1960) *The process of communication: an introduction to theory and practice,* New York: Holt, Rinehart & Winston.

Berlo, D. K., Lemert, J. B. and Mertz, R. J. (1970) 'Dimensions for evaluating the acceptability of message sources', in *The Public Opinion Quarterly,* 33, 563–76.

Birdwhistell, R. L. (1970) *Kinesics and context,* Philadelphia: University of Pennsylvania Press.

Blanchard, K. and Johnson, S. (1984) *The one minute manager,* London: Fontana/Collins.

Blondis, M. N. and Jackson, B. E. (1977) *Nonverbal communication with patients: back to the human touch,* New York: John Wiley.

Bloom, B. S. (ed.) (1956) *Taxonomy of behavioral objectives. Handbook I: Cognitive domain,* New York: McKay.

Bolton, R. (1979) *People skills: how to assert yourself, listen to others and resolve conflicts,* New York: Simon & Schuster.

Bond, C. F. and Robinson, M. (1988) 'The evolution of deception', in *Journal of Nonverbal Behavior,* 12, 295–307.

Boster, F. J. and Stiff, J. B. (1984) 'Compliance-gaining message selection behavior', in *Human Communication Research,* 10, 539–56.

Bostrom, R. (1984) *Competence in communication: a multidisciplinary approach,* Beverly Hills, California: Sage Publications.

——(1990) *Listening behaviour: theory and research,* New York: Guilford.

Braysich, J. (1979) *Body language,* Sydney: Joseph Braysich.

Brislin, R. W., Landis, D. and Brandt, M. E. (1983) 'Conceptualizations of intercultural behavior and training', in *Handbook of Intercultural Training Volume 1: Issues in Theory and Design,* Landis, D. and Brislin, R. W. (eds), New York: Pergamon Press.

Brown, L. (1982) *Communicating facts and ideas in business,* Englewood Cliffs, New Jersey: Prentice Hall.

Bruneau, T. J. (1973) 'Communicative silences: forms and functions', in *Journal of Communication,* 23, 17–46.

Burgoon, J. K. (1985) 'Nonverbal signals', in *Handbook of interpersonal communication,* Knapp, M. L. and Miller, G. R. (eds), California: Sage, 344–90.

Burgoon, M. and Bailey, W. (1992) 'PC at last! PC at last! Thank God Almighty, we are PC at last!', in *Journal of Communication,* 42, 95–104.

Callan, V., Gallois, C. and Noller, P. (1986) *Social psychology,* Sydney: Harcourt Brace Jovanovich.

Carey, J. W. (1992) 'Political correctness and cultural studies', in *Journal of Communication,* 42, 56–72.

Carver, C. S. and Scheier, M. F. (1982) 'Control theory: a useful conceptual framework for personality-social, clinical, and health psychology', in *Psychological Bulletin,* 92, 111–35.

Cashdan, A. and Jordin, M. (eds) (1987) *Studies in communication,* Oxford: Basil Blackwell.

Clark, H. H. and Clark, E. V. (1977) *Psychology and language: an introduction to psycholinguistics,* New York: Harcourt Brace Jovanovich.

Cook, M. (1973) *Interpersonal perception,* Harmondsworth, UK: Penguin.

——(1984) 'The good judge of others' personality: methodological problems and their resolution', in *Issues in person perception,* Cook, M. (ed), London: Methuen, 145–66.

Cooper, L. O. (1991) *Toward a theory of listening competency: the development of a two-factor model of listening in organisations*, unpublished PhD dissertation, Dept of Speech Communication, University of Illinois at Urbana-Champaign.

Cronkhite, G. (1976) *Communication and awareness*, Menlo Park, California: Cummings.

Cross, K. P. (1983) *Adults as learners: increasing participation and facilitating learning*, San Francisco: Jossey-Bass.

Crossley, D. J. and Wilson, P. A. (1981) *How to argue: an introduction to logical thinking*, New York: Random House.

Dance, F. E. X. (ed.) (1982) *Human communication theory: comparative essays*, New York: Harper & Row.

Davitz, J. R. (ed.) (1964) *The communication of emotional meaning*, New York: McGraw-Hill.

Davitz, J. R. and Davitz, L. J. (1959) 'The communication of feelings by content-free speech', in *Journal of Communication*, 9, 6–13. Reprinted in *Nonverbal communication: readings with commentary*, Weitz, S. (ed), New York: Oxford University Press, 1974, 99–104.

De Bono, E. (1985) *Conflicts: a better way to resolve them*, UK: Penguin.

Delbecq, A. L., Van de Ven and Gustafson, D. H. (1975) *Group techniques for program planning*, Glenview, Illinois: Scott Foresman.

Delia, J. G., O'Keefe, B. J. and O'Keefe, D. J. (1982) 'The constructivist approach to communication', in *Human communication theory: comparative essays*, Dance, F. E. X. (ed), New York: Harper & Row, 147–91.

Deming, W. E. (1982) *Out of the crisis*, Cambridge, Massachusetts: Cambridge University Press.

Dennis, E. E. (1992) 'Freedom of expression, the university, and the media', in *Journal of Communication*, 42, 73–82.

De Paulo, B. M. (1988) 'Nonverbal aspects of deception', in *Journal of Nonverbal Behavior*, 12, 153–62.

De Paulo, P.J. (1988) 'Research on deception in marketing communications: its relevance to the study of nonverbal behavior', in *Journal of Nonverbal Behavior*, 12, 253–73.

De Paulo, B. and Jordan, A. (1982) 'Age changes in deceiving and detecting deceit', in *Development of nonverbal behavior in children*, Feldman, R. (ed), New York: Springer-Verlag, 151–80.

DeVito, J. A. (1981) *Communication: concepts and processes*, Englewood Cliffs, New Jersey: Prentice Hall.

Dillard, J. P. (1993) 'Persuasion past and present: attitudes aren't what they used to be', in *Communication Monographs*, 60, 90–7.

Dillard, J. P., Hunter, J. E. and Burgoon, M. (1984) 'Sequential-request persuasive strategies: meta-analysis of foot-in-the-door and door-in-the-face', in *Human Communication Research*, 10, 461–88.

Donohue, W. A. and Kolt, R. (1992) *Managing interpersonal conflict*, California: Sage.

Downs, C. W., Smeyak, G. P. and Martin, E. (1980) *Professional interviewing*, New York: Harper & Row.

Dreher, D. (1991) *The Tao of peace: a modern guide to the ancient way of peace and harmony*, London: Mandala.

Dunphy, D. and Stace, D. (1990) *Under new management: Australian organizations in transition*, Sydney: McGraw-Hill.

Egan, G. (1985) *Change agent skills in helping and human service settings*, Monterey, California: Brooks/Cole.
—— (1988a) *Change agent skills A: assessing and designing excellence*, San Diego: University Associates.
—— (1988b) *Change agent skills B: managing innovation and change*, San Diego: University Associates.
—— (1991) *The pragmatics of business effectiveness*, Chicago: Gerard Egan.
—— (1993) *Adding value: a systematic guide to business-driven management and leadership*, San Francisco: Jossey-Bass.
Egan, G. and Cowan, M. A. (1979) *People in systems: a model for development in the human-service professions and education*, Monterey, California: Brooks/Cole.
Ekman, P. (1988) 'Lying and nonverbal behavior: theoretical issues and new findings', in *Journal of Nonverbal behavior*, 12, 163–75.
Ekman, P. and Friesen, W. V. (1975) *Unmasking the face: a guide to recognising emotions from facial clues*, Englewood Cliffs, New Jersey: Prentice Hall.
Ekman, P. Friesen, W. V. and Ellsworth, P. (1972) *Emotion in the human face*, New York: Pergamon.
Ekman, P., Friesen, W. V., O'Sullivan, M. and Scherer, K. (1980) 'Relative importance of face, body and speech in judgments of personality and affect', in *Journal of Personality and Social Psychology*, 38, 270–77.
Erikson, E. H. (1969) *Childhood and society*, 2nd edn, UK: Penguin.

Fairhurst, G. T. (1993) 'Echoes of the vision: when the rest of the organization talks total quality', in *Management Communication Quarterly*, 6, 331–71.
Fairhurst, G. T. and Wendt, R. F. (1993) 'The gap in total quality: a commentary', in *Management Communication Quarterly*, 6, 441–51.
Farace, R. V., Monge, P. R., and Russell, H. M. (1979) *Communicating and organizing*, Reading, Massachusetts: Addison-Wesley.
Fast, J. (1971) *Body language*, New York: Pocket Books.
Fearnside, W. W. (1980) *About thinking*, Englewood Cliffs, New Jersey: Prentice Hall.
Fensterheim, H. and Baer, J. (1989) *Don't say 'yes' when you want to say 'no'*, London: Futura.
Fisher, R. and Ury, W. (1986) *Getting to yes: negotiating agreement without giving in*, London: Hutchinson Business.
Forgas, J. P. (1985) *Interpersonal behaviour: the psychology of social interaction*, Sydney: Pergamon Press.
Fox, W. M. (1989) 'The improved nominal group technique (INGT)', in *The Journal of Management Development*, 8, 20–7.
Freud, S. (1938) *The basic writings of Sigmund Freud*, New York: Modern Library.
Friedman, H. S. (1979) 'The interactive effects of facial expressions of emotion and verbal messages on perceptions of affective meaning', in *Journal of Experimental Social Psychology*, 15, 453–69.

Gibb, J. R. (1961) 'Defensive communication', in *Journal of Communication*, 11, 141–48.

Glass, L. (1993) *He says, she says: closing the communication gap between the sexes*, Sydney: Bantam Books.

Glasser, T. L. (1992) 'Professionalism and the derision of diversity; the case of the education of journalists', in *Journal of Communication*, 42, 131–40.

Goffman, E. (1959) *The presentation of self in everday life*, New York: Doubleday Anchor.

Goldberg, S. and Rosenthal, R. (1986) 'Self-touching in the job interview: antecedents and consequences', in *Journal of Nonverbal Behavior*, 10, 65–80.

Goldman, A. (1992) 'Japanese managerial psychology: an analysis of cultural and organizational features of "total quality control"', in *Journal of Managerial Psychology*, 7, 17–20.

Greer, G. (1971) *The Female Eunuch*, London: Paladin.

Gross, L. (1992) 'There they go again', in *Journal of Communication*, 42, 105–12.

Grossberg, L. (1992) 'Being politically correct in a politically incorrect world', in *Journal of Communication*, 42, 148–49.

Gudykunst, W. B., Ting-Toomey, S. and Chua, E. (1988) *Culture and interpersonal communication*, California: Sage.

Hale, J. R. and Burgoon, J. K. (1984) 'Models of reactions to changes in nonverbal immediacy', in *Journal of Nonverbal Behavior*, 8, 287–314.

Hall, E. T. (1968) 'Proxemics', in *Current Anthropology*, 9, 83–108.

—— (1969) *The hidden dimension: man's use of space in public and private*, New York: Doubleday.

Harper, R. G., Wiens, A. N. and Matarazzo, J. D. (1978) *Nonverbal communication: the state of the art*, New York: John Wiley.

Harrison, R. P. (1973) 'Nonverbal communication', in *Handbook of communication*, de Sola Pool, I., Frew, F. W., Schramm, W., Maccoby, N. and Parker, E. B. (eds), Chicago: Rand-McNally, 93–115.

Havighurst, R. J. (1953) *Human development and education*, Chicago: Longmans, Green & Co. Ltd.

Heider, F. (1958) 'Perceiving the other person', in *Person perception and interpersonal behavior*, Tagiuri, R. and Petrullo, L. (eds), Stanford, California: Stanford University Press, 22–26.

Henderson, L. (1992) 'Paris is burning and academic conservatism', in *Journal of Communication*, 42, 113–22.

Heslin, R. (1974) *Steps toward a taxonomy of touching*, paper presented at the Midwestern Psychological Assn Annual Conference, Chicago.

Hirsch, R. O. (1986) *On defining listening synthesis and discussion*, paper presented at the meeting of the International Listening Assn, San Diego, California.

Hoffman, D. (1970) *How to be an absolutely smashing public speaker without saying anything*, New York: American Heritage Press.

Hofstadter, D. R. (1979) *Godel, Escher, Bach: an eternal golden braid*, Harmondsworth, UK: Penguin.

Hollwitz, J. and Wilson, C. E. (1993) 'Structured interviewing in volunteer selection', in *Journal of Applied Communication Research*, 21, 41–65.

Hurd, K. and Noller, P. (1988) 'Decoding deception: a look at the process', *Journal of Nonverbal Behavior*, 12, 217–33.

Huxley, A. (1932) *Brave new world*, London: Chatto & Windus.

—— (1959) *The doors of perception: and, heaven and hell*, Harmondsworth, UK: Penguin.

Hybels, S. and Weaver, R. L. (1986) *Communicating effectively*, New York: Random House.

Infante, D. A., Rancer, A. S. and Womack, D. F. (1990) *Building communication theory*, Illinois: Waveland Press.

Irwin, H. (1983) 'Interpersonal communication: contemporary issues and directions in theory and research', in *Australian Journal of Communication* , 3, 1–11.

—— (1985) 'Interpersonal communication competence revisited: current debates and research directions', in *Australian Journal of Communication*, 8, 25–31.

—— (1988) 'Current concerns in mainstream United States interpersonal communication research', in *Australian Journal of Communication*, 13, 16–30.

Izard, C. E. (1971) *The face of emotion*, New York: Appleton-Century-Crofts.

Jacobs, S. (1985) 'Language', in *Handbook of Interpersonal Communication*, Knapp, M. L. and Miller, G. R. (eds), California: Sage, 313–43.

Jensen, A. D. and Chilberg, J. C. (1991) *Small group communication: theory and application*, California: Wadsworth.

Johnson, D. W. and Johnson, F. P. (1975) *Joining together: group theory and group skills*, 1st edn, Englewood Cliffs, New Jersey: Prentice Hall.

—— (1982) *Joining together: group theory and group skills,* 2nd edn, Englewood Cliffs, New Jersey: Prentice Hall.

Jones, B. O. (1983) *Sleepers, wake: technology and the future of work*, UK: Oxford University Press.

Kanter, R. M. (1977) *Men and women of the corporation*, New York: Basic Books

Katzenbach, J. R. and Smith, D. K. (1993) 'The discipline of teams', in *Harvard Business Review*, March–April, 111–20.

Kaye, M. (1985) 'Applications of interpersonal communication theory to the field of training and development', in *Australian Journal of Communication*, 8, 41–47.

—— (1986) 'Nonverbal communication in lecturing: a constructivist perspective', in *Higher Education Research and Development*, 5, 15–29.

—— (1988) 'Methodological considerations in researching facial and paralinguistic cues', paper presented to Australian Assn for Research in Education Annual Conference, November-December, University of New England, Armidale.

—— (1991) 'Deception in communication between adult learners and teachers: implications for research and practice', in *Australian Journal of Communication*, 18, 115–31.

—— (1992) 'Communication competence', in *Developing a competent workforce: adult learning strategies for vocational educators and trainers*, Gonczi, A. (ed.), Adelaide: National Centre for Vocational Education Research, 80–104.

—— (1993) 'Multicultural and intercultural implications for training approaches to international communication', in *Representative readings in adult communication management*, Kaye, M. (ed.), Sydney: University of Technology, 263–72.

—— (1994a) 'Implementing change in Australian education systems: reflections on some practical strategies', *Unicorn*, 20, 52–62.

—— (1994b) 'Adult communication management: an Australian perspective for enhancing organisational effectiveness', in *Electronic Journal of Communication*, in press.

Kaye, M. and McArthur, S. (1993) 'The criterion of "good communication skills" in job advertisements', in *Representative readings in adult communication management,* Kaye, M. (ed.), Sydney: University of Technology, 85–100.

Kelly, G. (1955) *The psychology of personal constructs*, New York: Norton.

Kendon, A. (1967) 'Some functions of gaze direction in social interaction', in *Acta Psychologica*, 26, 22–63.

Key, M. R. (1972) *The relationship of verbal and nonverbal communication*, paper presented at Eleventh International Congress of Linguistics, Bologna.

Kim, Y. Y. (1988) *Communication and cross-cultural adaptation: an integrative theory*, Clevedon: Multilingual Matters.

—— (1990) 'Communication and adaptation: the case of Asian Pacific refugees in the United States', in *Journal of Asian Pacific Communication*, 1, 1–17.

Kim, Y. Y. and Gudykunst, W. B. (eds) (1988) *Cross-cultural adaptation: current approaches*, California: Sage.

Kim, Y. Y. and Ruben, B. D. (1988) 'Intercultural transformation: a systems theory', in *Theories in intercultural communication*, Kim, Y. Y. and Gudykunst, W. B. (eds), California: Sage.

Kincaid, D. L. (1988) 'The convergence theory and intercultural communication', in *Theories in intercultural communication*, Kim, Y. Y. and Gudykunst, W. B. (eds), California: Sage.

Knapp, M. L. (1972) 'The field of nonverbal communication: an overview', in *On speech communication: an anthology of contemporary writings and messages*, Stewart, C. J. and Kendall, B. (eds), New York: Holt, Rinehart & Winston, 57–71.

—— (1977) 'Nonverbal communication: basic perspectives', in *Bridges not walls*, 2nd edn, Stewart, J. (ed.), Reading, Massachusetts: Addison-Wesley, 74–85.

—— (1978) *Nonverbal communication in human interaction*, 2nd edn, New York: Holt, Rinehart & Winston.

Kress, G. (1988) 'Language as social practice', in *Communication and culture*, Kress, G. (ed.), Sydney: University of New South Wales Press, 79–129.

Kretschmer, E. (1925) *Physique and character*, New York: Cooper Square.

Laird, D. (1978) *Approaches to training and development*, Reading, Massachusetts: Addison-Wesley.

Lange, J. L. (1982) 'Toward a model of communication in process consultation', in *The Communicator*, 12, 47–68.

Latham, G. P. and Saari, L. M. (1984) 'Do people do what they say? Further studies on the situational interview', in *Journal of Applied Psychology*, 69, 569–73.

Leathers, D. G. (1978) *Nonverbal communication systems*, Boston: Allyn & Bacon.

Leichty, G. and Applegate, J. L. (1991) 'Social-cognitive and situational influences on the use of face-saving persuasive strategies', in *Human Communication Research*, 17, 451–84.

Lesikar, R. V. (1988) *Basic business communication*, 4th edn, Illinois: Irwin.

Levinger, G. and Snoek, J. D. (1972) *Attraction in relationships*, Morristown: General Learning Press.

Littlejohn, S. W. (1992) *Theories of human communication*, 4th edn, California: Wadsworth.

Lower, H. M. (1980) 'Fear of touching as a form of communication apprehension in professional nursing students', in *Australian Scan of Nonverbal Communication*, 1, 71–95.

Lyman, S. M. and Scott, M. B. (1967) 'Territoriality: a neglected sociological dimension', in *Social Problems*, 15, 237–41.

McAndrew, F. T., Gold, J. A., Lenney, E. and Ryckman, R. M. (1984) 'Exploration in immediacy: the nonverbal system and its relationship to affective and situational factors', in *Journal of Nonverbal Behavior*, 8, 210–28.

McComb, K. B. and Jablin, F. M. (1984) 'Verbal correlates of interviewer empathic listening and employment interview outcomes', in *Communication Monographs*, 51, 353–71.

McCroskey, J. (1978) *An introduction to rhetorical communication*, 3rd edn, Englewood Cliffs, New Jersey: Prentice Hall.

McKenna, J. F. and Yeider, R. A. (1991) 'Management development for an organisation in transition', in *The Journal of Management Development*, 10, 54–63.

McLagan, P. A. (1983) *Models for excellence: the conclusions and recommendations of the ASTD training and development competency study*, Washington, DC: American Society for Training and Development.

McLuhan, M. (1987) *Understanding media: the extensions of man*, London: Ark Paperbacks.

McLuhan, M. and Fiore, Q. (1967) *The medium is the massage*, UK: Penguin.

Malandro, L. A., Barker, L. L. and Barker, D. A. (1989) *Nonverbal communication*, 2nd edn, New York: Random House.

Marsh, P. (ed.) (1988) *Eye to eye: how people interact*, Massachusetts: Salem House.

Martin, J. N. (1986) 'Training issues in cross-cultural orientation', in *International Journal of Intercultural Relations*, 10, 103–15.

Maslow, A. H. (1970) *Motivation and personality*, 2nd edn, New York: Harper & Row.

Mehrabian, A. (1972) *Nonverbal communication*, Chicago: Aldine-Atherton.

Mehrabian, A. and Ferris, S. (1967) 'Inference of attitude from nonverbal communication in two channels', in *Journal of Consulting Psychology*, 71, 149–60.

Miller, G. R. and Burgoon, M. (1978) 'Persuasion research: review and commentary', in *Communication Yearbook 2: An Annual Review Published by the International Communication Association*, Rubin, B. (ed.), New Jersey: Transaction Books, 29–47.

Mintzberg, H. (1973) *The nature of managerial work*, New York: Harper & Row.

Mitchell, T. R., Dowling, P. J., Kabanoff, B. V. and Larson, J. R. (1988) *People in organizations: an introduction to organizational behaviour in Australia*, Sydney: McGraw-Hill.

Mohan, T., McGregor, H. and Strano, Z. (1992) *Communicating! Theory and Practice*, 3rd edn, Sydney: Harcourt Brace Jovanovich.

Monge, P. R., Backman, S. G., Dillard, J. P. and Eisenberg, E. M. (1982) 'Communicator competence in the workplace: model testing and scale development', in *Communication Yearbook 5: An Annual Review, International Communication Association*, Burgoon, M. (ed.), New Jersey: Transaction Books, 505–27.

Morris, D. (1985) *Bodywatching: a field guide to the human species*, London: Jonathan Cape.

Morris, D., Collett, P., Marsh, P. and O'Shaughnessy, P. (1979) *Gestures: their origins and distribution*, London: Jonathan Cape.

Murray, H. G. and Lawrence, C. (1980) 'Speech and drama training for lecturers as a means for improving university teaching', in *Research in Higher Education*, 13, 73–90.

Myers, G. E. and Myers, M. T. (1988) *The dynamics of human communication: a laboratory approach*, New York: McGraw-Hill.

Nichols, R. G. and Stevens, L. A. (1957) *Are you listening?*, New York: McGraw-Hill.

Nofsinger, R. (1991) *Everyday conversation*, Newbury Park, California: Sage.

Ogden, C. K. and Richards, I. A. (1969) *The meaning of meaning*, London: Routledge & Kegan Paul.

O'Keefe, B. J. (1992) 'Sense and sensitivity', in *Journal of Communication*, 42, 123–30.

O'Keefe, D. J. (1990) *Persuasion: theory and research*, California: Sage.

Orwell, G. (1949) *Nineteen eighty-four*, New York: New American Library.

Parks, M. R. (1985) 'Interpersonal communication and the quest for personal competence', in *Handbook of interpersonal communication*, Knapp, M. L. and Miller, G. R. (eds), California: Sage, 171–201.

Patterson, M. L. (1984) 'Nonverbal exchange: past, present, and future', in *Journal of Nonverbal Behavior*, 8, 350–59.

Patterson, M. L., Powell, J. L. and Lenihan, M. G. (1986) 'Perceptions of nonreciprocal touch in romantic relationships', in *Journal of Nonverbal Behavior*, 10, 41–50.

Pease, A. (1981) *Body language: how to read others' thoughts by their gestures*, North Sydney: Camel.

Penman, R. (1985) 'A rejoinder: interpersonal communication competence in another frame', in *Australian Journal of Communication*, 8, 33–35.

Peter, L. J. (1975) *Competencies for teaching: teacher education*, California: Wadsworth.

—— (1986) *The Peter Pyramid*, London: Unwin.

Peter, L. J. and Hull, R. (1975) *The Peter Principle*, London: Pan.

Peters, T. J. (1987) *Thriving on chaos*, London: Pan.

Peters, T. J. and Austin, N. (1989) *A passion for excellence: the leadership difference*, Glasgow: William Collins & Sons.

Peters, T.J. and Waterman, R.H. (1984) *In search of excellence: lessons from America's best-run companies*, New York: Harper & Row.

Piaget, J. (1973) *The child's conception of the world*, London: Paladin.

Pisano, M. D., Wall, S. M. and Foster, A. (1986) 'Touch, compliance, and interpersonal affect', in *Journal of Nonverbal Behavior*, 10, 29–40.

Plant, R. (1987) *Managing change and making it stick*, London: Fontana/Collins.

Postman, N. (1986) *Amusing ourselves to death*, London: Heinemann.

Powers, W. T. (1973) *Behavior: the control of perception*, Chicago: Aldine.

Putnam, L. L. and Roloff, M. E. (1992) *Communication and negotiation*, California: Sage.

Ralston, S. M. (1993) 'Applicant communication satisfaction, intent to accept second interview offers, and recruiter communication style', in *Journal of Applied Communication Research*, 21, 53–65.

Rand, A. (1970) *The new left: the anti-industrial revolution*, New York: Signet.

Rankin, P. T. (1926) 'Measurement of the ability to understand the spoken word', unpublished doctoral dissertation, University of Michigan.

Rasberry, R. W. and Lemoine, L. F. (1986) *Effective managerial communication*, Boston, Massachusetts: PWS-Kent.

Reardon, K. K. (1981) *Persuasion: theory and context*. California: Sage.

Redding, W. C. (1972) *Communication within the organization: an interpretive review of theory and research*, New York: Industrial Communication Council, 139–422.

Roberts, Y. (1984) *Man enough: men of 35 speak out*, London: Chatto & Windus, The Hogarth Press.

Rogers, C. R. (1951) *Client-centered therapy*, Boston: Houghton-Mifflin.

Rogers, C. R. and Roethlisberger, F. J. (1952) 'Barriers and gateways to communication', in *Harvard Business Review*, 30, 46–52.

Roloff, M. E. and Miller, G. R. (1987) *Interpersonal processes: new directions in communication research*, California: Sage.

Rosenfeld, H. M., Breck, B. E., Smith, S. E. and Kehoe, S. (1984) 'Intimacy-mediators of the proximity-gaze compensation effect: movement, controversial role, acquaintance, and gender', *Journal of Nonverbal Behavior*, 8, 235–49.

Rosenthal, R., Hall, J. A., DiMatteo, M. R., Rogers, P. L. and Archer, D. (1979) *Sensitivity to nonverbal communication: the PONS test*, Baltimore: Johns Hopkins University Press.

Roskos-Ewoldsen, D. R. and Fazio, R. H. (1992) 'The accessibility of source likability as a determinant of persuasion', in *Personality and Social Psychology Bulletin*, 18, 19–25.

Rotter, N. G. and Rotter, G. S. (1988) 'Sex differences in the encoding and decoding of negative facial emotions', in *Journal of Nonverbal Behavior*, 12, 139–48.

Rutter, D. R., Pennington, D. C., Dewey, M. E. and Swain, J. (1984) 'Eye contact as a chance product of individual looking: implications for the intimacy model of Argyle and Dean', *Journal of Nonverbal Behavior*, 8, 250–58.

Saarni, C. (1988) 'Children's understanding of the interpersonal consequences of dissemblance of nonverbal emotional-expressive behavior', in *Journal of Nonverbal Behavior*, 12, 275–94.

Salamon, G. (1979) *Interaction of media, cognition and learning*, San Francisco: Jossey-Bass.

Sapir, E. (1921) *Language: an introduction to the study of speech*, New York: Harcourt, Brace & World.

Scheflen, A. E. (1968) 'Human communication: behavioral programs and their integration in interaction', in *Behavioral Science*, 13, 44–55.

Scott, M. D. and Nussbaum, J. F. (1981) 'Student perceptions of instructor communication behaviors and their relationship to student evaluation', in *Communication Education*, 30, 44–53.

Shakespeare, W. (1951) *The complete works*, London: Collins.

Shannon, C. E. and Weaver, W. (1949) *The mathematical theory of communication*, Urbana, Illinois: University of Illinois Press.

Sheldon, W. H. (1954) *Atlas of man: a guide for somatyping the adult male at all ages*, New York: Harper & Row.

Sherwood, J. J. and Glidewell, J. C. (1973) 'Planned renegotiation', in *The 1973 annual handbook for group facilitators*, Jones, J. E. and Pfeiffer, J. W. (eds), California: University Associates.

Sieradski, Z. (1988) *Lateral thinking and convergence*, paper presented to the Australian Communication Assn Annual Conference, July, University of New England, Armidale.

Silverman, D. and Torode, B. (1980) *The material world: some theories of language and its limits*, London: Routledge & Kegan Paul.

Skinner, B. F. (1973) *Beyond freedom and dignity*, UK: Penguin.

Smith, M. J. (1984) 'Contingency rules theory, context, and compliance behaviors', in *Human Communication Research*, 4, 489–512.

Snyder, C. R. and Higgins, R. L. (1988) 'From making to being the excuse: an analysis of deception and verbal/nonverbal issues', in *Journal of Nonverbal Behavior*, 12(4), 237–52.

Stewart, C. J. and Cash, W. B. Jr. (1988) *Interviewing principles and practices*, 5th edn, Iowa: William C. Brown.

Stewart, J. and D'Angelo, G. (1976) *Together: communicating interpersonally*, Massachusetts: Addison-Wesley.

Taylor, A., Rosegrant, T., Meyer, A. and Samples, B. T. (1989) *Communicating*, 5th edn, Englewood Cliffs, New Jersey: Prenctice Hall.

Thayer, S. (1986) 'History and strategies of research on social touch', in *Journal of Nonverbal Behavior*, 10, 12–28.

The Holy Bible (1977) King James Version, Nashville: Thomas Nelson.

Thouless, R. H. (1976) *Straight and crooked thinking*, London: Pan.

Ticehurst, B., Walker, G. and Johnston, R. (1991) 'Issues in communication management in Australian organisations', in *Australian Journal of Communication*, 18, 81–97.

Timm, P. R. (1987) *Successful self-management: a psychologically sound approach to personal effectiveness*, California: Crisp.

Timm, P. R. and Peterson, B. D. (1982) *People at work: human relations in organizations*, St Paul: West Publishing Company.

Toffler, A. (1970) *Future shock*, London: Pan.

Tomkins, S. S. (1962) *Affect, imagery and consciousness: the positive effects*, vol I, New York: Springer.

Tomkins, S. S. and McCarter, R. (1964) 'What and where are the primary affects? Some evidence for a theory', in *Perceptual and Motor Skills*, 18, 119–58.

Tompkins, P. K. (1982) 'Human communication theory: comparative essays', in *Journal of Applied Communication Research*, 10, 78–81.

Tracy, K., Craig, R. T., Smith, M. T. and Spisak, F. (1984) 'The discourse of requests: assessment of a compliance-gaining approach', *Human Communication Research*, 10, 513–38.

Trenholm, S. (1986) *Human communication theory*, Englewood Cliffs, New Jersey: Prentice Hall.

Trenholm, S. and Petrie, C. R. (1980) 'Re-examining body accessibility', in *Australian Scan of Nonverbal Communication*, 1, 33–42.

Twomey, D. F. and Twomey, R. F. (1992) 'Assessing and transforming performance appraisal', *Journal of Managerial Psychology*, 7, 23–32.

Ury, W. (1991) *Getting past no*, London: Business Books.

Vecchio, R. P. (1988) *Organizational behavior*, Chicago: Dryden Press.

Verderber, R., Elder, A. and Weiler, E. (1976) 'A study of communication time usage by college students', unpublished study, University of Cincinnati.

Vonnegut, K. (1969) *Slaughterhouse-five or the children's crusade: a duty-dance with death*, New York: Delacorte Press.

Vroom, V. H. and Jago, A. G. (1988) 'Managing participation: a critical dimension of leadership', in *The Journal of Management Development*, 7, 32–42.

Vroom, V. H. and Yetton, P. W. (1975) *Leadership and decision-making*, Pittsburgh: University of Pittsburgh Press.

Watzlawick, P., Beavin, J. H. and Jackson, D. D. (1967) *Pragmatics of human communication*, New York: Norton.

Werner, H. (1957) 'The concept of development from a comparative and organismic point of view', in *The concept of development*, Harris, D. B. (ed.), Minneapolis: University of Minnesota Press.

Whitney, D. C. and Wartella, E. (1992) 'Media coverage of the "political correctness" debate', in *Journal of Communication*, 42, 83–94.

Whorf, B. (1956) *Language, thought and reality*, New York: John Wiley.

Wiener, M., Devoe, S., Rubinow, S. and Geller, J. (1972) 'Nonverbal behavior and nonverbal communication', in *Psychological Review*, 79, 185–214.

Wiio, O. (1979) *Wiio's laws of communication*, paper presented at Communication in the 21st Century World Communication Conference, Ohio University, April 27–May 4, 1979.

Wilkes, G. A. (1978) *A dictionary of Australian colloquialisms*, Sydney: Sydney University Press.

Williams, T. (1991) 'Socio-technical systems in the information technology age', in *Information technology in Australia: transforming organisational structure and culture*, Aungles, S. (ed.), Sydney: University of New South Wales Press, ch 1, 1–25.

Wolvin, A. and Coakley, C. (1988) *Listening*, 3rd edn, Dubuque, IA: Brown.

Woolfolk, A. E. (1981) 'The eye of the beholder: methodological considerations when observers assess nonverbal communication', in *Journal of Nonverbal Behavior*, 5, 199–204.

Yau, W. S. L. and Sculli, D. (1990) 'Managerial traits and skills', in *The Journal of Management Development*, 9, 32–40.

Name Index

Subject Index